"Rarely does scholarly work generate in me a feeling of excitement, but that's exactly what *New Body Politics* has done. Here is a book that redefines the limits and possibilities of comparative analysis and brings into brilliant conversation matters of race, ethnicity, ability, gender, and representation. Even better, it is written with verve and clarity."

—Steven Salaita, *Virginia Tech*

"A bold new foray into the exploration of corporeality and the sociopolitical through U.S. minority literatures: Therí A. Pickens brings together African American and Arab American cultural and literary expressions in a way that will not soon be forgotten. By putting these two complex traditions into conversation with one another, *New Body Politics* takes the reader through a dazzling array of topics, from the construction of minority subjecthood and family politics to illness and medical practices. This is a rare and important 'first' in American studies, disability studies, African American studies, and Arab American studies: a long-awaited yet desperately needed comparative analysis of two groups who are distinct, yet overlap with one another quite poignantly."

—Michelle M. Wright, *Northwestern University*

New Body Politics

In the increasingly multiracial and multiethnic American landscape of the present, understanding and bridging dynamic cross-cultural conversations about social and political concerns becomes a complicated humanistic project. How do everyday embodied experiences transform from being anecdotal to having social and political significance? What can the experience of corporeality offer social and political discourse? And, how does that discourse change when those bodies belong to Arab Americans and African Americans?

Therí A. Pickens discusses a range of literary, cultural, and archival material where narratives emphasize embodied experience to examine how these experiences constitute Arab Americans and African Americans as social and political subjects. Pickens argues that Arab American and African American narratives rely on the body's fragility, rather than its exceptional strength or emotion, to create urgent social and political critiques. The creators of these narratives find potential in mundane experiences such as breathing, touch, illness, pain, and death. Each chapter in this book focuses on one of these everyday embodied experiences and examines how authors mobilize that fragility to create social and political commentary. Pickens discusses how the authors' focus on quotidian experiences complicates their critiques of the nation state, domestic and international politics, exile, cultural mores, and the medical establishment.

New Body Politics participates in a vibrant interdisciplinary conversation about cross-ethnic studies, American literature, and Arab American and African American literature. Using intercultural analysis, Pickens explores issues of the body and representation that will be relevant to fields as varied as political science, African American studies, Arab American studies, and disability studies.

Therí A. Pickens is an assistant professor of English at Bates College. Her research focuses on Arab American and African American literatures and cultures, disability studies, philosophy, and literary theory. Her critical work has appeared in *Disability Studies Quarterly*, *Al-Jadid*, *Journal of Canadian Literature*, *Al-Raida*, and the groundbreaking collection, *Blackness and Disability: Critical Examinations and Cultural Interventions*.

Routledge Series on Identity Politics

SERIES EDITOR: Alvin B. Tillery, Jr., *Rutgers University*

Group identities have been an important part of political life in America since the founding of the republic. For most of this long history, the central challenge for activists, politicians, and scholars concerned with the quality of U.S. democracy was the struggle to bring the treatment of ethnic and racial minorities and women in line with the creedal values spelled out in the nation's charters of freedom. In the midst of many positive changes, however, glaring inequalities between groups persist. Indeed, ethnic and racial minorities remain far more likely to be under-educated, unemployed, and incarcerated than their counterparts who identify as white. Similarly, both violence and workplace discrimination against women remain rampant in U.S. society. The Routledge series on identity politics features works that seek to understand the tension between the great strides our society has made in promoting equality between groups and the residual effects of the ascriptive hierarchies in which the old order was rooted.

New Body Politics

Narrating Arab and Black Identity
in the Contemporary United States

Therí A. Pickens

Routledge
Taylor & Francis Group

NEW YORK AND LONDON

First published 2014
by Routledge
711 Third Avenue, New York, NY 10017

and by Routledge
2 Park Square, Milton Park, Abingdon, Oxon OX14 4RN

*Routledge is an imprint of the Taylor & Francis Group,
an informa business*

Library of Congress Cataloging-in-Publication Data
Pickens, Therí A.
   New body politics : narrating Arab and Black identity in the contemporary
United States / Therí A. Pickens.
      pages cm. — (Routledge series on identity politics)
   1. Arab Americans—Ethnic identity.   2. African Americans—Race
identity.   3. Human body—Social aspects—United States.   4. Human
body—Political aspects—United States.   5. United States—Ethnic
relations.   6. United States—Race relations.   I. Title.
   E184.A65P53 2014
   305.800973—dc23
   2013038263

ISBN: 978-0-415-73521-6 (hbk)
ISBN: 978-0-415-74904-6 (pbk)
ISBN: 978-1-315-81931-0 (ebk)

Typeset in Sabon
by Apex CoVantage, LLC

Dedicated to
Tristan H. Campbell
(1983–2010)
and
Christopher M. Bell
(1974–2009)
in loving and cherished memory

Contents

Figure

Acknowledgments

First, there is God. Without Him, I am nothing. I would rather have splinters at the foot of the cross than smooth hands on my own.

The people who ushered this project into completion did so without regard for public applause. I speak their names here as a partial way to express my gratitude for their tireless efforts and generosity of spirit. No project is undertaken alone and truly there is no way to ensure that everyone who has contributed in ways small and large gets included. Please blame my head and not my heart for oversights.

In some ways, this project started from intellectual obsessions and skills I developed as an undergraduate at Princeton. I am thankful to the various professors, TAs, staff, and fellow students who encouraged my four-year peripatetic: Andras Hamori, Anne Jamison, Carole Sutphin, Carolyn Rouse, Charif Shanahan, Cornel West, Cristina Rivera, Cynthia Pierre, Dale G. Caldwell, Daniel Heller-Roazen, Daphne Brooks, Darryl Smith, Deborah Blanks, Denis Feeney, Donnell Butler, Eddie S. Glaude Jr., Elliot Ratzman, Ernest J. Mitchell II, Frank Ordiway, Gladys Valdesuso, Howard Taylor, Hyeyoung Oh, Ikram Masmoudi, James Peterson, Janet Dickerson Stephens, Janet Neglia, Jeremy and Adriana Moore, Jonathan Schettino, Jonathan Walton, Kyndall Parker, Laurie Ann Hall, Michael Wood, Mikaela and Jaquan Levons, Nadia Ellis, Noliwe Rooks, Nyron and Ruth Burke, Patricia Fernandez Kelly, Paulina Ortíz, Rob Simmons, Sandra Bermann, Teng-Kuan Ng, Soyoung Oh, Thema Bryant-Davis, Tim Watson, and Valerie Smith.

I extend my heartfelt thanks to those who encouraged this project during its nascent stages at UCLA. First, my committee strengthened my resolve and my analysis in equal measure. I owe a deep debt of gratitude to Richard Yarborough (co-chair), Nouri Gana (co-chair), Helen Deutsch (PhDiva extraordinaire), and Shu-mei Shih (PhDiva extraordinaire). I didn't realize how much of a community I had during graduate school until I left. What a testament to the unnecessary nature of being a curmudgeon or stereotypical disgruntled graduate student! Thank you to the people who formed my community: Aamir Mufti, Amy (Cammack) Walker, Anna Ward, Arthur L. Little Jr., Ashley Richardson, Basirat Alabi, Billie Buchanan, Birgitta Johnson, Caitlin Rohn, Caroline Streeter, Chinyere Osuji, Chris "C.J." Emmons,

Christina Nagao, Christine Wilson, Claudia Kernan, Claudia Mitchell Kernan, Courtney Marshall, David Fieni, Deirdre and Bryan Cooper Owens, Dennis Tyler, Eboni Haynes, Erica (Powe) Onugha, Ester Trujillo, Evangeline Heiliger, Georgina Guzmán, H. Samy Alim, Harryette Mullen, James Fugate, Jeff Fox, Jeff Wong, Jennifer McMillan, Jenny Sharpe, JoAnn Dawson, Jordan Smith, Jovanni (Williams) Lota, Joyce Warren, Justin Lim, Katherine King, Katherine McCloone, Kathy Komar, Kirk Sides, Kirstie McClure, LaTonya Rease-Miles, Leila Pazargadi, Magdalena Edwards, Marian Gabra Kahsay, Marilu Medrano, Mark Brewer, Maryam Khan, Michael and Beth Flecker, Michael David Cooperson, Michael Malek Najjar, Mignon Moore, Muriel McClendon, Naomi Baldinger, Nasia Anam, Nikki Brown, Olivia Banner, Paul and Amy Neal, Perry Shieh, Priscilla Ocen, Rafael Perez-Torres, Reed Wilson, Ryan Kernan, Simchi Cohen, Spencer Jackson, Steven Nelson, Susanah Rodriguez-Drissi, Sylvie Inkindi, Valerie Popp, Wendy Belcher, and Yvette Martinez.

I am appreciative of the time I got to spend in the last outpost of LA County (Claremont, CA). Thank you to the people who quenched my thirst for intellectual friendship in the desert: Alicia Bonaparte, Darryl Smith, Deb Vargas, Erica Edwards, Evangeline Heiliger, Fred Lee, Imani Harris, Laura Harris, Rochelle Brown, Sandra Mayo, and Valorie Thomas. My students fed me with their intellectual curiosity, laughter, and keen wit. They also let me experiment on them pedagogically. (Thanks for seeing the links between Katt Williams and Ann Petry!) Thank you to Annie Brown, Ava Untermyer, Camille Goldstein, Daria Dulan, Elena Thomas, Gar Lauerman, kYmberli Corprue, Lucy Copp, Samantha Morse, Stephanie Migdail, Ti'esh Harper, and Tyriek White.

I am glad to call Bates College my intellectual home. My colleagues have given me the mentorship, warmth, support, time, and space to complete this project. I want to thank my colleagues in the English Department for their razor-sharp wit, wisecracking, and genuinely supportive atmosphere: Jess Anthony, Lavina Dhingra, Steven Dillon, Robert Farnsworth, Sylvia Federico, Sanford Freedman, Mollie Godfrey, Ruth Lexton, Tina Malcolmson, Lillian Nayder, Eden Osucha, and Robert Strong. Special thanks to my colleagues across the college for their reading of drafts, open doors, and models of thoughtful and successful scholarship: Alejandro Dellachiesa, Ali Akhtar, Balthasar Fra-Molinero, Charles "Val" Carnegie, Charles Nero, Cynthia Baker, Dale Chapman, Don Dearborn, Emily Kane, Erica Rand, Hilmar Jensen, Holly Ewing, Jim Parakilas, Joseph Hall, Joseph Tomaras, Lauren Vedal, Leslie Hill, Mara Tieken, Marcus Bruce, Margaret Imber, Matthew Pettway, Melinda Plastas, Micah Pawling, Phil Walsh, Rebecca Herzig, Steve Engel, Sue Houchins, and Thomas Tracy. I am thoroughly appreciative of the Humanities Rock Stars Writing Group: Bradley Proctor, Beata Niedzialkowska, Matthew Pettway, Mollie Godfrey, Lauren Vedal, and Ruth Lexton. My student researchers performed the grunt work so desperately needed for a project of this size: Akinyele Akinruntan, Leigh Michael,

Kathryn Ailes, and Rebecca Salzman-Fiske. Our support staff helped make this road a lot easier to travel down. You all often have a thankless, tiresome job. I am so honored to work with you: Alison Keegan, Christine Schwartz (and all the dining services staff), Clementine Brasier, Lori Ouellette, Kelly Perreault, Kerry O'Brien, Shareen Gustin, and Victoria Toppses. It's a great day to be a Bobcat, indeed.

Some of my colleagues and friends don't fit into any of these categories. They are a class all by themselves. To my "Sister Scholars" writing group, this was so much more than just reading drafts. You gave the soul-satisfying support and friendship so few people experience in an intellectual arena. A million thanks for your candor, wit, laughter, and insight: Courtney Marshall, Folashade Alao, Leslie Wingard, and Samaa Abdur-raqib. There is a great host of people whose intellectual and physical labor cannot be overlooked. Thank you for your tweets, Facebook posts, emails, reading of drafts, phone calls, intellectual curiosity, passionate critique, and more. You all have shaped my thinking and my outlook more than you know: Aaisha Tracy Lund, Aisha Lockridge, Ann Fox, Asia Pinckney, Ayesha Hardison, Beauty Bragg, Brandon Manning, Brenda Brueggemann, C. Riley Snorton, Cait Vaughn, Carol Fadda-Conrey, Charif Shanahan, Cherise Pollard, Cheryl Toman, Chris Baswell, Christina Sharpe, Christopher Freeburg, Cynthia Wu, David B. Green Jr., David J. Leonard, Daylanne English, Dennis Britton, Ean Lexton, Earl Brooks, Ebony Coletu, Elie Chalala, Ellen Samuels, Ernest J. Mitchell II, Evelyn Alsultany, Evie Shockley, Farah Jasmine Griffin, Francine Saunders, George Kelling, Hayan Charara, Herman Beavers, Hosam Aboul-Ela, Howard Rambsy II, Imani Perry, Jafari Allen, James Peterson, Jennifer James, John Jennings, Jonathan Walton, José and Linda Leiva, Joshua Bennett, Joshua Lukin, Kameelah Martin, Kerry Ann Rockquemore, Khaled Mattawa, Koritha Mitchell, LaMonda H. Stallings, Lanisa Kitchiner, Leila Pazargadi, Lori Harrison Kahan, Lovalerie King, Mark Anthony Neal, Mary Hubbard, Maryemma Graham, Meta DuEwa Jones, Michelle Jarman, Mikaela and Jaquan Levons, Mitchell Ross, Moya Bailey, Nirmala Erevelles, Petra Kuppers, Phillip Metres, Quentin Miller, Randa Jarrar, Reginald Wilburn, Robert W. Azubuike, Roger Cosineau, Sharon Holland, Siobhan Senier, Steven Salaita, Susan Burch, Susan Weeber, Takiyah Nur Amin, Terry Rowden, Thabiti Lewis, Tim Howard, Trudier Harris, Uri McMillan, Vaughn Rasberry, W. Lawrence Hogue, Wayne Fisher and Wilfredo Gomez. I call most often on my crew for intellectual and emotional support: Aaisha Tracy Lund, C. Riley Snorton, Courtney Marshall, and Leila Pazargadi, There are no words to express how much I appreciate your existence and presence in my life.

Thank you to my family whose love and support means so much. I honor my grandparents because they would have been so proud of me: Ursuleen A. Scott (Gramma), James Scott (Pop Pop), Roddie Pickens (Grandfather, Granpa), and Dorothy Pickens (Big Ma). To Lori A. Scott-Pickens: I take after your quick wit, quicker tongue, sharp mind, and sensitive spirit. I am so grateful that your bravery and commitment to excellence exists alongside your compassion and intelligence. A Ronald "Jefe" Parm: Siempre dices que no hay sorpresas cuando triunfo yo. Espero que no estes sorprendido otra vez. ¡Que no hay sorpresas nunca! Te amo y te aprecio de verdad. To Terryl L. Pickens: I am grateful that I inherited your love of knowledge and puzzles. Both have served me well! To Debora Parks Pickens: Thank you so much for your gentle spirit; it is beautiful to be around. I am grateful that you have always extended yourself in love and support.

At Routledge, I had such thoughtful and insightful reviewers. I appreciate their candor and commitment to making this an excellent project. I especially want to thank Natalja Mortensen for seeing the potential in my manuscript. Darcy Bullock, I am so grateful for your patient work on this project! I also appreciate that Alvin Tilley saw fit to include me in this series. It is an honor and a privilege. I extend my deepest thanks to Laura Magzis, Emily Lupton Metrish, Deepti Agarwal, and everyone who performed copyediting, indexing, and proofreading on this manuscript. Your labor is much appreciated!

This project was generously financially supported by the Woodrow Wilson Dissertation Fellowship, Lori A. Scott-Pickens, and Bates College. Earlier versions of this manuscript have appeared under the following titles: "To Be or Not To Be: The Question of Having a Body in Ethnic Studies." *Defying the Global Language: Perspectives in Ethnic Studies*. Eds. Cheryl Toman & Gilbert Doho. Amherst, NY: Teneo Press, Ltd., 2013. 19–44; "Feeling Embodied and Being Displaced: A Phenomenological Exploration of Hospital Scenes in Rabih Alameddine's Fiction." *MELUS*. 38.3 (2013): 1–19; and "Pinning Down the Phantasmagorical: Discourse of Pain and the Rupture of Post-humanism in Evelyne Accad's 'The Wounded Breast' and Audre Lorde's 'The Cancer Journals.'" *Blackness and Disability: Critical Examinations and Cultural Interventions*. Ed. Christopher Bell. Berlin: Lit Verlag, 2011. 75–94. Reprinted with permission.

Introduction

This project is obsessed with bodies, bodies that do what a body does, no matter how mundane or embarrassing or unpredictable. Since no body exists without its owner, and no one who owns a body exists outside social and political grounding, I channel that obsession to discuss the relationship between one's corporeality and one's sociopolitical position. Specifically, I ask, what can corporeality offer social and political discourse? How do those discourses change when the bodies in question belong to Arab Americans and African Americans? How can we place Black and Arab American embodied experience in conversation around salient social and political concerns?[1] By way of answer, I offer the following: within narratives by and about Blacks and Arabs, embodied experience, particularly when the body announces its fragility, becomes a vehicle through which they articulate their reflections on and critiques of the world we inhabit.

At the crux of this discussion is *embodiment* or *embodied experience*, moments of tangible, sensory living from which humans make sense of their world. I draw from Tobin Siebers's notion of "complex embodiment," which "views the economy between social representations and the body not as unidirectional [. . .] but as reciprocal."[2] That is, embodied experiences emanate from understanding and living what is sensory and tangible within social contexts. The flesh not only comprises the world and helps one make sense of that world but is also beholden to and constrained by that social, cultural, and political world. I turn to the quotidian flesh (breathing, touch, illness, pain, death) because, as Sharon Holland notes in *Erotic Life of Racism*, examining the everyday not only foregrounds the "messy materiality of the body" but is also critically useful for understanding how ordinary the practice and effects of virulent discourses have come to be.[3] The body so often (rightly or wrongly) stands in for the body politic and the family, and as an allegory for the nation-state. My analysis of the everyday embodiment of Arab and Black people within the United States questions how the quotidian aspects of subjectivity and making families (among other acts) affect the political discourses to which they are often wed. The seemingly mundane aspects of embodiment allow us to unpack some of the culturally conscripted ideology mapped onto Arab and Black bodies within the United

States. This is not to say that narratives about stereotypes like the supposed big Black buck or oppressed veiled Arab woman disappear. Rather, a discussion of the quotidian challenges us to consider how and where those narratives buckle. Moreover, embodiment opens up the possibility for cross-cultural conversation based on fundamental human sameness, even if said conversation remains fraught with the social and political concerns that prompt and sustain divisions.

Since "the embodied subject on which this book dwells is not ethereal, transcendent, or fixed, in either form or identity, but rather palpable, porous, and motile,"[4] I examine moments when embodiment highlights corporeal fragility. 'Fragility' here is synonymous with neither strength nor weakness, but rather the wear and tear caused by being both acted upon and agentive. The moments in my analysis call attention to the aforementioned relationship between social representation and the body, the world and the flesh. Such an interplay highlights how indebted this project is to the field of disability studies. Certainly disability studies is "a location and a means to think critically about disability, a juncture that can serve both academic discourse and social change."[5] However, the field also bears implications for understanding "the variations that exist in human behavior, appearance, functioning, sensory acuity, and cognitive process, but, more crucially, the meaning we make of those variations."[6] As a result, disability is both object of inquiry and analytic for this project. I examine what disability studies scholar Simi Linton terms "the critical divisions [made] in creating the normal versus the pathological, the insider versus the outsider, or the competent citizen versus the ward of the state."[7] I analyze them from the standpoint (or more accurately sitpoint) that embodied experience matters significantly to these distinctions and the rubrics upon which they are based.

Though I explore what it means to narrate African American and Arab American embodied experience in particular, I draw from several other modes of inquiry that undergird and complement the larger field of American studies: comparative ethnic studies, literary and cultural studies, gender studies, and phenomenology. I link these embodied ways of knowing as an avenue to making sense of Black and Arab American embodied experience based on the terms delineated by the writers themselves. As such, this project's aims align with the imperative to "write or be written"[8] as articulated by Barbara Nimri Aziz in the edited collection *Scheherezade's Legacy*. She challenges Arab American writers to create their own stories or risk having others do so for them. As Aziz notes, the same injunction has existed for African American writing. Her injunction recalls Alain Locke's challenge to the new Negro of the early twentieth century or the Black Arts Movement's specific aims for creating and sustaining black art. Langston Hughes's desire to depict the beauty and the ugly too echoes here as a refrain for Arab American and African American writing. In the words of Khaled Mattawa and Munir Akash: "If the image of us [Arab Americans] is truly being created by the American imagination, the time has come to invalidate that image and render it unrecognizable both to ourselves and to the world."[9] The critical conversations with which this book dialogues emphasize the social and cultural politics at stake when choosing to narrate raced, gendered, classed, and abled quotidian experience.

I contend that Arab American and African American narratives announce the body's fragility as a way to open up sociopolitical discourse. In contrast to the depiction of the raced and gendered body as exclusively able, exceptionally strong, or visibly threatening, these writers spotlight their bodies' fragility as compelling for sociopolitical commentary. These authors and cultural producers' ideas emphasize the tenuousness and unruliness of quotidian embodied experience, finding critical utility in the following conundrum: the body is an inherently mercurial object of inquiry that, at times, does not change the conversations in which people participate; nevertheless, the discussions must begin with the body itself. Each of the figures I examine attempts to debunk the idea that their embodied experiences are solely an individual matter. Instead, their work becomes an empowering and transgressive space, viable for examining and contesting their "condition[s] of alterity."[10] They take for granted that, regardless of how others view them, they make sense of the world, in phenomenological terms, "through processes and logic of sense–making that owe as much to [their] carnal existence as they do to [their] conscious thought."[11] To my mind, their work privileges the radical potential within the diegetic capacity of embodiment, harnessing ordinary embodiment as a starting point for understanding and critiquing institutional and social practices.

Elsewhere I have argued for the utility of phenomenology as a close reading methodology for narratives by Arabs and Blacks. Since "the thought of ethnic others as simply bodies [objects] is the lingua franca in projects of global domination," these works require "criticism that emanates from embodied experience, criticism that privileges the body as a primary space of interpretation, because [humans'] simultaneity as subjects and objects demands it."[12] In this project, I read narratives with a phenomenological eye, focusing on the body as "the first way of access to the world."[13] In other words, the experiences of the body, such as breathing, touching, or feeling pain, are what one perceives first prior to interpreting those feelings. The clarion cry of phenomenologists is to get to the things themselves,[14] but it is impossible to reduce experience completely because we require language to describe it.[15] Nevertheless, I analyze how these authors describe and invoke their perception, or rather their way of accessing the world through their bodies. My readings also emphasize the body as "both an objective subject and a subjective object: a sentient, sensual, and sensible ensemble of materialized capacities and agency that literally and figuratively makes sense of, and to, both ourselves and others."[16] An objective subject is one who acts upon others; a subjective object is acted upon. The body remains both simultaneously, which results in a reversibility and reciprocity within interaction wherein the objective subject constitutes and is constituted by the subjective object and vice versa.[17] As Charles Johnson notes, it is a general rule for phenomenology that there is never an object, even a subjective object, without a corresponding subject, even an objective subject.[18] That is, one cannot escape being socially and historically grounded in the world. As Du Bois's *Souls of Black Folk* and Fanon's *Black Skin, White Masks* illuminate, the raced and gendered body must be conscious of itself in terms of how others understand it as well as how it understands itself. In short, the flesh matters.

As examples of how an emphasis on embodiment opens up the critical possibilities of reading Arab American and African American literature, I point to Ralph Ellison's novel *Invisible Man* (1952) and Joseph Geha's short story collection *Through and Through* (1990). While the characters' corporeality refutes their social invisibility, their corporeality also reveals the logics by which the characters are made socially invisible. Ellison's unnamed narrator struggles with how he is seen and understood in the context of Jim Crow America, claiming in the familiar line, "I am invisible because people refuse to see me."[19] In the preceding sentence, he acknowledges the irony of this invisibility in terms of his body saying, "I am a man of substance, of flesh and bone, of fiber and liquids—and I might even be said to possess a mind."[20] Here, Ellison's unnamed narrator wrestles against the disjuncture between the tangibility and the materiality of his body and its social fungibility and invisibility. Geha's short fiction collection mirrors Ellison's novel in that Geha's characters demonstrate the simultaneity of being seen and not seen. In "Monkey Business," Asfoori, a deaf, palsied neighborhood vagrant, remains visible, as he is a fixture on the street, but invisible, since others generally ignore his presence. Much as in Ellison's novel, the street becomes the space of contested selfhoods. Neither man receives acknowledgment of his material presence as part of a unique subjectivity. By the end of both narratives, Asfoori is dead and the unnamed narrator is underground. Unlike the latter's community, the neighborhood does mourn Asfoori, but his funeral cannot grant him the subjectivity he has been denied all along. As David Mitchell and Sharon Snyder might describe, Asfoori's disabilities make him a "symbolic vehicle for meaning-making and cultural critique."[21] The tragedy of Asfoori's death is that he remains invisible and largely symbolic even when his dead body is the impetus for the occasion. In Ellison's novel, it is the psychological trauma of being understood as invisible despite being physically visible that forces the unnamed narrator underground.

Ellison's and Geha's works evince the disjuncture between the way the body is understood by others and how it is experienced by the one who inhabits it. Moreover, when read in concert, their works proffer a critique of the logics that determine who gets to be a subject. For instance, Ellison contests the credibility of the world outside in determining the parameters of community and citizenship, two significant vehicles for defining a subject. Yet, even with the presence of a community, as with Geha's short story, the neighborhood can still be a profoundly alienating space. Though Asfoori has found a place in the community, his character's symbolic function would indicate that space was not carved out by him but for him instead—according to the logic that invisibilizes his presence. I would venture that Geha's "Monkey Business" comments on the choice available to Ellison's unnamed narrator because Asfoori brings into sharp relief a clustered identity that includes ethnicity, gender, immigrant status, and disability. While Ellison's narrator can assert his agency by going underground, Geha's work asks, how does agency operate when bodily impairment forecloses certain possibilities? If we are to consider that Geha and Ellison also comment on the making of masculinity, then we learn that being flesh and bone significantly, but only partly, constitutes one's subjectivity, community is contested, and ability status must be foregrounded.

Reading Geha and Ellison alongside each other becomes an instructive example for how Black and Arab authors interrogate the liberatory possibility of both conceptualizing oneself in terms of embodied experience and mobilizing that conception to be at stake in wider conversation. To rely on the body as a primary way of accessing the world and to highlight the reciprocity of human interaction counters and distorts existing notions about Black and Arab savagery, licentiousness, pain, and fungibility (among other narratives). The artists I examine take for granted that "departures from the norm are seen as threats to the mainstream body politic"[22] and envision a polity that contests the accepted standard of normality, crafted as it was in the crucible of the Enlightenment. Relying on "a theory in the flesh"[23] that believes "the reality of identities often comes from the fact that they are visibly marked on the body itself,"[24] I view their work as a challenge to and engagement with these classical ideas. They mobilize the broken, fragile, scatological, and impaired body to explode the Cartesian underpinnings of racism, sexism, and ableism.

In pairing Arab American and African American narratives, this book constructs a new cultural history of the two groups in conversation with each other. Current conversations circumscribe their relationship to one of three historically based but limited options: competition, hierarchies of whiteness, or replacement paradigms. With a brief sketch of Arab and African Americans' intertwined history, it is clear how the narratives came to be. During the twentieth century, the two groups navigated the American racial, cultural, and economic landscape, seemingly pitted against each other for resources. In the beginning of the twentieth century, Arabs in America fought to be considered legally white so that they could immigrate to the U.S., a series of juridical battles that socially and legally distanced them from Blacks.[25] Black worry regarding immigration dates prior to this time. The debates regarding immigrants, which included Arabs during the late 1800s and early 1900s, were rehearsed in the writings of Booker T. Washington[26] and splashed across the pages of the NAACP's *The Crisis* in Jessie Fauset's *The Sleeper Wakes*.[27] During the era of Jim Crow segregation, it became clear that the relationship between the two communities seemingly rested on a specific converse idea. Blacks had access to citizenship but not economic capital, while Arabs in America had access to economic capital but not citizenship.[28] Certainly, the terms of this inversion were vexed as African American citizenship was decidedly second-class and Arabs in America had access to the economic capital that placed them in Black neighborhoods. For instance, Nadine Naber notes that, according to Arab American businesspeople in California's Bay Area, "there is a tendency to view Arab business owners as violent and that this [limits] their business opportunities."[29] These same businesspeople could not receive government assistance because they were not recognized as minorities. San Francisco was the first to recognize them as minorities and provide the business opportunities that accompany that status.[30] The result of such vexed competition was a growing set of tensions between the two communities, particularly in areas where they were in close contact. As Sohail Daulatzai notes, some of this competition has been manufactured. He writes, "When [America] emerged from the Cold War and the Red Scare of communism in the aftermath of World War II, Civil Rights assumed that the United States' moral standing in winning the hearts and minds of the decolonizing nations of Africa and Asia (which includes what is now the 'Middle East') was linked to its treatment of Black peoples."[31] As a result, "the Civil Rights establishment supported an aggressive U.S. foreign policy in the name of anticommunism."[32] I do not conflate immigrant struggles with Arab American struggles lightly. However, until the third wave of Arab American immigration beginning in 1967, most of the Arab American population comprised immigrants or children of immigrants, so competition between the communities was formed (and continues, in part) on this basis.

Yet, scrutiny of this competition narrative assumes a constancy regarding Arab American economic power and African American access to citizenship that is not true. Such a formulation ignores the Arab American poor, lack of cultural competency within health care agencies for both groups, and structural inequalities that prevent African Americans from accessing resources.[33] Moreover, the competition paradigm elides the way that Orientalism and racism become strange bedfellows with regard to citizenship and economic capital. Without relying on fiction as sociological treatise, I find it useful to point out the way fictive works have imagined these narratives and laid bare the discrepancy within them. For instance, in Mohja Kahf's novel *The Girl in the Tangerine Scarf*, resentment of immigrant ambition and racial hatred collide in American suburbs; the results of such hostility are rapacious violence and constant harassment. The Muslim Cultural Center within Kahf's novel becomes one site of useful, albeit uneasy, cross-cultural unification. In urban areas where African and Arab Americans share geographical proximity, like Houston, Texas, the Greater Detroit Metropolitan Area, Michigan, and Paterson, New Jersey, xenophobia and racial prejudice can combine to deny both groups access to resources. Rabih Alameddine's *Koolaids: The Art of War* briefly depicts a friendship between two men (one Arab and one Black) during the height of the HIV/AIDS epidemic. Though the novel does not explicitly mention battles with social services, it does point to the possibility of building community in a tense and fraught social landscape.

During the mid-twentieth century, a shift in demographics prompted a change in the cultural climate such that Arab Americans forged some bonds with Blacks. Specifically, the 1967 War (also referred to as the Six-Day War) brought an influx of Arab immigrants,[34] many of whom were more politically engaged with the Arab world, and who were more culturally aware of their status as "not quite white."[35] However, the juridical battles that classified Arab Americans as legally white seemed to position the two groups along a hierarchy of whiteness with Blacks at the bottom. Michelle Hartman has refuted this paradigm by pointing out the way Arab Americans have used "political organizing [as] one of the primary locations for these solidarities [with African Americans]"[36] and articulated "identification with African American arts, literature, and creative production more generally."[37] Hartman is not alone in these ideas, since her scholarship draws from Therese Saliba,[38] Helen Samhan,[39] and Lisa Suhair Majaj,[40] and dialogues with Andrea Shalal-Esa.[41] Subscribing to the belief that the two groups exist along a hierarchy of whiteness erases the way racialization of Arabs and Blacks operates along the same volatile fault lines within U.S. political discourse. For instance, Daniel Patrick Moynihan not only authored the infamous "Moynihan report" that pathologized Black families but also lobbied the United Nations General Assembly to rescind resolution 3379, which linked Zionism with South African apartheid.[42] Moynihan's uncomplicated view of both the Israel/Palestine conflict and Black life highlights the commonalities between anti-Black and anti-Arab racism stemming from an impoverished view of both cultures and histories.

I do not seek to dismiss the way the perception of the two groups along a hierarchy of whiteness has social implications and repercussions for their interaction with each other. In fact, I take up that concern at several points within this book. However, continuing to think about them within an unquestioned hierarchy of whiteness ignores the stringent critiques that both groups make *vis-à-vis* white privilege. Danzy Senna's work consistently draws attention to the way whiteness is configured as standard. In her first novel, *Caucasia*, the main protagonist, Birdie, has a Black father and a white mother and others assume she is white based on appearance. When she and her mother must go on the run from the authorities, Birdie assumes a white Jewish identity. Birdie questions the implications of her choice, not simply because it is a lie, but also because her silence allows others—her friends and possible paramour—to articulate Blackness as an aberration. *Caucasia* frustrates the idea of whiteness as normal because Birdie has difficulty assuming whiteness internally and externally (she is assumed to be other ethnicities). It makes clear Richard Dyer's assertion that "white power [. . .] reproduces itself regardless of intention, power dynamics, and goodwill and overwhelmingly because it is not seen as whiteness but as normal."[43] Diana Abu Jaber's novel *Arabian Jazz* takes up the same question when one of her

Arab American characters, who others assume is white, affirms her connection to African Americans. Critic Steven Salaita's statements clarify how Diana Abu Jaber's and Danzy Senna's works unsettle white privilege in relation to national narratives of inclusion and belonging. He defines "imperative patriotism" as a narrative that "assumes (or demands) that dissent in matters of governance and foreign affairs is unpatriotic and therefore unsavory."[44] For him, ethnic studies and literature by people of color (including Arab Americans) "challenge[s] centers of traditional (White) American power."[45] Of Arab American literature, he specifically notes that the genre discusses the vexed position Arab Americans hold within the American polity, concurrently embedded within and yet isolated from it. Authors like Danzy Senna, Diana Abu Jaber, and others function as flies in the ointment of national patriotic narratives. The way that "traditional (White) American power" can determine who is and is not legitimately American remains fundamentally tied to whiteness as it authorizes white privilege, making it antithetical to inclusion. When viewed together, Senna and Abu Jaber's fictional works create a cross-cultural conversation about the workings of white privilege. Whiteness as a standard and arbiter of national identity deposes both Arab and African Americans from citizenship and repositions them as subordinate to whites within the national narrative.

After 9/11/2001 and the election of the first African American president, Barack Obama, media depictions of Arab Americans and the Patriot Act led some to believe that Arab Americans have replaced Blacks as the most disenfranchised group in America or that social relations in America had transformed such that the country was now supposedly post-racial. There are several objections to the pervasive idea that African American and Arab Americans currently exist in a replacement paradigm in which Arab is the new Black. The first objection is based in history. Arab Americans have been in the U.S. since the Wahab family in the 1400s and steadily came to the country beginning in the late nineteenth century.[46] Such a long history within the United States couples with a longer history of Orientalism to suggest that Arab Americans have always occupied a vexed racial position. It also elides the way the aforementioned shifts in demographic compound the hyperinvisibility of Arab Americans within the American racial landscape.[47] The second objection extends the first and questions the replacement paradigm on the basis of Arab American struggles with assimilation. Evelyn Shakir notes that some Arab American authors capitalized on their phenotypical proximity to whiteness to assimilate during the mid-twentieth century.[48] True, assimilation requires eliding multiple factors of one's identity, but it can often rest on one's physical ability to pass for white. The fact is that the preference for white skin in America allowed for and encouraged some Arab Americans to erase their specific ethnic identity in favor of a white Protestant identity. Some Arab American writers, including Abu Jaber (noted above), point out that this passing can be involuntary. In short, the replacement paradigm obscures the way that white skin privilege and assimilation facilitates the invisibility of Arab American identity. Moreover, the replacement paradigm—couched as it is in the language of fashion—adopts a progressive view of history for Blacks in America. It assumes that Black history moves forward from slavery to Barack Obama, viewing the latter as indicative of eradicated structural inequality despite Obama's consistent recourse to conservative racial politics.[49] It also assumes that liberal fights for equality have not been without their problematic homophobic, misogynist, ableist, and even racist underpinnings. Not only does a progressive view of history obfuscate the complicated nature of history itself, but it also presupposes that there have been no setbacks in the journey toward equality. As Moallem and Boal note, "[r]acialization remains a deep current in the politics of inequality. It has generated severe historical contradictions to the point of crisis for liberal nation-state formations, which must reconcile racial logic with the universalistic aspirations of Enlightenment ideology."[50]

This project, by rethinking the vicissitudes of living in a Black or Arab body, unpacks the problematic ideology at the heart of our conception of the nation-state. I pair Black and Arab narratives because rethinking this ideology challenges the doxic seduction of whiteness, maleness, and able-bodiedness masquerading as normalcy. To be clear, midwifing a conversation between Blacks and Arabs makes clear the "heterogeneous nature of racism's ideological underpinnings."[51] Specifically, anti-Arab and anti-Black racism share the same "complicated (and usually discordant) discourse of oppression and resistance, capitalism and egalitarianism, stereotype and self-representation."[52] The two groups' relationship with institutions ranging from the medical establishment to the nation-state forces a consideration of how race, racialization, and racial hierarchy work within the United States. These conversations are made more exigent and more difficult because the two groups are not always in agreement and the opposition proves revelatory. When Michelle Hartman rightly asks how Arab Americans engage with blackness, such a question "reformulate[s] the positioning of Arab Americans within US racial hierarchies."[53] Here, Hartman's analysis draws on Arab Americans as being situated within a probationary whiteness both legally and socially. Toni Morrison makes clear how Blacks born in America become suspicious of the privilege (however vexed) that relationship to whiteness affords: namely, because the price of the ticket into American culture is maltreatment of Blacks born in America. In Morrison's words, "a hostile posture toward resident blacks must be struck at the Americanizing door before it will open."[54] As scholars seek to explore race within the United States, they cannot ignore the tension between how Arabs and Blacks have been mutually constituted, at times in opposition to one another. In scholastic terms, conversations between Blacks and Arabs challenge the way we discuss the larger fields with which this project is engaged (and I would imagine many others). In American studies and comparative ethnic studies, a robust comparison of this sort refuses to participate in the invisibilizing of Arabs and Arab Americans, constituting them as part of the American narrative.[55] Ken Warren's purposefully provocative *What Was African American Literature?* (2011) prompted scholars of African American literature to consider how to read the tradition of African American literature in the late twentieth and early twenty-first century. I would argue that reading African American literature now requires a set of cross-cultural conversations that examines the wide range of influences this art has as well as the inspiration it receives from others.

As I noted, a cross-cultural conversation between Blacks and Arabs could be contentious because of the way both groups have been enfolded and implicated within the "hegemony of normalcy."[56] Within the crevices, we find that "white supremacy is an equal-opportunity employer; nonwhite people can become active agents of white supremacy as well as passive participants in its hierarchies and rewards."[57] More specifically, Arab American battles with racism reveal African American complicity with intolerance. African American battles with racism also reveal Arab American complicity with intolerance. It becomes urgently necessary to unpack the "significant linkages that enable us to understand possibilities for social change" without "position[ing] racialized groups or individuals as somehow inadequately politicized or underdeveloped."[58] On the one hand, African American studies occupies a peculiar, advantageous position within ethnic studies as the long established tradition from which most scholars, critics, and authors draw inspiration. That peculiar advantage has several impacts on existing scholarship. First, it would be easy to remain solipsistic about African American issues as if they were not in dialogue with other communities. In addition, it becomes taboo to discuss African American complicity with intolerance. Lastly, when Black studies is placed into a privileged position over other ethnic studies fields, Blackness is erased even as it is relied upon as a resource to articulate progressive politics or readings. Arab American studies as a nascent field challenges this so-called advantage and forces African American studies to reconsider how it engages race and racism post–Civil Rights. On the other hand, African American studies has the potential to question the Arab American relationship to whiteness and the historical distance between the two communities economically and socially. Integral to mining these cross-cultural discussions for their potential is the knowledge of the way Arabs and Blacks have already sought to traverse the historical and cultural distance of difference. For instance, Alice Walker, Angela Davis, Gina Dent, Robin D. G. Kelley, June Jordan, and other Blacks have been heavily involved in boycott, divestment, and sanctions (BDS) activism against Israel. Arab American and African American women writers find common ground in their explorations of intersectional identity. Andrea Shalal-Esa notes that Arab American writers "deriv[e] strength from feminists, black theorists, and post-colonial thinkers [. . .] to chronicle decades of racism, oppression, and marginalization in the United States."[59]

Instead of creating a narrative of "cross-racial dysfunction,"[60] I examine how both groups critique the national and cultural narratives that sustain various politics of inequality. This conversation does have a caveat. It assumes that "the psychic life of racism can best be read in the context of the United States in the space where black and white intersect."[61] I concur with the idea that "regardless of how far modernist binaries may be deconstructed, regardless of how unstable their bare understanding of oppositional difference, they cannot be simply dismissed: their power may be based on an illusion, but its operation is all too real."[62] However, my stance regarding the Black/white binary does not assume that the only way to approach a discussion of that "psychic life" is through the depiction of Black/white relations. Scholarship must explore how that binary affects other racial and ethnic groups. In the words of Andrea Smith, we must "address the nuanced structure of white supremacy" without assuming that "if we just include more people, then our practice [and our scholarship] will be less racist."[63] I am interested neither in erasing Blackness nor in moving beyond it but rather seeking to understand how Blackness remains in dialogue with the racial landscape that includes Arab Americans and how Arabness remains in dialogue with a racial landscape whose foundation is the Black/white binary. At varying points in this book, I place Blacks at the center of conversation or Arab Americans at the center of conversation. They remain interlocutors with each other and within these strange and interlocking discourses of race, gender, and ability.

This cross-cultural conversation maintains embodied experience at its center to appreciate the wide range of social and political analysis from Arabs and Blacks in America. Since I argue that these authors announce the body's fragility as an inroad to critique, I have organized this book to address quotidian embodiment moving from basic life function like breathing to end of life. These mundane experiences shift narratives from being merely individual concerns to bearing implications for larger social and political issues. I turn to respiration, touch, illness, pain, and death because these experiences of the flesh cut across identity even as they become politicized.

The first two chapters investigate the liberatory potential of bodily function and bodies in contact. They each explore how fleeting embodied experiences, breathing and touching, respectively, promulgate critiques of war, poverty, and the nation-state. Chapter 1, "Respirating Resistance: Suheir Hammad's Invocation of Breath" examines Arab American Suheir Hammad's poetry and interviews for the way she mobilizes breath as a way to challenge the circumstances surrounding occupied Palestine. Her critiques gain critical utility based on the centrality of respiration to living. The logic undergirding her metaphor is that if a Palestinian breathes, one can disavow the idea that Palestinians do not exist. Hammad draws on Black feminist poetics, specifically those of June Jordan, and hip hop aesthetics to make her point. In addition to referencing Black women in epigraphical form, Hammad draws on hip hop conventions like signifying. Her poetry not only challenges the idea of remaining in silos during struggle but also examines the difficulty in building cross-cultural bridges.

Within the first chapter, breath as metaphor foregrounds the ephemeral nature of life itself, emphasizing the value of the lives of people of color and women worldwide. In the second chapter, "Try a Little Tenderness: Tactilic Experience in Danzy Senna and Alicia Erian," I examine how touch works, despite its ephemerality, to underscore the liberatory potential of bodies in contact. I read Alicia Erian's novel *Towelhead* (with its filmic adaptation) alongside Danzy Senna's novel *Symptomatic*, arguing that the tactile functions to construct these protagonists according to the shifting illogic of racism and sexism. In contrast to the violent touches they experience at the hands of others, their recuperative touches become a fail-safe so that they can begin to construct themselves. Both writers rely on the experiences of middle-class bicultural and biracial characters to query the way Arab American and African American identities have been positioned within a racial hierarchy where whiteness resides at the apex. Their writing suggests that adhering to whiteness as a standard curtails a more complicated conversation about the intertwined nature of race/ethnicity and gender. In addition, these two *bildungsromane* challenge the way white privilege—even in liberal form—displaces Arab Americans' and African Americans' claims to an inclusive national narrative.

The next two chapters move from ephemeral embodied experience to explore how illness opens up space for complicated critique. The third chapter, entitled "Unfitting and Not Belonging: Feeling Embodied and Being Displaced in Rabih Alameddine's Fiction," surveys all of Arab American author Rabih Alameddine's fiction, finding that the hospital emerges as a space to engage and understand feelings of exile and displacement. I frame my discussion with W. E. B. Du Bois, who, in *Souls of Black Folk*, voices the salient but unarticulated question asked of Blacks—"How does it feel to be a problem?"—and Moustafa Bayoumi, who asks the same question of Arabs in America approximately one century later. Much like the answers offered in Du Bois's and Bayoumi's work, Alameddine's characters push back against the idea that normalcy or belonging is a state to which they should aspire, regardless of whether that norm or belonging is constituted in sexual, bodily, or mental terms. They also challenge the ableist underpinnings of Du Bois's original statement, proffering their answers from within the space of a hospital. Du Bois's question interpellates an other as one in need of being fixed even as it fixes the person as a permanent problem. Within Alameddine's work, the hospital space becomes the starting point for the characters to negotiate this conundrum. The characters and stories suggest that healing and belonging are neither desirable nor necessary.

In Chapter 4, "Beyond 1991: Magic Johnson and the Limits of HIV/AIDS Activism," I examine a rich archive of Magic Johnson's autobiographies, magazine articles, and educational pamphlets to understand how he uses his body in narrative to dispel rumors and create awareness about HIV/AIDS. Much like the other (arguably more literary) narratives, Johnson foregrounds the double-edged sword of making social and political meaning out of quotidian embodied experience: namely, the same diegetic tools that open up critical conversation can also undermine it. As Toni Morrison reminds us about national narratives, "underneath the commodified story [. . .] is a cultural one."[64] Two prevailing ideas shadow Johnson's cultural narrative. The first is a problematic conception of health that relies on visible manifestations of sickness and the second is the stereotype of hypersexualized, super-able Black male athletes. As a result, Johnson could only advocate for HIV/AIDS education and prevention temporarily. His efficacy as an advocate was curtailed by his somatic appearance as a plump, smiling, Black male athlete, since he did not appear to be fragile. In sum, Johnson's reliance on his healthy body to promote prevention curtailed his ability to remain an advocate.

By way of conclusion, the final chapter weaves together previous discussions about touch, existing narratives, and paradoxes of representation to discuss Audre Lorde and Evelyne Accad's cancer memoirs. In this chapter, entitled "The Big C Meets the Big O: Pain and Pleasure in Breast Cancer Narratives," I contend that the two women mobilize pain to unmake the medical establishment. Not only are they seeking comfort in their nonnormative bodies (like Alameddine's characters), but they also choose to place those bodies on display in an effort to critique the medical establishment that acts upon them. In addition, they deploy sexual pleasure as an antidote to the pain inflicted by cancer treatment and to counteract those who attempt to silence them. In other words, these women remain aware of their bodies as objects and images, manipulating both in service of their critiques. What makes their critiques more palpable is the discourse of pain. Linguistically, pain forces the body to disappear, since pain carries no object in a grammatical sense. It is only with this rhetorically disappeared body that Lorde and Accad can promulgate critique and allow their bodies to emerge on their (sexual) terms.

This project also opens up a discussion between and about Blacks and Arabs in America on a wide range of issues including Palestine, hierarchies of whiteness, double consciousness, communally sanctioned silence around illness, and the medical establishment. I examine narrative (broadly defined) because stories are never divorced from the circumstances that create them, neither can they be cleaved from the circumstances upon which they comment, nor can they be delinked from the embodied experience that architects them. I have chosen to discuss a variety of social and political concerns because politicized flesh appears in multiple places. To narrow the conversation to one topic dismisses the wide range of critiques these authors and figures make. Moreover, this project is, I hope, the beginning of scholarship that addresses the intersection of Blackness and Arab identity.

NOTES

1. Gene Andrew Jarrett writes a provocative entreaty to scholars regarding the use of "politics" in discussions of literature in his introduction to *Representing*

the Race. He draws a distinction between formal political engagement and informal politics within aesthetic documents, cautioning against a slippage between the two. In my project, I contend that authors advocate for certain formal political engagement within informal media. Their aesthetic engagements, though informal, should not be easily shunted aside. See Gene Andrew Jarrett, *Representing the Race: A New Political History of African American Literature* (New York, NY: NYU Press, 2011).

2. Tobin Siebers, *Disability Theory* (Ann Arbor, MI: U of Michigan Press, 2008), 25.

3. Sharon Holland, *Erotic Life of Racism* (Durham, NC: Duke University Press, 2012), 26–27.

4. William A. Cohen, *Embodied: Victorian Literature and the Senses* (Minneapolis, MN: U of Minnesota Press, 2008), xvi.

5. Simi Linton, *Claiming Disability: Knowledge and Identity* (New York, NY: NYU Press, 1998), 1.

6. Ibid., 2.

7. Ibid., 2.

8. Barbara Nimri Aziz, *Scheherezade's Legacy: Arab and Arab American Women on Writing.* Ed. Susan Muaddi Darraj (Westport, CT: Praeger, 2004), xii.

9. Khaled Mattawa and Munir Akash, *Post-Gibran: Anthology of New Arab American Writing* (Syracuse, NY: Syracuse University Press, 1999), xi.

10. Daphne Brooks, *Bodies in Dissent: Spectacular Performances of Race and Freedom* (Durham, NC: Duke University Press, 2006), 4.

11. Vivian Sobchack, *Carnal Thoughts: Embodiment and Moving Image Culture* (Berkeley, CA: U of California Press, 2004), 4.

12. Therí A. Pickens, "To Be or Not to Be: The Question of Having a Body in Ethnic Studies," *Defying the Global Language: Perspectives in Ethnic Studies.* Eds. Cheryl Toman and Gilbert Doho (Amherst, NY: Teneo Press, Ltd., 2013), 21–22.

13. Maurice Merleau-Ponty, *Phenomenology of Perception.* Trans. Colin Smith (New York, NY: Routledge, 2008), 102.

14. George Alfred Schrader, ed. *Existential Philosophers: Kierkegaard to Merleau-Ponty* (New York: McGraw-Hill, 1967).

15. This is also known as the impossibility of phenomenological reduction. See Schrader.

16. Sobchack, *Carnal Thoughts*, 2.

17. See Maurice Merleau-Ponty, *The Visible and Invisible.* Trans. Alphonso Lingus (Evanston, IL: Northwestern University Press, 1969); Luce Irigaray, *An Ethics of Sexual Difference.* Trans. Carolyn Burke and Gillian Gill (Ithaca, NY: Cornell UP, 1993); Elizabeth Grosz, *Volatile Bodies: Toward a Corporeal Feminism* (Bloomington, IN: Indiana University Press, 1994).

18. Charles Johnson, "A Phenomenology of the Black Body," *Male Body: Features, Destinies, Exposures.* Ed. Laurence Goldstein (Ann Arbor, MI: U of Michigan Press, 1997), 122.

19. Ralph Ellison, *Invisible Man* (New York, NY: Vintage, 1980), 3.

20. Ibid., 3.

21. David Mitchell and Sharon Snyder, *Narrative Prosthesis, Disability, and the Dependencies of Discourse* (Ann Arbor, MI: U of Michigan Press, 2000), 1.

22. Christopher M. Bell, "Doing Representational Detective Work," *Blackness and Disability: Critical Examinations and Cultural Interventions.* Ed. Christopher M. Bell (Berlin: Lit Verlag, 2011), 1.

23. Cherríe Moraga, "Entering the Lives of Others: Theory in the Flesh," *This Bridge Called My Back: Writings by Radical Women of Color.* Eds. Gloria Anzaldúa and Cherríe Moraga (Berkeley, CA: Third Woman Press, 2002), 21.

24. Linda Alcoff, *Visible Identities: Race, Gender, and the Self* (New York, NY: Oxford University Press, 2005), 1.
25. See Nadine Naber and Amaney Jamal, *Race and Arab Americans before and after 9/11: From Invisible Citizens to Visible Subjects*. Eds. Amaney Jamal and Nadine Naber (Syracuse, NY: Syracuse UP, 2008); Sarah Gualtieri, *Between Arab and White: Race and Ethnicity in the Early Syrian American Diaspora* (Berkeley, CA: U of California Press, 2009); Michelle Hartman, " 'this sweet/ sweet music': Jazz, Sam Cooke, and Reading Arab American Literary Identities," *MELUS*. 31.4 (2006): 145–66; Lisa Suhair Majaj, "Arab American Ethnicity: Locations, Coalitions and Cultural Negotiations," *Arabs in America: Building a New Future*. Ed. Michael Suleiman (Philadelphia, PA: Temple UP, 1999), 321–36; Andrea Shalal-Esa, "Arab-American Writers Identify with Communities of Color," *Al-Jadid*. 9.42–43 (2003): 24–26. In Nadine Naber's introduction to *Race and Arab Americans before and after 9/11*, she details the Arab American relationship to whiteness in legal and social terms. Amaney Jamal follows up her points in the conclusion. Sarah M.A. Gualtieri has detailed this relationship extensively in her text *Between Arab and White* regarding the first half of the twentieth century. Other scholars have started with the Arab American relationship to blackness as a point of departure, notably Michelle Hartman, Lisa Suhair Majaj, and Andrea Shalal-Esa.
26. Booker T. Washington, *Up from Slavery* (Boston, MA: Bedford–St. Martin's, 2003)
27. See Elizabeth Ammons, "Black Anxiety about Immigration and Jessie Fauset's *The Sleeper Wakes*," *African American Review*. 42.3–4 (2008): 461–76.
28. See Andrew Shryock, "The Moral Analogies of Race." *Race and Arab Americans before and after 9/11*; Sawsan Abdulrahim, "Whiteness and the Arab Immigrant Experience." *Race and Arab Americans before and after 9/11*; Helen Heran Jun, *Race for Citizenship: Black Orientalism and Asian Uplift from Pre-Emancipation to Neoliberal America* (New York, NY: NYU Press, 2011). Shryock details the Arab American relationship to citizenship when he analyzes the way Arab Americans define their relationship to whiteness. Abdulrahim makes this point abundantly clear when discussing the base consumers of businesses in Dearborn. Helen Heran Jun's book *Race for Citizenship* underscores how blacks' relationship to citizenship and economic capital becomes a contentious part of that community's relationship with Asian Americans. Though Jun's book mainly focuses on Chinese Americans, her analyses are instructive for thinking through this idea.
29. Nadine Naber, *Arab America: Gender, Cultural Politics, and Activism* (New York, NY: NYU Press, 2012), 57.
30. Ibid., 57.
31. Sohail Daulatzai, *Black Star, Crescent Moon* (Minneapolis, MN: U of Minnesota Press, 2012), xi.
32. Ibid., xi–xii.
33. Barbara Aswad, "Attitudes of Arab Immigrants toward Welfare," *Arabs in America: Building a New Future*. Ed. Michael Suleiman. (Philadelphia, PA: Temple UP, 1999), 177–92.
34. See Tanyss Ludescher, "From Nostalgia to Critique: An Overview of Arab American Literature," *MELUS*. 31.4 (2006): 93–114. Scholars have pointed to this wave of immigration as the "third wave." Tanys Ludescher describes the third wave's political awareness's effect on literature. Nadine Naber details the shifting demographic in California's Bay Area in *Arab America: Gender, Cultural Politics, and Activism*. Nadine Naber also points to this phenomenon in terms Arab Americans' the vexed relationship with whiteness in the introduction to *Race and Arab Americans before and after 9/11: From Invisible Citizens to Visible Subjects*.

35. Helen Samhan, "Not Quite White: Race Classification and the Arab-American Experience," *Arabs in America: Building a New Future*, 209.
36. Hartman, "'this sweet/sweet music'," 146–47.
37. Ibid., 147.
38. Therese Saliba, "Resisting Invisibility: Arab Americans in Academia and Activism." *Arabs in America: Building a New Future*, 304–19.
39. Helen Samhan, "Politics and Exclusion: The Arab American Experience," *Journal of Palestine Studies*. 16.2 (1987): 11–28.
40. Specifically, Hartman refers to Majaj's article "Arab American Ethnicity: Locations, Coalitions and Cultural Negotiations." I would add that Majaj's other work highlights these connections as well. See "Arab Americans and the Meaning of Race," *Postcolonial Theory and the United States: Race, Ethnicity and Literature*. Ed. Amritjit Singh and Peter Schmidt (Jackson, MS: U of Mississippi Press, 2000), 320–37; and "New Directions: Arab American Writing at Century's End." *Post-Gibran: Anthology of New Arab American Writing*. Eds. Munir Akash and Khaled Mattawa (Syracuse, NY: Syracuse UP, 1999), 66–77.
41. Andrea Shalal-Esa. "Arab-American Writers Identify with Communities of Color," 24–26.
42. Steven Salaita, *Anti-Arab Racism: Where It Comes From and What It Means for Politics Today* (Ann Arbor, MI: Pluto Press, 2006), 151.
43. Richard Dyer, "The Matter of Whiteness," *White Privilege: Essential Readings on the Other Side of Racism*. 4th edition. Ed. Paula Rothenberg. (New York: Worth Publishers, 2012), 12.
44. Steven Salaita, "Ethnic Identity and Imperative Patriotism: Arab Americans before and after 9/11," *College Literature*. 32.2 (2005): 154.
45. Salaita, "Ethnic Identity and Imperative Patriotism," 146–47.
46. See Randa Kayyalli, *The Arab Americans* (Westport, CT: Greenwood Press, 2006); Gregory Orfalea, *The Arab Americans: A History* (Northampton, MA: Interlink Books, 2006); Rosina J. Hassoun, *Arab Americans in Michigan* (East Lansing, MI: Michigan State University Press, 2005).
47. See Evelyn Alsultany, *Arabs and Muslims in the Media: Race and Representation after 9/11* (New York, NY: NYU Press, 2012).
48. See Evelyn Shakir, "Mother's Milk: Women in Arab-American Autobiography," *MELUS*. 15.4 (1988): 39–50; Evelyn Shakir, "Arab Mothers, American Sons: Women in Arab-American Autobiographies," *MELUS*. 17.3 (1991): 5–15; Evelyn Shakir, "Pretending to Be Arab: Role Playing in Vance Bourjaily's 'The Fractional Man,'" *MELUS*. 9.1 (1982): 7–21.
49. During the fiftieth anniversary that commemorated the March on Washington, Barack Obama lambasted Blacks for putatively poor behavior, citing that their complaint about racial injustice divided the country. He has routinely criticized Black men regarding their role in family life.
50. Minoo Moallem and Iain A. Boal, "Multicultural Nationalism and the Poetics of Inauguration," *Between Woman and Nation: Nationalisms, Transnational Feminisms, and the State*. Eds. Caren Kaplan, Norma Alarcón, and Minoo Moallem (Durham, NC: Duke University Press, 1999), 244.
51. Salaita, *Anti-Arab Racism*, 10.
52. Ibid., 6.
53. Hartman, "'this sweet/sweet music'," 145.
54. Toni Morrison, "On the Backs of Blacks," *Time*, Fall 1993, 57–58.
55. Lisa Suhair Majaj calls for this kind of discussion in her article "Arab American Ethnicity: Locations, Coalitions, and Cultural Negotiations," realizing that this is difficult and fraught territory.
56. Lennard Davis, *Enforcing Normalcy* (London: Verso, 1995), 49. I reference this phrase here to draw out how the concept of normalcy relies on what

disability studies scholar Rosemarie Garland-Thomson, in *Extraordinary Bodies*, has called the normate, "the constructed identity of those who, by way of the bodily configurations and cultural capital they assume, can step into a position of authority and wield the power it grants them." See Rosemarie Garland-Thomson, *Extraordinary Bodies: Figuring Physical Disability in American Culture and Literature* (New York, NY: Columbia University Press, 1996).

57. George Lipsitz, *The Possessive Investment in Whiteness* (Philadelphia, PA: Temple University Press, 2006), viii.

58. Jun, *Race for Citizenship*, 4.

59. Andrea Shalal-Esa, "Arab American Writers Identify with Communities of Color," 24.

60. Jun, *Race for Citizenship*, 4.

61. Holland, *Erotic Life of Racism*, 7.

62. Margrit Shildrick, *Dangerous Discourses of Disability, Subjectivity and Sexuality* (New York, NY: Palgrave Macmillan, 2009), 3.

63. Andrea Smith, "Heteropatriarchy and the Three Pillars of White Supremacy: Rethinking Women of Color Organizing." *The Colour of Violence: The Incite! Anthology.* Ed. Andrea Lee Smith (Cambridge, MA: South End Press, 2006), 70.

64. Toni Morrison. Introduction. *Birth of a Nation 'Hood: Gaze, Script, and Spectacle in the O.J. Simpson Case.* Eds. Toni Morrison and Claudia Brodsky-Lacour (New York, NY: Pantheon, 1997), xvii.

1 Respirating Resistance
Suheir Hammad's Invocation of Breath

In 2001, Suheir Hammad closed the premiere episode of *Russell Simmons Presents DEF Poetry* by reading her poem "first writing since." The last lines were:

> there is life here. Anyone reading this is breathing, maybe hurting,
> but breathing for sure. And if there is any light to come, it will
> shine from the eyes of those who look for peace and justice after the
> rubble and rhetoric are cleared and the phoenix has risen.
>
> affirm life.
> affirm life.
> we got to carry each other now.
> you are either with life, or against it.
> affirm life.[1]

For me watching on television, it was a profound moment because Suheir Hammad voiced what it meant to be an Arab American woman watching "those / buildings collapse on themselves like a broken heart."[2] She spoke poignantly about being simultaneously politically aware and grief-stricken. She also alerted everyone listening to the necessity of affirming life at a time when ideology and rhetoric could overcome compassion and critical thinking. Moreover, she reminded mourning Americans of the danger posed by permitting "the obsessive focus on the Self in the United States [to obscure] the violence against the Other."[3]

The *DEF Poetry* stage emerged as a multicultural and multiethnic site of artistic and political collaboration. The show, which would last six seasons and spark the Tony Award–winning Broadway production, featured a cast of poets who represented a variety of gender presentations, ages, sexual identities, geographies, races, ethnicities, occupations, and, broadly speaking, life experiences. During the first episode, Hammad performed after Nikki Giovanni and Benjamin Bratt, the latter of whom performed a poem by the late Miguel Piñero entitled "Lower East Side." She also performed after Steve Colman, Georgia Me, Lemon, and Black Ice, all of whom would become her costars on *Russell Simmons Presents DEF Poetry on Broadway*.[4]

By featuring Mos Def (now Yasiin Bey) as its host and foregrounding Russell Simmons as its producer, *DEF Poetry* (and the later Broadway production) championed the poetic traditions of hip hop and slam as culturally and commercially viable forms of art. One critic and slam poet commented that with *DEF Poetry* "the marriage between hip-hop and spoken word was finally consummated."[5] Despite the clear multicultural influences within hip hop and slam, the two art forms have been understood as Black American music and poetry. The show fought against that by encouraging various traditions and poetic forms from its artists. The first episode's multicultural lineup serves as a testament to that endeavor,[6] even though critics like John S. Hall felt that *DEF Poetry* was simply slam poetry without scoring.[7] *DEF Poetry* sought to craft a layered and multifaceted definition of poetry and poets for the future while creating a capacious genealogy of multiethnic forebears.

Considering that *DEF Poetry* re-created this context for a televisual medium on a national stage, it is important to note that most of the poets, like Suheir Hammad, had been writing or performing in similar spaces for a number of years. Russell Simmons admits to a *New York Times* critic, "I don't pretend to discover ideas. [. . .] By the time I get hold of something, it's already hot. I bring it to HBO, or Hollywood, or records, and it may be the first time that people have heard it outside of the core, but these people are already cultural heroes in their community."[8] Suheir Hammad had already surfaced as a figure and a writer who not only contributed to that cross-cultural conversation but also enacted it in her own writing. She draws heavily from her experiences as an Arab American from Brooklyn and Palestine. Hammad was born in October 1973 in Jordan. Her family later immigrated to the United States and lived in Sunset Park, Brooklyn, where Hammad experienced the multiethnic space that fundamentally shapes her verse. In interviews, she has described her peers and their experience as a muse for how she shapes counter narratives within her poetry and essays. She notes, "The poorer you are, as in any situation in the world, the less access you have to your own history. I'm a product of the New York City public school system so I can definitely relate to one dominant narrative being projected onto a multi-ethnic, religious, gendered group of people."[9] Hammad's writing is "conscious of the connections among people from different backgrounds and ethnic groups."[10]

Integral to the conversation within this project is the way that Hammad's poetry and essays sustain cross-cultural conversations amid a transparent struggle with language and words. First, language as inadequate or scarce is wedded to the medium of poetry in general and, certainly, spoken word poetic traditions in particular. Though Suheir Hammad is not exclusively a spoken word or performance poet, her affiliation with *DEF Poetry* and hip hop influences how others define her and her work. Hammad also performs at venues (college campuses and others) across the country, solidifying the expectation that her work straddles the page and the stage. The medium of spoken word tends to be considered ephemeral given that performances usually last less than five minutes, or three minutes in slam competitions. The brevity of the performances and the color of the performers often leads reviewers to be reductive, saying "there is a lot of rage on the stage"[11] or that the poetry is merely commentary,[12] or to call the performance a "gathering of angry young poets."[13] What lurks beneath the reviewers' comments is that the poetry does not travel past the stage and that poets are simply speaking from experience rather than crafting a dynamic work of art. Certainly, it is important to acknowledge that Hammad's and other poets' work remains temporally bound to the performance, but it is important to note that their poetry circulates based on the poets' relationship to one another and their audiences. For instance, Lemon mouths the words of other poets while he is onstage with them during group pieces. On the HBO television program, at least two people recited poetry from other poets, including comedian Tracy Morgan and poet/actor Lemon, who chose to perform Etheridge Knight's "Feeling Fucked Up" and "I Sing to Thee of Shine," respectively. At a spoken word venue, it is not uncommon for poets to perform their contemporaries' work as a form of homage or for audience members to recite along with the poet. In short, the ephemerality of the stage performance is not an obstacle, but the beginning of an ongoing conversation.

Second, Hammad draws explicit links between hip hop, Arab oral poetic traditions, and American literature writ large. In one interview, she invokes working-class white male poet Walt Whitman, making it clear that she is part of an oft-forgotten multivalenced narrative.[14] Whitman functions as shorthand for signaling that she and other voices like hers have been excluded from a largely white male (and presumed middle class) narrative about American poetry specifically. Walt Whitman's working-class background surfaces in this context though it has been ignored in others. Hammad's robust set of multicultural influences points to a sentiment expressed by Arab American literary critic Lisa Suhair Majaj: namely, that "contemporary Arab-American literature increasingly reflects the awareness of the need to forge connection beyond the insular boundaries of group identity."[15] Yet, the commentary about American poetics extends beyond the realm of the literary to how we think about inclusion. To be sure, Hammad's claims about language engage with the semiotic question of how words maintain social and political meaning and who determines that meaning. As Edward Said has remarked, the ability to prevent certain stories "from forming and emerging is very important to culture and imperialism, and constitutes one of the main connections between them."[16] In other words, one cannot have domination of bodies without domination of discourse. Hammad focuses on the exclusion of various racialized, gendered, and classed voices. She claims that the result is language that remains ill-equipped to describe, define, or discuss everyone's concerns. Hammad openly discusses the "transparent struggle that [she has] with the poem about finding appropriate language."[17] She recasts words like 'occupation,' 'liberation,' and 'terrorist' to examine why they are automatically ascribed to Arabs and Muslims. For instance, in "first writing since," she asks, "When we talk about holy books and hooded men and death, / why do we never mention the kkk?"[18] Moreover, Hammad points out that people of color do not "have the power of the narrative" so their claims on language and meaning-making remain tenuous.[19] As a result, their words can be "neutralized under the terms 'victim art' and 'political correctness,' [so that their] incursion into territory usually secured for whiteness can momentarily be tolerated and quickly dismissed."[20]

Yet Hammad continues to mobilize the ephemeral to explain and explore concerns that are so easily and summarily dismissed. Turning again to her appearance on *DEF Poetry,* I wish to highlight how she understands breathing as integral to the act of affirming life. Within the logic of poem, those who are breathing make clear that "there is life here." Hammad writes, "anyone reading this is breathing" despite their hurt. She repeats "breathing" and emphasizes it with "for sure." When she underscores that life is present, she explicitly links the heft of existing after this trauma to the quotidian nature of breathing. Her call to "affirm life" is also a call to breathe and to honor those who do so. Notably, Hammad's emphasis on living and breathing does not negate the fragility of either. Instead, her injunction relies on breathing and living as evidence of all our ephemerality. Despite the clear fragility of those actions, Hammad insists upon them as urgent and necessary counterbalances to injustice and pain.

In this chapter, I turn to Hammad for two reasons. First, she mobilizes breath—as metaphor, image, idea, and action—as an act of resistance. Within Hammad's oeuvre, fragility does not need to be overcome or compensated for, but rather embraced as a way to reconstitute the past and move into a politically and socially progressive future. Second, her poetry and essays facilitate cross-cultural conversations between Blacks and Arabs about myriad social and political issues. As noted above, she enacts these conversations within her work based on the influences of hip hop, Arab oral poetic tradition, and spoken word. Of Hammad's invocation of African American jazz traditions, critic Michelle Hartman notes that she "establishes an [Arab American] identity based on a shared cultural feature."[21] In addition, Hammad draws inspiration from Black feminist traditions, particularly June Jordan and Audre Lorde.[22] Hammad finds Jordan's work "powerful and transformative" because Jordan wrote poetry about injustice in Nicaragua and Guatemala during the 1980s and linked it to other injustices in Palestine and the United States.[23] Hammad recalls that reading Jordan transformed her understanding of what poetry can do and who can have a voice. Hammad's poetry takes up a project similar to Jordan's, discussing global injustice and also explicitly linking it back to U.S. domestic issues with race, class, and gender.

Hammad's "first writing since" made her famous both as a spoken word artist and as an artist responding to 9/11/2001. The latter tends toward a partial erasure of Hammad's oeuvre. Positioning herself as indebted to June

Jordan and others places Hammad within a lineage of Black and Brown feminism and activism. Her first collection, *Born Palestinian, Born Black* (1996), and her memoir, *Drops of this Story* (1996), explore the complex interracial landscape of the United States and what it means to write one-self into existence within such a milieu. *Born Palestinian, Born Black* especially illuminates that the issues brought into sharp relief by the attacks on the World Trade Center have long histories. Her first collection includes poems that discuss and critique a wide range of issues, including interracial sexual politics, the Israeli/Palestinian conflict, and the politics of fashion. Shadowing the collection are the vexed terms of visibility that surface only to "silenc[e] critiques of state violence and the structural inequalities that produce hatred and racism."[24] Hammad's poetry works against the erasure through her use of breathing and respiration as a constant image and action, which insists on visibility and tangibility of a different sort.

The readings below make use of phenomenology as a way to access the texts' use of breath. Incorporated (and I use that verb deliberately) into the metaphor of breathing is the act itself. Since phenomenology understands the body as the "first way of access to the world,"[25] I read the metaphors of breathing by focusing on the way their function as part of embodied experience dictates how the metaphors perform in Hammad's poetry. So, before thinking through how Hammad mobilizes breathing as poetic tool, it is important to consider the physiological aspects of the action. Breathing involves both voluntary and involuntary processes. The brain stem controls both since breathing is essential for life function. We breathe to exchange oxygen for carbon dioxide, ridding ourselves of excess heat and water. The respiratory process involves not only the respiratory system but also the nervous system and the circulatory system since breathing helps to regulate the heartbeat, and requires that the nervous system send pulses to the dia-phragm so that it can expand and contract at the appropriate time. Humans have some control over when and how much to breathe so that we can control speech or participate in activities like exercise and singing. Control-ling one's breath is also integral to avoiding inhalation of noxious gases and participating in certain religious practices. As a result, respiration involves physiological processes and bears implications for cultural production. Hammad's poetry highlights the interplay between breathing as a natural phenomenon and as evidence of cultural practice.

In the piece "argela remembering,"[26] the speaker watches the father recon-stitute memory as he smokes an *argela* (water pipe). The act of breathing governs the rhythm and the logic of the poem. When one smokes an *argela,* one must inhale and exhale the smoke, taking care not to allow the smoke into the lungs. It is a process that relies on both the voluntary and involun-tary aspects of breathing. As the father in the poem speaks, he remembers and retells certain aspects of history, the result of which is the tearful end of the poem. The father's breathing sets up the rhythm of the poem, "exhaling Mediterranean breezes / mid east sighs / him telling me." The father expels air both to exhale the smoke of the *argela* and to sigh. His sigh prompts the stories within the poem. On the page, the stories, which begin with the first person plural pronoun, are center justified such that the page's layout performs the exhalation. In other words, the left-justified text appears to exhale the centered text. Since "w" is a labial consonant and requires an exhale, the poem also forces a reader to perform a round of inhalations and exhalations every time the speaker mentions "we."

What subtends the poem is the idea that the foundational story of Israel leaves out the Palestinians. In other words, the inhalation or acceptance of one story is tempered with the exhalation of another. The centered stories, the exhaled stories, present the loss of Palestine. The inhaled stories, or the left-justified verse, points to the acknowledgement of the current situation. After a series of center-justified text, the left-justified text reads:

> inhaling strawberries through argelas
> we've become a people of
> living room politics and tobacco
> stained teeth painfully
> reminding each other.[27]

Echoing the page layout, the speaker inhales in order to tell a different story. Unlike the center-justified verse, this stanza is about the present, not the past. The inhalation is a painful moment of memory and, like the repetitive act of breathing, will be reenacted. It is important to note that the inhalation within the poem is by necessity. It occurs before and after "we" and as a result of moving between center-justified and left-justified text. Since the reading of the poem forces one to return to exhalation, the poem foregrounds it as the more forceful and powerful action. Nonetheless, there cannot be one without the other. However short the inhalations, they remain an opposed but necessary action for maintaining the rhythm of the poem. Here, the poem evokes the tension between Israel's story of its own foundation and Palestinian remembrance. The rhythm suggests that, unlike some real breathing, the pattern of inhale and exhale on the page is not an even exchange. Much more like the process of smoking an *argela,* the history of Palestine has gone through a process of uneven acceptances and articulations.

In "argela remembering," respiration indexes the cultural practice of smoking water pipes as evidence of Palestinian existence. The poem dovetails with Hammad's larger critique of the discourse regarding the Israel/Palestine conflict. Elsewhere, Hammad speaks of Palestinian life as a challenge to the existence of the state of Israel. She points to Golda Meir's statement, made exactly one year before her birth, "I cannot sleep at night knowing how many Arab babies are being born this night."[28] Hammad contends that Meir's statement configures Palestinian existence as a "nightmare for the Israeli enterprise."[29] As a result, she views her birth and all others since as an indication of Palestinian humanity in the face of the desire to deny it. In the poetry, breathing moves the poem along but it still remains metonymic for the other acts that distinguish the human from the inhuman. Not surprisingly, Hammad spotlights independent and critical thought as central to her ability to live. She writes, "In feminist circles, where the fear of anti-Jewish racism has become a muzzle on any critique of Zionism, I can't not be me—a Palestinian whose ancestry traces itself to the 1948 territories, whose existence undermines the legitimacy of the state of Israel."[30] The double negative "can't not" emphasizes that her understanding of herself as a Palestinian is not a choice but an embodied reality. Immediately after her statement, she anticipates the silencing rhetoric that would attempt to erase her and her critique by asking and answering, "Complicated? Not really."[31]

Within the logic of Hammad's oeuvre, the act of breathing constitutes a rebellion since it indicates life. She expresses this sentiment in her poem "talisman" in her second collection, *ZaatarDiva* (2005). She writes:

> It is written
> the act of writing
> is holy words are
> sacred and your breath
> brings out the god in them[32]

The talisman in the poem is the words themselves, but this talisman cannot be carried by paper alone. It has to be coupled with the breath, sacred as she terms it, that gives it divinity. She links words, breath, and power in a triad to stress the idea that they are coextensive. In other words, the talisman (the word) is not powerful without the sacred act of breathing. According to the logic of the poem, the word garners its strength from being inside a living body, a body she acknowledges as unique and powerful. Her link between the power of the word and the sacred nature of the body dovetails with other poems in the *Born Palestinian, Born Black* collection. In "open poem to those who rather we not read. . . or breath [sic]," Hammad links Arawak and Taino peoples to descendants of African slaves and children of exiles who "carry continents in our eyes" and "demand recognition of our humanity."[33] Her poem condemns the historical processes by which people became exiles or slaves and lauds those who have survived: "fascism is in imperial fashion / but we be style [. . .] fashion is passing / style is everlasting."[34] Positioning fascism as temporary and the aforementioned people groups as permanent challenges the notion that fascism and imperialism (and their effects) will remain ad infinitum and also presents hope in the face of what could appear to be enduring oppression.

In contemplating Hammad's use of breathing and embodiment as sacred, the question arises as to whether the delicacy of the body itself counteracts the narrative she attempts to create. Physically speaking, the body and its breath are inherently breakable and temporary. It would seem that a narrative based on them would also be tenuous. Nonetheless, I would argue that Hammad's work does not seek to negate the nature of embodiment but rather uses its delicacy as evidence of its value. Her poetry critiques the idea that fragility equals fungibility. This becomes most clear in her poems about the dead and in her third collection, *Breaking Poems* (2008). In "dead woman," she writes about someone who is doomed to die both spiritually and physically. With the piece, she collapses physical death, the emotional tomb caused by trauma, and people presumed dead. The links between the three are not clear as they seem to be causally related or ironic commentaries. Not only can you "tell a dead woman by the way she walks / going no where a little / too fast," but you can also "smell the death of a woman / on her sister's breath / as the story of her people's / sad laughter is told."[35] In this poem, the dominant narrative and those in power have overwhelmed women (and their people) such that they are counted dead while they are still alive. The reference to a putative dead woman walking acknowledges the fact that the body can do only so much to resist. However, "dead woman" evinces a kind of hope in this fragility. The speaker identifies with the titular character, saying, "I am a dead woman / until we inhale our collective / breath healing / our pierced lungs."[36] To claim this identity in the face of certain demise constitutes a specific act of defiance. It makes clear that the speaker believes the position of the so-called dead more justifiable than the would-be murderers. What appears is a kind of moral rectitude on the part of the speaker. Furthermore, the act of breathing surfaces again as a moment of living defiance. The poem reads "won't breathe / will not breathe / unless my very breath / is a sacred / act of prayer."[37] The speaker's vow to use breath and, by extension, living as a willful act of survival suggests that the fragility of one's body is what makes it an all the more powerful site of resistance. In her poem about honor killings, "of woman torn," the speaker describes the victims: "you join and now those who won't leave / the Earth haunt my sleep / who watch my back / whenever I lay."[38] Their deaths do not point to the evanescence of their life but rather illuminate the influence they hold over the speaker since their memory propels the speaker to action. Memory functions here, not as a simple, discrete moment, but rather a more permanent reservoir from which to draw. It is precisely because of its fragility that the women's lives have an impact.

In *Breaking Poems,* Hammad's poetry creatively mines the limitations of the body to expose the way violence ruptures human experience. Many of the poems break words apart and sounds apart as a way to get through to meaning. She relies on puns and what Lennard Davis has termed the "deaf moment of reading" in which readers must hear the words inside their heads rather than rely on sonic cues to determine meaning.[39] He writes, "All readers are deaf because they are defined by a process that does not require hearing or speaking [. . .] reading is a silent process, and although anyone can vocalize what he or she reads, the vocalization is a second-order activity."[40] The "deaf moment" defamiliarizes one's relationship to text because it privileges sight over sound. Hammad's collection likewise defamiliarizes one's relationship to the text, not only because it privileges sight over sound, but also because it requires one to engage sight to understand sound. The text is often broken apart, indicating that the typeface and the sound create multiple and, at times, varied meanings. For example, the titles all include "break" in some way, usually at the front (i.e., "break (clean)") and sometimes in between words (i.e., "wind(break)her"). "Wind(break)her" sonically refers to the jacket that often shields wearers from environmental elements like wind or rain and provides some warmth. Textually, the title meditates on the possible relationship between a woman, brokenness, and the wind. Separate from, but reliant on, this "deaf moment" is the title's reliance on the literal broken body as an image. Some poems force the reader to impose a structure on the words to determine meaning. Given that all of the poems contain Arabic, which may be unfamiliar to some of her readers, the structures one can impose vary greatly depending on one's linguistic knowledge. Specifically, the last four poems don't follow a deliberate poetic structure as they are rendered in paragraph form and rely on the reader to link the words together however one sees fit. The mere act of doing so creates a rupture, forcing the reader to linguistically enact what has already been done to the people, countries, and places she discusses.

Subtending *Breaking Poems* and, for that matter, all of Hammad's work is the idea that systems of oppression are related, the corollary of which is that people under those systems must seek solidarity and cross-cultural coalition. As mentioned before, Hammad takes her cue from June Jordan, who linked the United States' involvement in Nicaragua in the 1980s to the Israel/Palestinian conflict and racism and sexism within the United States. Specifically, June Jordan's poem "Moving Toward Home" declares

> I was a Black woman
> and now
> I am become a Palestinian
> against the relentless laughter of evil
> there is less and less living room
> and where are my loved ones?
> It is time to make our way home.[41]

Though this is the oft-quoted portion that most impacted Hammad, Jordan's poem in its entirety speaks to the ethical implications of being born into one identity and seeking solidarity with another. To have "become a Palestinian" means that Jordan goes beyond finding commonalities with Palestinians to understand their struggle as her own. This should not be confused with cooptation and simplistic analogies that use one people group's struggle as a metaphor for one's own and erase the other in the process. Instead, Jordan's poem calls for the responsibility to "speak about living room"[42] and create that living room (meaning the room to live and the intimacy of the living room space) in a world where atrocity occurs. Jordan's poem contains a litany of violent acts that she discusses via paralipsis, using the phrase "I do not wish to speak about" and "Nor do I wish to speak about." The latter half of the poem positions her desire to "speak about living room" as an antidote to the activities that she does not want to discuss. Making one's way home occurs despite the unspeakable and because one seeks a space to call home. Furthermore, Jordan's poem implies what Therese Saliba articulates regarding the risk of identifying as Palestinian. Saliba describes the logic behind the stringent attacks on white American activist Rachel Corrie after her death: "She has become Palestinian, and she will be attacked in the same way the Palestinians have always been attacked and their struggle discredited. She will be called a terrorist or a terrorist-sympathizer."[43]

Hammad builds on Jordan's statement in the preface to *Born Palestinian, Born Black* by expanding the definition of Black to include herself. She lists fifteen different usages, including "the coal diamonds are birthed from," "the Arabic expression 'to blacken your face' meaning to shame," "the opposite of white," "Africans in America," "Palestinians in Israel," and "the face of God."[44] In the 2009 reprint of *Born Palestinian, Born Black*, she reprises these definitions, relating them to the poems within the collection, calling the poems "a new embroidery, stitched in june jordan's dark."[45] Not only does she incorporate Palestinians into the definitions she provides, but she also complicates that relationship by highlighting the Arabic phrase regarding shame: 'to blacken your face.' This usage of Blackness opposes other definitions Hammad provides, including "relative purity" and "the face of your grandmother."[46] When Hammad lists all of these usages, she opens up the space to critique the connotations and histories of words. More specifically, the Arabic phrase clarifies that no one's relationship to language is innocent or apolitical. Though someone can identify as Black, that does not immunize that person from perpetrating (linguistic) violence against others who share that identity. Important to this discussion is the way that phrase in particular highlights a possible tension between the various groups of people who could identify as Black, including but not limited to African Americans and Arab Americans. In her words, "We need to own our definitions and live by them. We need not to be afraid to adapt or change them when necessary."[47] Such is the beginning of her interrogation of what it means to be born Palestinian and born Black.

Her other collections add further complexity to the intersections of Arab (specifically Palestinian)[48] and African American identity. Her second collection, *ZaatarDiva*, uses Mahalia Jackson's singing "Walk in Jerusalem" as an epigraph: "Lord knows I'm gonna walk in Jerusalem / talk in Jerusalem / be in Jerusalem / sing in Jerusalem / High up in Jerusalem when I die."[49] Invoking Black transcendental experience, Hammad makes literal the symbolism of this song. "Walk in Jerusalem" is an up-tempo song that expresses joy at the certainty of being in the promised land after death. Hammad's concern with Palestinian self-determination adds a literal aspect to the song in that

there is also joy at being able to walk, sing, and exist in Jerusalem literally—
especially because it is not a possibility for some. Considering that spirituals
like "Walk in Jerusalem" have specific ties to the subjugation of the Black
body, Hammad's epigraph reminds readers that the struggle for Palestinian
liberation is analogous to struggles against racism in America. She not only
indexes Black soul to think through Palestinian occupation but also references the Black body to parallel the Palestinian one.

Breaking Poems foregrounds ruptured linguistic and bodily experience,
blending hip hop and Arab traditions such that they break in waves upon
one another.[50] The 'breaking' in the title refers to one of the four elements
of hip hop—break dancing. Within the poems, Hammad riffs on some of
hip hop's most prominent Black artists, including Nas, the Notorious B.I.G.,
and Erykah Badu. In "break (bayou)," she uses a style reminiscent of Mahmoud Darwish's "Take Care of the Stags, Father"[51] (originally in Arabic)
in that she repeats sounds and words not only for emphasis but also to
dislodge them from being associated with a singular meaning. She repeats
"check" so that it is simultaneously an injunction to investigate, a marker
of completed action, a call to restraint, and evidence of arrested motion. In
that same poem, she signifies on Langston Hughes's "The Negro Speaks of
Rivers" when she writes, "We rhyme of rivers / swim in vernacular."[52] Hammad becomes the deejay of a poem that mixes African American and Arab
American poetic traditions. Her poem spins the two together to create a
cross-cultural conversation about a "soul [that] has grown deep like the rivers"[53] even while one says, "I am from there, I am from here, / but I am neither there nor here."[54] Participants in this conversation also include Michael
Jackson, Nina Simone, June Jordan, Um Kalthom, Fairuz, and others.

Though Hammad midwifes cross-cultural conversations about a wide
variety of topics, she focuses on "uncovering racism and sexism in her
essays and poetry [. . .] urg[ing] women of color to accept themselves as they
are."[55] I would add that her work is not solely about acceptance but also
about fighting against patriarchy. She underscores her message with a focus
on the way women's bodies produce and reproduce in physical and cultural
terms. Her message to women is not just about their own uniqueness as
individuals but also their integral and powerful roles as part of a collective.
Her stance dovetails with Arab American feminist thought that understands
women, queer, and transgender "experiences [as] situated within multiple
overlapping and intersecting structures of power and privilege."[56] Hammad
understands feminism as a quest for a more "socially just and imaginative
world"[57] and views her commitment to various collectives as part of that
quest. Hammad finds kinship with other Arab women writers like Ahdaf
Soueif and Hanan al-Shaykh signaling that she can do it all, meaning retain
her femininity while having a career. Their experiences echo Hammad's own
encounter where she "explored [her] otherness among mostly Black and
Latina girlfriends, [and] began to understand that what [she] wanted to do
most was write [her] stories."[58] Fomented in the crucible of her mother's

creativity and a cadre of girlfriends, Hammad articulates her desire to write about people of color as a particularly feminist enterprise.

Within her conversation with Gloria Steinem for *New York*, Hammad complicates Steinem's understanding of feminism. Hammad's collective has a slightly different constituency than Steinem's and those constituencies have specific needs. Steinem's collective rejects the association of the feminine with the bodily and sees choices against motherhood, for abortion and the like as a victory. Hammad describes a group that is already "more of a body if English isn't the first thing people hear"[59] and so embraces the body as an act of reclamation, making room for motherhood and modesty. In contrast, Steinem does not express sophisticated knowledge about the complexities that choice can bring. She recalls her encounter with women from the Indian subcontinent: "When I visited India, I thought, *Am I going to tell the truth or not?* because they were very traditional young women in the poor part of Mumbai. But I told the truth, which was: not for a millisecond [did I regret not having children]."[60] Steinem's hesitation based on the women's nationality and class position suggests a lack of imagination about what reproductive choices could be and could mean for poor Indian women. She also assumes that the women lead, in Chandra Talpade Mohanty's words, "truncated lives"[61] circumscribed by poverty, education, tradition, domesticity, family, and victim narratives. Steinem's surprise—"and they applauded!"—at their reaction also implies that she had not (yet?) considered the wide array of relationships her audience could have to the idea of motherhood. Hammad follows up: "You know, it's complicated [. . .] there's the possibility of feeling regret about the decisions you've made."[62] Hammad's commentary nuances Steinem's experiences by contemplating that the availability of choice is not the only issue at stake for women of color worldwide. Global feminism must also consider the repercussions after the choice has been made. Hammad's interjections spotlight her commitment to a feminism that forges connections between women of color while it critiques the idea that there is a universal woman's experience.

In Hammad's poetry, she turns to embodied experience as a way to imagine women's collective despite varied experiences. For instance, her poem "exotic" (performed on *DEF Poetry Jam*) echoes the sentiments of two poems that come before it in *Born Palestinian, Born Black*, "delicious" and "may I take your order." All three pieces consider the absurdity of thinking of women's bodies with food metaphors. These ideas are not limited to American women and American foods, but rather extend to Indian, Arab, and Chinese fare. Read in succession, they promulgate the idea that all women share this strange conundrum within patriarchal norms. She questions the consumption of women's bodies in this fashion, asking "why is it men / describe our colors / as edible."[63] The answer—"is it / beacuse [sic] they are / always ever / so ready to // eat us?"—is phrased as another question where 'eat us' is placed in a different stanza. The eating not only connotes consumptive sexual acts like cunnilingus, anilingus, and biting but also queries the way this kind of consumption doubles as violence and erasure. The suitor of "may I take your order" appears desperate for someone he does not understand. The female speaker becomes the "white boy's spam / to be processed diluted canned / so his tender digestion can / take it" even though she gives it a "south of the border tang / w/ jalepeño hips & guacamole looks."[64] When read alongside "delicious," "may I take your order" condemns the politics of desire at work in all three poems. The white male gaze compounds the general male gaze in "delicious" as it brings to bear the power and privilege of race alongside patriarchy. As a corollary, her disavowal of this system in "exotic" calls on a cadre of ethnically stereotyped women and historical figures:

harem girl	geisha doll	banana picker
pom pom girl	pum pum shorts	coffee maker
town whore	belly dancer	private dancer
la malinche	venus hottentot	laundry girl[65]

Her use of the collective points to her understanding that 'la malinche' and 'venus hottentot' have much in common with their sisters the 'banana picker' and the 'geisha doll.' All of the women are exploited and consumed for the pleasure of men who don't understand that "the beat of [their] lashes against each other / ain't some dark desert beat / it's just a blink."[66] The implication of these three poems is that these women's bodies constitute a collective that fights against these ideas, not only by existing in opposition to them, but also by actively rejecting the system in which these ideas flourish.

Hammad refuses to forge connections without asking others to interrogate their relationships to the systems of oppression in which they find themselves. Just as she repeats this work in her preface to *Born Palestinian, Born Black* where she turns a critical eye toward the multiple, conflicting, and offensive uses of Blackness, Hammad asks readers to consider the world beyond their immediate geopolitical space. She expands her critique beyond acknowledging systemic oppression to point out how those systems do not distinguish between one person of color and the next. In "fly away," the speaker addresses a young man living in New York City who wishes to go into the military as a way to cope with poverty, police brutality, and violence. The speaker elucidates a deep irony in the analogies between warfare in urban areas and warfare in other nations. The speaker recounts the conversation: "out my mouth trail the places / america's military has visited" and "out his mouth trail the faces / the young dark faces [. . .] / American society has enlisted."[67] The two remain at an impasse. The speaker laments:

young brother don't wanna
hear bout nuclear bombs and
world domination

he's gotta support his moms
give up donations
for the next funeral

someone else's child died too soon

nurse his uncle
keep his sister outta trouble

all while watchin his back
you never know who's carryin a piece
my words of
revolution and peace
can't get through his cloud[68]

The homonyms—piece and peace—give a sense of the duplicitous nature of both types of warfare. The rhymes also create a sonic correlation between ideas: domination/donation, bombs/moms, and funeral/trouble. The pairs suggest that the two elements are intertwined. World domination must be linked to the necessity of monetary donations. Bombs over there affect moms over here. Or, as Hammad would later write in her poem "first writing since," "over there is over here."[69] The speaker's correlation between the two situations culminates in the line "might as well stay in the city." The young man notes the tragic ironic difference: "at least up in the sky / you got an / eject button / ain't nothing like that down here."[70] The possible eject button offers a suicidal option, metonymic for the military itself and the dangers it poses as a solution to urban blight.

In "fly away," Hammad's poetry performs cultural work similar to her list of the usages of Black. In both, she lays the groundwork to evaluate the conflicting ideas and stances within cross-cultural relationships. Within her work, readers are not allowed to forget the way that conversations between people of color should not "obscur[e] the realities of power differentials [. . .] that make such collaborations and the stories we tell about them fraught."[71] "Fly away" turns a critical eye on the way poverty within the United States forces people of color into being agents of United States military aggression overseas. Yet even as the speaker in the poem urges the young man to consider the implications of being "a techno pegasus with sneakered feet,"[72] the speaker understands that choosing between the air and the concrete feels like no choice at all. The analysis here is not as stringent as that of another poem, "taxi," in which the speaker claims, "its bigger than / our hoods and our heads / it ain't all about this poem / and it ain't all about / taxis / and little white women."[73] One might read "taxi" as an implicit prioritizing of Palestinian concerns over the daily racism that occurs within the United States (i.e., white women who clutch their purses as Black men walk by or the inability of a Black man to hail a taxi in NYC). In that case, both "fly away" and "taxi" lump racism into a category of what people have disdainfully described as so-called first world problems, concerns experienced only by the privileged and wealthy in industrialized nations. Yet the tone of both is plaintive ("fly away" more so than "taxi") and understanding. The speaker implores the listener or reader to critically examine global concerns, balancing that entreaty with an admission that racism and sexism are quotidian and intimate practices that demand one's full engagement.[74]

Her poem "letter to anthony (critical resistance)" links the intimate nature of racism and sexism to their quotidian praxis while it draws connections between Palestinians in Israel and Blacks in America. "Letter to anthony (critical resistance)" has two parts: the first is flanked by the language used in a phone call from a prison and the second discusses the prison industrial complex and other related systems more directly. The poem explores how intimacy between people can be created even when that intimacy is mitigated by narratives about criminality. Similar to her other poetry, Suheir Hammad links intimacy and the ruptures thereof to the body. She writes, "a woman will tell you / every home she has ever inhabited / has been broken into / starting with her body."[75] The woman of this stanza is not an 'every woman' but describes the women that the speaker (presumably Hammad) works with to "place words together / into rhymes or lines."[76] The violation of their bodies, their homes, speaks to a rupture of intimacy that occurs with some degree of frequency. As she notes, "their stories / are not original or fictional."[77] The intimacy between the speaker and Anthony contrasts with the coldness of the outside world. The speaker describes Anthony's letter as "a dozen / handwritten double sided single / spaced muslim oil scented legal / sheets" that juxtapose "polyester hotel rooms."[78] The single-spaced pages have a physical proximity between the words, one that cannot be duplicated by typewritten pages. Moreover, the familiarity of handwriting and the sensuality of the olfactory allows for emotional closeness despite physical distance.

That intimacy breaks when an automated voice interrupts—"this call is from a federal prison"—and reminds them that their conversation is mitigated and monitored by prison authorities.[79] Even the intimacy of being able to hail someone by name severs when Hammad has to include Anthony's prison number alongside his given name, or the names he has chosen for himself (i.e., Nymflow-9 or Nazim). Hammad not only places those phrases within the body of the poem but also turns to a discussion of prisons and criminals in the second part of the poem. She writes:

> i have always loved
> criminals and not only the thugged
> out bravado of rap videos and champagne
> popping hustlers but my father
> born an arab baby boy
> on the forced way out

of his homeland his mother exiled
and pregnant gave birth in a camp[80]

Ending the line with "thugged" takes advantage of the way "thugged" can function as past tense verb and imply passive voice or part of the adjectival phrase "thugged/out." In the former instance, "thugged" emphasizes that criminals are constructed. The latter usage points to the embrace of a criminal persona. The two are not mutually exclusive. In contrast to the thugged-as-made criminal (by self or others), the speaker positions her father as one born into a narrative of criminality. Elsewhere in the poem, she links her father's existence to her own, ventriloquizing Golda Meir, who stated that there is no such thing as a Palestinian.[81] The corollary, which Hammad highlights, is that she too would be considered a criminal. As she sums up, "i have always loved criminals / it is a love of self."[82]

By self-identifying as a criminal constructed by systems and ideologies, Hammad drives home the point that anti-Arab racism and anti-Black racism perform a similar function within nationalist narratives. Steven Salaita describes anti-Arab racism in terms similar to the descriptions of anti-Black racism. He writes that anti-Arab racism is "a phenomenon that, placed in the comprehensive framework of American exceptionalism, is traceable to the very origin of the United States."[83] He links the two more explicitly and his writing is worth quoting at length:

> The origin of American racism is a combination of European colonial values and interaction with Blacks and Indians; [which] became uniquely American as the relationship among White settlers and slaveowners and those they subjugated evolved from a seemingly one-sided display of power to a complicated (and usually discordant) discourse of oppression and resistance, capitalism and egalitarianism, stereotype and self-representation.[84]

In line with the logic of Salaita's argument, Hammad's poem makes clear that the construction of the criminal Palestinian also has its origins in the creation of the state of Israel. Two aspects of their social positioning link the two groups: first, they are constructed as criminals based on the logics of cultural or geopolitical nationalism (or both); second, they experience the repercussions of this narrative in ways that break apart quotidian moments of intimacy like talking or interpellation.

Recall that reading Hammad's poems "exotic," "delicious," and "may i take your order?" in tandem makes clear how the politics of desire works similarly across racial lines and opens up the space for women to speak to each other about their experiences. Similarly, reading "fly away," "taxi," and "letter to anthony (critical resistance)" makes explicit links between impoverished people of color in the United States and disenfranchised people of color across the globe. These three poems also ask, what can the

Palestinian struggle for liberation and self-determination say to the struggles of people of color within the United States and vice versa? As with most poems, Hammad's work does not propose answers, but it does open up the space for conversation. Of course, Hammad gives this conversation some parameters. First, she makes it clear that the two struggles are not in hierarchical relationship to one another, but rather exist simultaneously. She links the thugged-out rappers with those born Arab in much the same way that she equalizes the stereotypes of women in "exotic." Here, her sparse style functions much in the style of Langston Hughes's work, which one scholar described as "simple but not simplistic" verse that puts forward a "strategic move both for keeping fresh an awareness of ongoing betrayal and for asserting the betrayed's refusal to be defined or defeated by that betrayal."[85] Second, she lays bare that systems of oppression rely on similar logics in order to function. Both anti-Arab and anti-Black racism rely on the criminalization of the other in order to create nationalist narratives about belonging. Just as Salaita drew parallels to African American and Native studies scholarship to craft his exploration of anti-Arab racism, Hammad links systems of oppression because they all function by bestowing privileges on one group while justifying the (violent) exclusion and dehumanization of another. Third, she highlights that we are all implicated in the perpetuation of these systems. This idea is most salient in the critique of "fly away" and the solipsism undergirding "taxi." It also surfaces in Hammad's spotlight of the Arabic phrase meaning 'to shame,' translated as 'to blacken one's face.' In Hammad's oeuvre, resistance to the lure of the military or highlighting global oppression or changing one's language would function similarly to Audre Lorde's army of one-breasted post-mastectomy women marching on Capitol Hill (which I discuss in chapter 5).[86] One would protest as an ethical response to the pain of others and in the face of one's own pain.

Contemplating the parameters for this cross-cultural conversation returns us to the salient features of Hammad's poetic enterprise. She insists upon people as valuable based on their embodied fragility and despite the narratives and histories that attempt to erase their experience. Here, their flesh, their breathing, become political acts of resistance and reclamation. In "break (clean)," Hammad mobilizes the vulnerability of the broken body to suggest that these acts of living and resisting are neither discrete nor divorced from the creation of history. Much of the poem focuses on the metaphorical and literal meanings of the term 'clean break.' Such a formulation suggests that rupture can be neat and, by extension of the metaphor, easy to repair. Instead, the poem suggests that breaking and healing always hurt and, after, there are consistently and simultaneously multiple forms of breaking and healing. For instance, one of the subjects of the poem is a woman who has had her heart broken. It reads, "healing swell then bruise then harden cuts heal like hearts please God this hurt do not calcify."[87] Here the physical cut and a broken heart conflate as they both risk healing inappropriately or with residue embedded. The natural process delineated by swelling, bruising, and hardening suggests that the body and the heart undergo analogous processes that forever alter the places where they have been broken. So it is not altogether impossible to imagine that "each hurt sings own song"[88] and that the breaks will never be clean.

Given what it implies about breaking and healing, "break (clean)" is also a praise song for the nonviolent. Praise songs are typically recited in times of celebration and include a set of laudatory remarks about one particular place, person, or event. Hammad's version functions similar to Elizabeth Alexander's "Praise Song for the Day" (read at President Obama's 2008 inauguration). Both celebrate a cluster of people and their survival. Hammad's poem begins with a recitation of the setting: "dawn sky midnight long past lightening dusk rose horizon."[89] These could be several temporal settings, including dusk, dawn, and midnight. Given that references various points in the evening, the speaker suggests that this poem takes place anywhere, implying that the temporal setting becomes inconsequential because those who are broken exist regardless of it. Much of the poem details how and why a heart or a body is broken by saying "radio reports growing exodus west bank life no future" and asking about the terms under which a heart and body could be broken: "how many times can you refugee?"[90] In forming the question, the speaker sets the stage for those who live despite trauma, those who "break new dream," or those who, in other words, attempt to imagine a future. When the speaker explains with an oath, "w'allah even in war women cry over hearts broken / wa even in privilege women want," the implication is that life continues in multiple forms during war and that the machinations of human emotion do not stop in the face of atrocity. By the time we arrive at the end of the poem, when the speaker declares "god bless the non-violent / ooooh God bless them,"[91] what becomes clear is that the entire poem has been seeking those who would allow for the possibility of healing clean amid chaos. The poem becomes an homage to and celebration for those whose nonviolence opens up the possibility of healing.

"break (clean)" explicitly links the embodied experiences of healing and brokenness with the various kinds of brokenness forced by war. Hammad writes with the same ironic posture toward transitioning in "break (transition)," noting that the idea of a 'smooth transition' belies the violence embedded in shifts of power. She invokes the language of magic to draw attention to a more sinister manipulation regarding the disappearance of bodies, people, and histories in the state of Israel. The poem begins with a sleight of hand saying,

There is no body
no matter

i gave it away wila it was taken w'allah what i had
what i had wanted to say was

w'allah if someone touches me
i will break open sesame abracadabra arab cadavers posted[92]

The idea that there aren't any bodies misleads one into believing the sentiment of the next line, which is that the body (or lack thereof) is not important. Yet the next stanza invokes a common phrase known to signal a lie or equivocation, "what had happened was,"[93] by hesitating in its language as it explains the reasons why there is no body. The third stanza erupts with a swear ('w'allah' means 'by God') and a promise borne out of volatile emotion, so unpredictable that it will break open. The subsequent references to magic prompt a reconsideration of the initial sleight of hand. Is it true that there is no body or no matter? Is it true that the question does not matter? The references to magic continue to fluster the notion of what is true. The speaker says, "once there was path here habibi / once there was road" and ends with the statement "I left my body somewhere / I remember rooms / bas i don't remember walls."[94] Conceiving this question of the body or the missing body as a magic trick crystallizes the importance of reconsidering the logic attributed to the settler patterns of Israel. Was it a land without a people for a people without a land? The poem hints that it was not and that the state's existence was built on the disappearance of bodies. Naming the poem "break (transition)" also mocks the conception that this transition was peaceful or smooth. Instead, the poem implies that it was a fundamental rupture, not just of rooms and roads, but also of truth and lies.

Both "break (clean)" and "break (transition)" drive home several key components of Hammad's work. She links the fragility of the body and the temporary nature of embodied experience with the construction of narratives about people groups. For her, bodily presence is neither incidental nor accidental, but rather evidence of the fundamental value of human life. She ruptures language to force a re-examination of commonly used words and their attendant meanings for nationalist and imperialistic projects. Hammad's work also proposes a set of cross-cultural conversations about what people of color across the globe can say to one another despite being implicated in the domination of one another often imposed by nation-states in their name (and without their permission). Nonetheless, Hammad's work raises two important questions that undergird the next chapter. First, if the body is a site of resistance, what happens when that body is violated? Second, how does ephemeral embodied experience (that leaves lasting effects) transform social and political discourses of representation?

NOTES

1. Russell Simmons, director, *Russell Simmons Presents DEF Poetry Season 1* (2001; New York, NY: HBO Home Video, 2004). DVD.
2. Ibid.
3. Nirmala Erevelles, *Disability and Difference in Global Contexts: Enabling a Transformative Body Politic* (New York, NY: Palgrave Macmillan, 2011), 121.
4. Simmons, *DEF Poetry Season 1*.
5. Cristin O'Keefe Aptowicz, *Words in Your Face: A Guided Tour through Twenty Years of the New York City Poetry Slam* (New York, NY: Soft Skull Press, 2008), 262–63.

6. Steve Colman is white. Georgia Me, Black Ice, and Nikki Giovanni are African American. Benjamin Bratt is Peruvian American. Bratt performed poetry by Puerto Rican poet Miguel Piñero. Lemon has explicitly identified as Puerto Rican, though he also identifies himself as mixed race in the final episode of *DEF Poetry*.

7. See Aptowicz, *Words in Your Face*; Simmons, *DEF Poetry Season 1*.
Poets in the series draw from a wide variety of influences, including but not limited to praise songs, comedy, blues, rap, hip-hop, slam formats, Caribbean storytelling, Arab poetry, soliloquy, and beat poetry. In Aptowicz's book, John S. Hall commented in an interview that slam poetry is an art form that encourages one simplistic style. His comments seem to stem from the idea that New York City slam, as affiliated with the Nuyorican Poetry Café, discusses primarily identity politics, which he seems to believe are exclusively the domain of non-white people.

8. Jon Pareles, "A New Platform for the New Poets," *New York Times*. 10 November 2002. Section 2: 1.

9. Marcy Jane Knopf-Newman, "Interview with Suheir Hammad," *MELUS*. 31.4 (2006): 74.

10. Andrea Shalal-Esa, "Arab American Writers Identify with Communities of Color," *Al-Jadid*. 9.42–43 (2003): 26.

11. Lynda Richardson, "From Amman, Jordan, to Broadway, Via Brooklyn," *New York Times*. 14 March 2003. Section B: 2.

12. Elysa Gardner, "'Def Poetry Jam' Is All Relative," *USA Today*. 15 November 2002. 7.

13. Ben Brantley, "Theater Review; Untamed Poetry, Loose Onstage," *New York Times*. 15 November 2002. Section E: 1.

14. Pareles, "A New Platform for the New Poets," 1.

15. Majaj, "Arab-American Ethnicity: Locations, Coalitions, and Cultural Negotiations," 326.

16. Edward Said, *Culture and Imperialism* (New York, NY: Vintage, 1994), xiii.

17. Knopf-Newman, "Interview with Suheir Hammad," 75.

18. Suheir Hammad, *ZaatarDiva* (New York, NY: Cypher Books, 2008), 100.

19. Knopf-Newman, "Interview with Suheir Hammad," 80.

20. Jill Dolan, "Utopia in Performance," *Theatre Research International*. 31.2 (2006): 168.

21. Hartman, "'this sweet/sweet music'," 159.

22. See Michelle Hartman, "A *Debke* Beat Funky as P.E.'s Riff: Hip Hop Poetry and Politics in Suheir Hammad's *Born Palestinian, Born Black*," *Black Arts Quarterly*. 7.1 (2002): 6–8; Suheir Hammad, *Born Palestinian, Born Black* (New York, NY: Harlem River Press, 1996). Hammad notes this influence herself in interviews and within *Born Palestinian, Born Black*. Michelle Hartman has discussed it also.

23. Knopf-Newman, "Interview with Suheir Hammad," 78.

24. Naber and Jamal, *Race and Arab Americans before and after 9/11*, 3.

25. Merleau-Ponty, *Phenomenology of Perception*, 102.

26. Hammad, *Born Palestinian, Born Black*, 31–34.

27. Ibid., 32.

28. Knopf-Newman, "Interview with Suheir Hammad," 72.

29. Ibid., 72.

30. Suheir Hammad, "Composites," *Signs: Journal of Women in Culture and Society*. 28.1 (2002): 471.

31. Ibid.

32. Hammad, *ZaatarDiva*, 59.

33. Hammad, *Born Palestinian, Born Black*, 81.

34. Ibid., 82–83.

35. Ibid., 53.
36. Ibid., 54.
37. Ibid., 54.
38. Hammad, *ZaatarDiva*, 76.
39. Lennard Davis, *Enforcing Normalcy*, 100–108.
40. Ibid., 4.
41. June Jordan, *Directed by Desire*. Eds. Jan Heller Levi and Sara Miles (Port Townsend, WA: Copper Canyon Press, 2007), 400.
42. Ibid., 399.
43. Therese Saliba, "On Rachel Corrie, Palestine, and Feminist Solidarity." *Arab American Feminisms: Gender, Violence, and Belonging.* Eds. Rabab Abdulhadi, Evelyn Alsultany and Nadine Naber. (Syracuse, NY: Syracuse UP, 2011), 187.
44. Hammad, *Born Palestinian, Born Black*, x.
45. Hammad, *Born Palestinian, Born Black and the Gaza Suite* (New York, NY: UpSet Press, 2010), 9.
46. Hammad, *Born Palestinian, Born Black*, x.
47. Ibid., x.
48. It is important to note that Suheir Hammad has eschewed identification as Arab American, saying, "I mean, I didn't grow up Arab American—what the fuck is Arab American? I grew up Palestinian and Brooklyn, really specifically." See Knopf-Newman. Elsewhere I discuss the reason why I use the term 'Arab American' to describe her and her work. See Therí A. Pickens, "'Mic Check: Can You Hear Me?': Suheir Hammad and the Politics of Spoken Word Poetry," *Al-Raida*. 124 (Winter 2009): 8–14.
49. Hammad, *ZaatarDiva*.
50. I am aware that hip hop is not an exclusively black art form. However, it is important to note that several aspects of the music racialize it as black: the music's ties to African American traditions of jazz, blues, and African diasporic traditions of reggae, dancehall, and salsa; the subject matter that depicts the urban poor, who tend to be disproportionately black and brown; the media association of rap and hip hop with black people; and the racial identity of many prominent hip hop artists. For a fuller history of hip hop, see Jeff Chang, *Can't Stop Won't Stop: A History of the Hip-Hop Generation* (New York, NY: Picador, 2005).
51. I have chosen to reference the English translation here, though the original Arabic version, especially when performed, best showcases the point I wish to make. The title of the poem in Arabic, "Rabbi Al-Aya'il Ya Abi Rabbiha" (Raise the Stags, Father, Raise Them), repeats the command, showcasing the multiple valences of the word. See Mahmoud Darwish, *If I Were Another*. Trans. Fady Joudah (New York, NY: Farrar, Straus and Giroux, 2011), 9–15; Fady Joudah, Email message to author. July 9, 2013.
52. Hammad, *Breaking Poems* (New York, NY: Cypher Books, 2008), 25.
53. Langston Hughes, "The Negro Speaks of Rivers," *The Norton Anthology of African American Literature*. Eds. Henry Louis Gates, Jr., and Nellie Y. McKay (New York, NY: W.W. Norton & Company, 1996), 1254.
54. Mahmoud Darwish, "Counterpoint." *If I Were Another: Poems*, 183.
55. Shalal-Esa, Andrea. "Arab American Writers Identify with Communities of Color," 26.
56. Rabab Abdulhadi, Evelyn Alsultany, and Nadine Naber, eds. *Arab American Feminisms: Gender, Nation, and Belonging* (Syracuse, NY: Syracuse UP, 2011), xxv.
57. Emily Nussbaum, "In Conversation: Gloria Steinem and Suheir Hammad: A Feminist Rising Star on the Sexual Revolution, the Booty-Call Nineties, and the Superwoman Myth." *New York* (2008). http://www.nymag.com.

58. Suheir Hammad, "In My Mother's Hands." *Essence*. 29.1 (1998): 70.
59. Nussbaum, "In Conversation."
60. Nussbaum, "In Conversation."
61. Chandra Talpade Mohanty, "Under Western Eyes: Feminist Scholarship and Colonial Discourse." *The Women, Gender, and Development Reader*. Eds. N. Visvanathan, L. Duggan, L. Nisonoff, and N. Wiegersma (London: Zed Books, 1997), 80.
62. Nussbaum, "In Conversation."
63. Hammad, *Born Palestinian, Born Black,* 61.
64. Ibid., 67.
65. Ibid., 70.
66. Ibid., 69.
67. Ibid., 45.
68. Ibid., 46.
69. Hammad, *ZaatarDiva*, 102.
70. Hammad, *Born Palestinian, Born Black*, 47.
71. Carolyn Sorisio, "Introduction: Cross-Racial and Cross-Ethnic Collaboration and Scholarship: Contexts, Criticism, Challenges," *MELUS*. 38.1 (2013): 2.
72. Hammad, *Born Palestinian, Born Black*, 45.
73. Ibid., 14.
74. The idea that racism and sexism are quotidian practices is not new, but in forming this idea, I lean on Sharon Holland's work in *The Erotic Life of Racism,* which asks us to construct new relationships between queer theory and race theory. Her work begins from the standpoint that the two are intimately linked.
75. Hammad, *ZaatarDiva*, 65.
76. Ibid., 64.
77. Ibid., 65.
78. Ibid., 64.
79. Ibid., 65.
80. Ibid., 66.
81. Golda Meir, "Mrs. Meir Bars Any 'Deal' for Israel's Security." *The Washington Post*. 16 June 1969. Section A: 15.
82. Hammad, *ZaatarDiva*, 67.
83. Salaita, *Anti-Arab Racism*, 5.
84. Salaita, *Anti-Arab Racism*, 5–6.
85. Karl Henzy, "Langston Hughes's Poetry and the Metaphysics of Simplicity," *Callaloo*. 34.3 (2011): 915–27.
86. In *The Cancer Journals*, Black feminist thinker and activist Audre Lorde calls for an army of one-breasted women to march on Capitol Hill as a way to protest environmental policies that allow for the spread of carcinogens. See Audre Lorde, *The Cancer Journals* (San Francisco, CA: Aunt Lute Books, 1997).
87. Hammad, *Breaking Poems*, 41.
88. Ibid., 41.
89. Ibid., 41.
90. Ibid., 41.
91. Ibid., 41.
92. Ibid., 46.
93. Ibid., 46.
94. Ibid., 46.

2 Try a Little Tenderness
Tactilic Experience in Danzy Senna and Alicia Erian

This chapter turns from one ephemeral experience to another, from breathing to touching. As Suheir Hammad's poetry has shown, the mundane and precarious nature of bodily functions, like breathing, opens up the space for coalition building and shared political enterprise. As her poem "letter to anthony (critical resistance)" makes clear, racism and sexism disrupt not only the ability to breathe freely but also the possibility of creating intimacy. Following that logic, the question arises as to how we understand touches between people with politicized flesh. Considering that touch affirms one's existence, how does touch function when one's presence remains fraught?

By way of partial answer, I examine two *bildungsromane* about mixed race protagonists for the way that their stories of growth trouble national narratives of belonging.[1] As Werner Sollors notes in *Neither Black nor White yet Both*, the subject of Black/white love and relationships "elicit[s] censure and high emotions, or at least a certain nervousness."[2] Of the representations, he notes "what is subjected to socially approved, attempted or legalized bans in real life is often also censored, suppressed, denied or rejected."[3] Yet as the sheer volume of his tome (and others' work) demonstrates, representations of Black/white relationships and their resulting progeny have not been scarce. The presence of mixed race individuals forces the questions Rebecca Walker so adroitly asks: "Which multiracial narrative fits our ethos of triumph over great odds? Which reaffirms our hopeful belief that our country really is a place everyone can call home?"[4] The commonplace narrative that mixed race people are caught between two worlds points to an anxiety within the national consciousness about the nature of belonging and the significant racial and ethnic tension that exists between multiple groups. The other, ostensibly more hopeful, narrative, that mixed race peoples symbolize hope and progress, obfuscates the fact that, in the words of poet Sarah Jones, "the revolution does not happen between [one's] thighs."[5]

As Michelle Elam and others have argued, these formulations put pressure on the mixed race subject to function in primarily, if not exclusively, representative terms.[6] In short, these narratives call mixed race protagonists to exist solely in the service of others' aims and desires, "between [. . .]

competing hagiographic and apocalyptic impulses."[7] Other scholars have argued that Black/white biracials in particular have been mobilized as figures to perform this kind of critical work, but that the figure of the mulatto, to use a historically situated term, evinces more about racial anxiety than the possibility of harmony. According to Hortense Spillers, "the 'mulatto/a,' just as the 'nigger' tells us little or nothing about the subject buried beneath them, but quite a great deal more concerning the psychic and cultural reflexes that invent and invoke them."[8] Such understandings of this figure are not simply relegated to the late nineteenth or early twentieth century in America, but rather, according to Michelle Elam and Werner Sollors, expand to include other parts of the globe, the late twentieth century, and the early twenty-first century.[9] Yet, the anxiety about the fate of multiracials remains as new invocations of biracialism "call for challenges to the unimpeachability of sight and recognize that the obsession with seeing race is also a necessarily flawed search for ontological gratification."[10]

It is worth noting how the Arab American literary tradition has engaged differently than the African American one with regard to mixed race. Whereas Black literature has consistently showcased protagonists who have one Black parent and a parent of a different race, Arab American writing developed a different literary tradition *vis-à-vis* mixed race subjectivity. For the sake of brevity, I must discuss the Arab American tradition in broad terms. I acknowledge that there are outliers and exceptions to the schema below, but I seek to provide a way to understand how this tradition discusses mixed race identity. For scholars of Arab American literature, mixed race may appear to be a dubious way of describing a tradition that deals primarily with biculturality as one of its main tropes. More specifically, the narratives about Arab Americans refer primarily to their biculturality as being both American, by virtue of living within the borders of the United States, and Arab, because of kinship and heritage ties to the Arab world. Many writers consider themselves Arabs in America, retaining the culture and customs of the Arab world while trying to adjust to the United States to varying degrees. They point out the troublesome nature of being forced to choose sides and the difficulty of navigating the spaces between, when the nations that represent those spaces have an antagonistic relationship. These writers discuss the differences between the cultures in the Arab world and those of the United States; most often, their texts traverse the United States and the Arab world (and sometimes Europe) to do so.

We can trace this trope from the first published Arab American novel and first Arab American work published in English, Ameen Rihany's *The Book of Khalid* (1911), wherein the main character traverses the United States and Lebanon in search of a spiritual connection to either place. He decides to live in Lebanon because that is the place he can comfortably call home. Ameen Rihany's contemporaries, including Mikhail Naimy and Kahlil Gibran, explored similar themes of homeland and exile. Vance Bourjaily's *Confessions of a Spent Youth* (1961) tells the story of a man who learns about his connection to his Arab heritage while fighting in World War I. Evelyn Shakir labels Bourjaily's work paradigmatic of the concerns held by the children of the first wave of Arab immigrants to the United States. The children attempted to make sense of their heritage, though their parents chose to assimilate.[11] Writers of this generation include the novelists William Peter Blatty and Eugene Paul Nassar, as well as the poets Sam Hamod, Sam Hazo, D. H. Melham, and Lawrence Joseph, though not all of these writers articulated the same concerns. The use of biculturality as a trope continued into the 1990s; one such example is Joseph Geha's *Through and Through* (1990), a collection of short stories that depicts an Arab American community's ties to the Arab world and the pressure of living in the United States. Certainly, writers who have published after Geha continue thinking of Arab American identity in the very interesting and fruitful terms associated with biculturality. J. Kadi's edited collection *Food for Our Grandmothers* explicitly seeks to "[offer] landmarks, signposts, names, and directions not only for Arab-American and Arab-Canadian communities but for other communities of color and our allies."[12] Other writers engaged in describing and depicting biculturality include (and this list is by no means exhaustive) Pauline Kaldas, Suheir Hammad, Susan Muaddi-Darraj, Rabih Alameddine, Randa Jarrar, Laila Halaby, and Mohja Kahf.

In recent years, some Arab American writers have shifted their focus from biculturality to an idea that resembles biraciality or mixed race identity. 'Biracial' is a useful but problematic term, as Arab is legally (and in some social circles) considered an ethnic white identity, though it has been racialized. Diana Abu Jaber's *Arabian Jazz* (1993) and *Crescent* (2003) feature protagonists with one Arab parent and one American parent, paying particular attention to how they understand their dual heritage. Laila Halaby's debut novel, *West of the Jordan* (2003), Rabih Alameddine's *I, the Divine: A Novel in First Chapters* (2001), Pauline Kaldas's *Letters from Cairo* (2007), and Alicia Erian's *Towelhead* (2005) have minor and major characters who have one Arab parent. I don't want to overstate the difference between the use of the bicultural and mixed heritage tropes, but I do want to point out that having one American parent shifts the conversation about immigrant status and rights to a conversation about kinship and blood ties to America. The latter, much more similar to the African American tradition's engagement with mixed race, explicitly grants the characters a heritage from and, therefore, an inheritance from the United States. Citizenship requires that one "be read as unreadable" in order to participate by "pass[ing] as invisible by fading into equivalence."[13] Arab American mixed heritage characters have a great deal in common with their African American counterparts in that they spotlight the way others' "fractured projections"[14] bear implications for national narratives of inclusion. In line with Steven Salaita's aforementioned arguments in *Anti-Arab Racism in the USA*, troubling race and racial formation for Arab Americans and African Americans strikes at the heart of the foundational narratives of the United States.[15]

In Alicia Erian's *Towelhead* (and director Alan Ball's filmic interpretation) and Danzy Senna's *Symptomatic*, the tactile emerges as a way to navigate the touching of the mixed race characters' bodies. At the hands of others, they experience violent touching that attempts to corral them into narratives that fetishize or exoticize. Under their own hands, recuperative touch becomes a fail-safe so that they can begin to construct themselves. Both texts rely on the experiences of middle-class mixed race characters to query the position of Arab American and African American identities within a national racialized hierarchy where whiteness resides at the apex. The narratives suggest that adhering to whiteness as a standard curtails a more complex conversation about the intertwined nature of identities and nationhood. Moreover, these two *bildungsromane* challenge the way white privilege—even from liberals—displaces Arab American and African American claims to an inclusive national narrative.

The unnamed narrator in *Symptomatic* is a recent college graduate living in New York City who has an African American father and a white mother. Based on her phenotype, her body is interpreted as white by others.[16] She has romantic encounters, professional friendships, and acquaintances that end or become complicated by the other parties' assumptions about her racial background. In navigating those relationships, the unnamed narrator uses her social savvy to avoid disclosing the truth of her parentage, out of a desire that it not be a focal point in her relationships. Her romantic entanglement with Andrew, a wealthy young white man, goes sour after his friends make racist jokes in her presence. She seeks friendship with an older biracial woman, Greta (also known as Vera), who is resentful of racial and gender politics. Even when the narrator is recognized as biracial, she feels she must openly strive to finagle out of the common and simplistic ideas about biraciality.

Jasira, the 13-year-old protagonist in *Towelhead*, is also of mixed heritage: her father, Rifat, is Lebanese American and her mother, Gail, Irish American. However, she is not as socially savvy as the unnamed narrator in *Symptomatic*, a trait that crystallizes when she makes many of her observations about race and sex. Her observations are all the more unsettling because she appears so woefully immature, if one is being generous, or stupid, if one is reading less charitably. Jasira's naïveté about sexuality leads her into an inappropriate sexual relationship with her army reservist neighbor, Mr. Vuoso, and another sexual relationship with her Black classmate, Thomas Bradley. My readings, by necessity, focus not only on Jasira but also on how others, namely Vuoso, interact with her and read her body. Her lack of social savvy makes her understanding of her experiences inaccessible through the text. Rather than conjecture, I turn to Vuoso's actions. His bodily experience reveals the disjuncture between the way Jasira is understood by others as one who is acted upon (subjective object) and the way Jasira understands herself as one who acts (objective subject).

In keeping with the phenomenologically grounded readings of this project, it is important to note the way the tactile functions. It is in the act of touching and being touched that we exhibit how much we are simultaneously a subjective object (one who is perceived as an object that is acted upon) and an objective subject (one who is a subject who acts upon others). As Elizabeth Grosz and Margrit Shildrick have noted, touch requires reciprocity, reflexivity, and reversibility.[17] One cannot touch without touching. Given that relationship, touch enacts the dissolution of the boundaries between self and other. By touching something, we understand it to be an object separate from ourselves and understand ourselves as distinct from it even while our touching binds us to it physically. This is not altogether different from acts of vision, but tends to be viewed as impoverished because of the way Western philosophical tradition privileges vision and sight. Given that touch is constitutive, who touches whom and when and why governs the possibilities of a self-determined subjectivity. In *Towelhead* and *Symptomatic*, there are multiple kinds of touches and all have their distinct methods of constituting the touched. The grab is different from the caress is different from the tap. The unwanted and rapacious touch is different from the missed opportunity for touch, which is also different from the touch fueled by desire. As Shildrick explains, "We do not all engage with [the] world on an equal basis and some of us experience greater restraints on touching than others."[18] In *Towelhead*, Jasira's experiences question whether touch ought to be viewed as impoverished, as it is the basis of how she is constituted by others. Her father's abuse, Mr. Vuoso's rape, and, her boyfriend Thomas's caress have a hand, so to speak, in making and unmaking her. *Symptomatic*'s unnamed narrator takes for granted that touch is as important as other senses because she avoids and makes use of it to create and re-create herself. Elizabeth Grosz's discussion of the touch as a gendered endeavor highlights how contact with young women's bodies becomes part of an explicitly gendered narrative of touch. She writes, "The coding of femininity with corporeality in effect leaves men free to inhabit what they (falsely) believe is a purely conceptual order while at the same time enabling them to satisfy their (sometimes disavowed) need for corporeal contact through their access to women's bodies and services."[19]

Since these texts work against the visual as a reliable marker of racial identification, it is not surprising that sight takes on an impoverished quality. Irigaray, in her revision of Merleau-Ponty, notes that the visual cannot be collapsed into the tactile.[20] She explains, "[t]he eye objectifies and it masters. Sits at a distance and maintains a distance."[21] In these texts, narratives about gender and race abet that distance and maintain it. Some characters, namely Vuoso and Andrew, force themselves to look from their distance as white men to gain clarity. Yet their focus and observations remain incomplete because they cannot be corroborated by touch. In opposition to ideology and stereotype, the boundaries of the body itself, constituted by touching and being touched, make and remake these young women's subjectivities.

Though touching does not wholly replace the visual as a way to make sense of the world, the characters confirm that "the visible needs the tangible."[22] By challenging the relationship between vision and touch, the characters upend the ideas about race and national belonging that hinge on vision as a privileged sense. These characters enact what bell hooks terms the "oppositional gaze," one that opens up the space for agency in looking back but also reinterpreting the looks of others.[23] In sum, the emphasis on the tactile as a primary sense-making modality confronts an "equality [. . .] predicated on exclusion and visibility [as] the 'optic' to read citizenship."[24] If we can no longer rely on what we see to determine who belongs, these works question whether our criteria for belonging make sense.

In *Symptomatic*, vision is the impoverished sense and the tactile must corroborate it in order for the characters to understand each other. The unnamed narrator attempts to explain this phenomenon by discussing contexts as necessary for what is visible to become clearly interpreted. For her, context attempts to map a set of narratives on one's body that isn't always entirely true. She says, "Every day in this new city I was trying to live in the purity of the present, free from context. Contexts, I knew, were dangerous: Once you put them in the picture, they took over."[25] Drawing on the literary definition of the term, this unnamed narrator suggests that other texts precede and follow her, the original passage, such that determining meaning rests with understanding the portions that come before and after. For her, context confines and, unlike contexts in literary studies, limits the interpretation available. Specifically, she seeks freedom from racial identification and wants her body to become a set of unreadable facts. Being an unnamed narrator references other African American literary works that explicitly explore racial invisibility, like James Weldon Johnson's and Ralph Ellison's unnamed narrators in *Autobiography of an Ex-Colored Man* and *Invisible Man*, respectively. She also looks to her career as a journalist to free her from contexts as well, so that she can "disappear[] into somebody else's story."[26] While in the "purity of the present," she can avoid the objectification of her body according to the so-called legible facts of race. Yet, she is never without a set of legible ideas with regard to race. Her strategy fails because it brings into sharp relief what the main protagonist of Senna's first novel has already adroitly stated: "They say you don't have to choose. But the thing is, you do. Because there are consequences if you don't."[27] To use the logic of Arab American writer Barbara Nimri Aziz's "Write or be written,"[28] Senna's characters understand that one must speak or be spoken for.

When the unnamed narrator in *Symptomatic* breaks up with her white boyfriend, Andrew, their failed touch and his eye rubbing crystallizes how little he understands her. She decides to break up with Andrew after his friends demonstrate they are ignorant about race and their own privileged position to Blackness. Andrew's complicity disturbs her and she begins to make plans to move out. When he discovers that she is leaving him, he asks her, "Who are you?"[29] His reach for her in the dark attempts to create intimacy between them despite the fact that she's moving out, but this failure speaks to the fact that the intimacy is already gone, the relationship already over. The emotional distance solidifies because the touch remains unconsummated.

This scene brings to bear the difficulty of vision alongside the estrangement of the thwarted touch. For both of them, vision is an incomplete sensory experience because it yields nothing in terms of interpretation. Here, Andrew rubs his eyes. When he touches his eyes, the action seems to imply that he must literally force his eyes to reinterpret what he has already seen.[30] She looks out the window even as he looks at her. During their exchange, "there are multiple instantiations of looking, and seeing, but also equal amounts of blurring and misreading."[31] In all of this looking, they perceive (in a phenomenological sense) very little. Much of this visual exchange relies on their memories of each other and the narrator's memory of past lovers. Instead of the immediacy of perception, they each appeal to memory, an act that denies them the ability to see, standing forth from a cluster of data, what is present and immediately significant.[32] For both of them, vision fails as a means to understand each other. The unnamed narrator invokes her oppositional gaze and chooses not to use vision as a medium for understanding. She avoids looking at Andrew, choosing to focus on her memories rather than the present moment. Andrew conjures up memories of their relationship in an effort to perform the kind of mastery usually available to him when he looks at her. He remembers looking at someone that he understands. Now, she is unfathomable. As a result, he resorts not just to his memory, but also to staring, an act that one turns to "when ordinary seeing fails" because it is "an interrogative gesture that asks what's going on and demands the story."[33]

In the final scene between herself and Andrew, his inability to touch her and her avoidance of his gaze allow her to remake herself. Here, she confirms herself now as someone who controls the disclosure of her racial identity and who knows how little that information provides in terms of explanation. That is, the appeal to the visual is only liberating in theory. The unnamed narrator contemplates the opportunity to trouble the way Andrew understands race by providing a context with which he can understand biraciality, because in so doing, she would disrupt his idea of whiteness. Such an act would also disrupt the supposedly context-free moment and provide a space in which she could explain and teach him. Her choice to not capitalize on this putative opportunity indicates that she does not consider it an opportunity at all. When she says she's tired, the double entendre indicates her fatigue of objectifying her body for the racial education of others. She repudiates the common conception that illustrating one's racial difference is always liberating. To view "[her] body, the lesson,"[34] as she terms it, as an opportunity assumes not only that explaining is liberating, but also that providing a visual object is useful for disrupting whiteness. She would need more than the visual objectification of her material body to change the way Andrew thinks of her as an objective subject.

Moreover, the desire to understand herself anew becomes an imperative. In contrast to the failed touching and seeing with Andrew, the unnamed narrator experiences a different tactile and visual moment that allows her to contemplate herself. After she moves into her own apartment, she cannot sleep and decides to take a bath. She examines her body in the tub:

> I took note of its features like a doctor examining a patient for the first time: broad shoulders, narrow hips, teardrop breasts that didn't quite match. One breast was small, prepubescent, with a pale pink nipple, the other slightly fuller, with a deeper mauve nipple. Like they belonged to two different women. I ran a hand across my mismatched breasts, then down across my belly, my thighs, and through the dark hair between my legs. I felt a surge of pity for this body—as if it were something separate from myself rather than something I lived inside. I pitied it as if it were a child I had just taken a dangerous toy away from, to spare it some potentially lethal accident.[35]

Unlike the thwarted touch in Andrew's apartment, her touch of herself aids her in understanding herself more fully. Despite the fact that the touch is fleeting, it corroborates that she feels as though she were two different people, trying to reconcile what she knows of herself and what others see. Rather than construct her as a fully formed subject, this fleeting touch allows her to constitute herself in a state of ambivalence and confusion. Her inability to engage with the touch as an elongated moment of perception forecloses the possibility of her gleaning anything concrete about herself. The ephemerality of touch also hints that she does not "identif[y] with an unhealthy sense of fragmentation"[36] as part of her being mixed race. Instead, touch as a fleeting act indicates that the unnamed narrator constitutes herself very specifically in this moment as ambivalent, rather than understanding herself as an ambivalent subject. Unlike the touch that Elizabeth Grosz describes wherein the interaction of the flesh implies the inseparability of the touched/touching,[37] the narrator's fleeting touch can do nothing more than emphasize her feeling split between her touch and her touched flesh.

In this moment, her use of her own vision disrupts the inseparability of the touched object (her body) and the touching (her hand). She doesn't actually perceive her body, but gazes at it with the particular eye of a medical professional. The medical gaze creates a distance between the viewer and the body as it insists that the body is an object that needs to be fixed and examined. In taking on this gaze, she eviscerates herself, evicts herself from her own body, and hints that she needs to be cured of something. In keeping with this idea, she feels a "surge of pity" rather than the erotic surge associated with the caress she describes. This scene certainly dovetails with the general premise of the novel, that racism is an illness that damages the bodies of those it contaminates.[38] Furthermore, her medical gaze troubles her ability to think of herself as an objective subject, one who inhabits her body as well as uses it as a tool. She can only imagine herself as a thing, an object that needs disciplining.

The toy to which she refers seems to be Andrew, the man she leaves supposedly for her and his own good. In conceptualizing her breakup as a form of racial discipline, she makes it clear that contexts are dangerous, but contradicts herself because they cannot be avoided. Regardless of the futility of her desire to live without context, she does move toward a particular understanding of her own subjectivity. As aforementioned, her understanding of herself as ambivalent or split should not indicate that she does not work toward forming herself as a unique "I." She becomes herself in this moment while being doubly conscious (pace Du Bois!) of how she looks to others as well as how she understands herself. The distinction here between the way the unnamed narrator views her body and the way others view it echoes in Senna's other work. Senna's first novel, *Caucasia*, intimately links the main character's raced and gendered self-awareness to her cycles of intimacy with and distance from her body. As Brenda Boudreau notes, "so much of a girl's identity is intricately linked to her physical body, and it is on the physical body that we expect racial identity to make itself visible."[39] In referring to Andrew as a toy, the unnamed narrator of *Symptomatic* voices a speculation that Andrew would not be able to understand her for who she is, as he would only concentrate on the racial identifications that construct her. Her own medical gaze enacts the kind of distancing necessary for her to become aware of herself as understood by others, a subjective object.

Alicia Erian's *Towelhead* presents a series of violent touches and failures of sight. Like *Symptomatic*, they attest to the imbrication of the tactile and the visible in constituting one's subjectivity. Jasira, the protagonist, foregrounds this relationship based on the naïveté within the first-person narration. Jasira can name the context in which she operates but, unlike Senna's narrator, does not appreciate the extent to which it governs her experience. For instance, she understands that her mother is Irish and her father is Lebanese, but she does not understand why others identify her solely with her Arab heritage. She understands that the Gulf War is happening, but does not express any sophisticated knowledge about the war itself or the narratives that supply what Erian calls "a low level pressure to the human drama."[40] One could question the extent to which any 13-year-old understands politics, and certainly that would be an apt way to approach this character. However, the convention for narratives with Arab American teenage protagonists is that they are significantly politically aware.[41] These protagonists usually find themselves trying to live up to "the idealized concepts of Arab culture that [circulate] in their families and communities" because the "stakes of culture and family respectability [are] so high in America."[42] As a result, they are usually able to articulate in some rudimentary form the politics of the day and the presence of Orientalism. In contrast, Jasira remains unaware of the way that the Gulf War makes her legible in Houston, Texas, as different. She also grasps that her pubescent body makes her a girl changing into a woman, but she does not fully comprehend the way Orientalism and exoticism influence others' behavior toward her developing body.

Specifically, Jasira experiences violent, sexually aggressive touches at the hands of her army reservist neighbor, Mr. Vuoso. During these abuses, the tactile corroborates the visual despite Vuoso's desire that they not do so. For instance, in his first act of sexual aggression, Vuoso rapes Jasira with his fingers. He arrives at her house after Jasira has hit his son, Zack, for calling her a "towelhead," a "camel-jockey," and a "sand-nigger." Vuoso demands that Jasira give back the *Playboy* magazine he has given her, but will not let her go to complete that task. The text reads,

> "Go and get that fucking magazine," he said and I tried to, but he wasn't letting go. Instead, he moved his hands off my shoulders and slid them down over the front of me, over my breasts. He started squeezing them. I tried to move again, but the more I pulled away, the tighter he held me. [. . .] Now his hands moved further down the front of me, into my jeans. [. . .] he wasn't listening. He was putting his fingers inside my underwear, then moving them down between my legs. [. . .] He just kept going further down. He started to rub me then.[43]

In sum, he turns her around, reaches into her pants, massages her clitoris and thrusts his fingers inside her vagina. When he pulls his bloodied fingers out of her pants, he hurriedly washes his hands and apologizes. The act of turning her around might appear to be simply logistic in that he demands that she retrieve his magazine and forces her, by turning her, to do so. However, turning her accomplishes more than pointing her in the direction of the magazine—it diminishes his ability to see her face. At that point, all he can see is hair and clothing. With his hands, he can feel her breasts, stomach, pubic hair, clitoris, and the blood and vaginal fluid. Vuoso's tactile experience appears to corroborate his visual experience. That is, he sees a woman and he touches a woman. Nevertheless, he is soon reminded that Jasira is not a woman. Though he feels her struggling against him and hears her pleas for him to stop, he does not stop until she begins to cry. He also is jarred from his fantasy by seeing her blood on his hands.

In this rape scene and the second one, Vuoso's experience with the visual and the tactile exposes how his fantasy of her as an exotic Arab woman relies on willful acts of vision and revision. Technically, Vuoso perceives Jasira as a woman in that moment based on the corroboration of his visual and tactile experiences. The visual and the tactile do not typically separate from each other except in cases of neurological damage,[44] but Vuoso's behavior suggests that the two can be made to separate when one seeks a particular end. Vuoso's forcing Jasira to turn around willfully makes his visual experience corroborate his tactile one. It is only the integration of another sensory experience—sound—that makes him aware of his actions.

After that moment, he has another visual experience that jolts his perception of the tactilic. He looks at his bloodied hands and recognizes that he has raped her.

Before he rapes her the first time, it is clear that Vuoso becomes aroused by touching Jasira. For him, she loses the specificity of being his teenage neighbor and becomes a sexually available Arab female body. In two previous scenes, he caresses her bottom and her breasts. In these particular scenes, he denies himself the visuality of looking at her adolescent face, choosing instead to concentrate on her breasts and buttocks. When Zack and Jasira peruse *Playboy* and find an "Arabian Princess" centerfold, Zack reveals to Jasira that Vuoso "even thinks [she's] pretty" because "[she's] going to have a lot of boyfriends, and [her] dad's going to lock [her] up."[45] Keeping in mind the stereotypes about Arab men who keep their women in harems, and the backdrop of the 1991 Gulf War, these comments and their context mark Jasira in sexual and ethnic terms and highlight that "anti-Arab racism is in no way removed from other, more deeply rooted instances of hate, discrimination, and xenophobia."[46] When Vuoso touches her, he must deny himself the experience of looking into her face. He cannot, based on visual experience, reconcile his knowledge and his tactile experience. Based on touch, Jasira must become his embodied fantasy.

In light of Vuoso's sexualized and Orientalized view of Jasira, the disjuncture between his visual experiences—bloodied hands, her head full of hair—and his tactilic ones reveals that he has willfully constructed Jasira according to his fantasy. Maintaining that view of her requires a continuous privileging of the tactile. The tactile, then, becomes a compulsion for Vuoso, one he must continue to sate to sustain his fantasy. When the two go to Houston's famous Mexican restaurant Ninfa's, he continuously rubs his eyes as Jasira speaks.[47] In the restaurant, he rubs his eyes after she mentions the first rape incident and stares at him, then he excuses himself to go to the restroom. Much like the bloodied hands, Jasira's stare and her preceding statement prompt him to remember her age and the gravity of his actions. In addition, they force him to confront the fiction of his fantasy. The difficulty Vuoso has in reconciling his visual and tactile experience foregrounds the reversibility of touch and his willful negotiation of sensory experience to suit his own desires. His actions rely on the fact that touch "figures both an indistinction between the limits of one body and another, and, thereby, the potential for the transfer of impurity."[48] Bearing in mind that Vuoso already has a degraded view of Jasira's sexuality based on her Arab heritage, his touch of her implicates him as sexually degraded as well. His continued eye rubbing manifests his desire to physically make the visual coincide with the tactile because allowing the reciprocity of touch to do its work unabated would facilitate his own psychological undoing. He must create the fantasy. He must attempt to use his touch as he would use his vision. Only there can the danger he feels in intimate contact with Jasira not immediately result in "self-dissolution."[49] In the second rape scene, which occurs several weeks after their trip to Ninfa's, the primary focus on his tactile experience would suggest that Vuoso has given into his fantasy. As a result, his touch no longer carries the danger of ethnic or pedophilic contagion. He forces her to fellate him and penetrates her in the rear entry position. Unlike the missionary or standing position, both positions keep her face turned away from his; in these positions, he can concentrate on the experience of touch rather than the visual. He has effectively policed his fantasy such that he no longer feels (and I use that verb deliberately) encumbered by the reversibility of the tactile.

In 2008, Alan Ball directed a film version of *Towelhead*, which complicates the visual and tactile understanding of these scenes. The scenes in *Towelhead* provide ample interaction between the tactile and the visual to understand how the two become mutually constitutive in Vuoso's fantasy. The filmic depiction of the second rape scene focuses largely on Vuoso through perspective and sound. After having observed Thomas leaving Jasira's home through his front window, Vuoso leaves his home under the pretext of looking for his son's lost cat. Vuoso tells Jasira that he has been summoned to Iraq in his capacity as an army reservist. She lets him come inside her house. He sits down on the couch and motions for her to join him, patting the sofa next to him. He asks her to strip for him. The camera cuts between Jasira and Vuoso as she undresses. This is not shot as a typical eyeline match as though they were in face-to-face conversation, but rather the eyeline match is between Vuoso's eyes and Jasira's torso. From his perspective, the camera is at a slightly low angle, though it avoids much of her breasts. The slightly low camera angle approximates Vuoso's point of view from the couch, but because the camera point of view remains objective, the film undercuts an identification with Vuoso. The stark *mise-en-scène* of the rest of the moment echoes in the sound production; during this scene, there is nothing but the sound of Vuoso's mildly labored breathing and swallowing. He makes several comments: when she begins undressing: "That's the most beautiful thing I've ever seen" and, twice, "You are so beautiful."[50] Because the eyeline match is between his eyes and her torso, it is not clear that he is looking at her face. After watching her strip, he tells her to get on the floor. Then, the camera cuts to the exterior of the house, where there is no sound but the clanging of the flagpole in the front yard. After the rape, the camera cuts to the interior of the house where Jasira sits curled in the fetal position on the floor, now dressed, and Vuoso, buttoning his pants, gets up off the floor and roughly kisses her on the top of the head, saying that he'll think of her in Iraq. In a flashback, we see Vuoso's head and neck as he thrusts into her, a camera angle that might suggest a missionary position (in contrast to the novel) if it is Jasira's memory and not the objective view of the camera.

By focusing on Vuoso's interiority through sound and camera angles, the film suggests much the same relationship between Vuoso's fantasy and his sensory experience: he sees her knowing she is a teenage girl, touches her, and then can see her as the object of his desire. It would seem that his sight is an act of will over and against his perception. However, that would presume that his immediate perception of her is that she is a teenage girl. I would argue that his perception is less clear than that and, in order to make it clear, he must impose the vision he wants to see. His vision, which in the film is based on his sight and touch of her torso, conforms to his imagining her as a sexually knowledgeable Arab woman rather than a naïve American teenager.

The problem with Vuoso's touch is that it takes on the impoverished quality to which Elizabeth Grosz refers as it must be corroborated by sight. Yet, since Vuoso's sight must be altered and manipulated, the novel implies that his perception is fundamentally flawed. In *Towelhead*, this quality surfaces in male touch and vision in a way that it does not in women's perception. For instance, Rifat hits his daughter and though he does not perform the same kind of eye-rubbing as Vuoso, he still does not see Jasira as a teenage girl. In fact, Rifat's touch operates similarly to Vuoso's when Rifat uses his violent touch to discipline Jasira into adhering to his understanding of good behavior. When Jasira comes to the breakfast table in pajamas, he smacks her across the face for not being appropriately dressed. Later, Rifat finds Jasira's *Playboy* and punches her roughly on the thigh as punishment for "not living in the moral universe" because, according to him, she is "not normal."[51] In both instances, Rifat's disciplining touch stems from an assumption about Jasira's intention to be highly sexualized and he acts on that principle. Like Vuoso, he uses one sense to corroborate another.

In stark contrast to the impoverished male touch that wounds, the women's touches help to reconstitute Jasira. These touches sometimes function somewhat like that of the unnamed narrator's in *Symptomatic* in that they illustrate confusion rather than cohesion. Nevertheless, they allow Jasira to determine how she understands herself rather than having that understanding mapped onto her. When Jasira discovers masturbation, she begins by pressing her thighs together, forcing the two lips to touch, an act to which Irigaray alludes in *The Sex Which is Not One*. When she masturbates more deliberately, she says, "I didn't press my legs together. Instead, I lay back on the bed, let my legs fall open, and touched myself while I looked at the pictures. I touched my nipples, too."[52] Unlike her father's violence or Vuoso's sexual aggression, Jasira doesn't feel scared, confused, or ashamed. In this instance, she feels as though "[her] body is the most special thing in the world. Better than other bodies, even."[53] Her masturbatory touch is only fleetingly satisfying as she must continue to reinvent the fantasy, but while it lasts, she understands herself as in control. In addition to sexual curiosity, what drives her to masturbate is the loss of control she experiences literally at the hands and demands of her father.

Earlier in this discussion, I examined the touch of *Symptomatic*'s unnamed narrator in terms of how it allows her to escape what she understands to be the confining context of race. Similarly, Jasira's own touch of herself permits her to reconstitute herself in contrast to the sexualized and Orientalized contexts assumed by her father and neighbor. Inasmuch as these characters' choices make sense in that they can escape the problematic narratives in which they are mired, the choices do not provide a great deal of granularity for them. In *Symptomatic*, the narrator can only caress herself into ambiguity. In *Towelhead*, masturbation becomes a sanctum, but fades after the orgasm. Even the caresses of Jasira's boyfriend appear to be only temporarily satisfying. It appears that touch retains its utility for escaping some moments, but it is only partially and temporarily constitutive. As they attempt to make and remake themselves based on their own touches, they still have to contend with the touches of others as well as being constituted as subjective objects through others' sight as well. Their recuperative touches rescue the young women from some of the repercussions of dangerous touching even though those same recuperative touches cannot whisk them away completely.

As hinted above, these tactilic moments eschew the idea fragmentation inheres in mixed race subjectivity. Jasira's masturbation and the unnamed narrator's self-caress place agency in their grasp, if only temporarily. They rely on the intimate reciprocity of touched and touching flesh to remake themselves in the wake of physical and emotive violence. Moreover, the narratives give the lie to equating visibility with truth. When the characters encounter mirrors, they make clear their distrust of the visual field and seek wholeness in touching or the possibility thereof. Lacan's mirror theory posits that the looking glass is the first place where children begin to perceive of themselves as whole beings apart from their parents. In front of the mirror, they develop a sense of themselves as individuals. Yet the mirror tends to consistently surprise the one who gazes into it because, as Judith Oster notes, "there is some discrepancy between the actual, surface, external mirror image that any onlooker could see and some sort of interior, mental self."[54] The mirror becomes a way to make sense of one's self and reconcile external appearance and interiority.

At times, the mirror does assist in this feat of reconciliation. However, this understanding of the mirror presupposes that what is external expresses some degree of truth. In these novels, it becomes imperative to reimagine how and why the mirror can be deceptive. Vivian Sobchack's discussion of her prosthetic leg clarifies how misrecognition, or in Lacanian terms *méconnaissance*, functions. Her essay "Is Any Body Home?" offers her experience of learning to use her prosthetic. She recounts that her therapist put her in front of a mirror so that she could adjust her body according to her image. Yet, that image could not help her. She writes:

> As a film scholar expert in evaluating visible images and a phenomenologist versed in (and often averse to) Lacanian psychoanalytic theory, it was truly epiphanic that the mirror was for me—from the first—a highly charged and negative site of *méconnaissance*, or misrecognition. That is, my visibility in it taught me nothing.[55]

The misrecognition not only made her hostile to the image, frustrated with it, it also illuminated how important her sensory experience would be in learning to walk again. She recalls that she had to feel her body and understand it in its own space, an act that cannot be abetted by the mirror.[56] In other words, she had to prioritize the touch of her own flesh and the prosthetic. Her experience suggests the importance of inhabiting the body and understanding it phenomenologically as opposed to understanding it visually. The mirror confuses rather than illuminates the understanding of the self, and so it becomes necessary to privilege the experience of being in a body over merely looking at it.

Both Jasira and *Symptomatic*'s unnamed narrator reject the mirror because of the wholeness it attempts to impose or the truths it seeks to tell about their images. In their cases, the looking glass holds putative truths about race, gender, and sexuality. Jasira rejects the mirror after Vuoso rapes her the second time in an effort to avoid reconciling the external image with her emotions. During the second rape in the novel, Vuoso forces Jasira to fellate him and ejaculates on her face. She describes her actions afterward.

> I put my hands to my face to keep it from dripping onto the carpet. I could feel it starting to fall from my skin. I walked to the bathroom naked, holding the drips, then got in the tub without looking in the mirror. I didn't want to see myself like that.[57]

Jasira avoids the mirror for a few reasons. The first, and perhaps most obvious, is shame. Her waning trust in Vuoso, until that point, did not diminish her attraction to him. But it is after this moment that she feels embarrassed. She is too naïve to understand her experience in terms of rape, so part of her shame stems from believing that she has had consensual sex. What surfaces when she reports him to the police is that he has called her a "slut" and asked her whether she liked it while he raped her.[58] Second, what accompanies her shame is confusion. She does not understand why her body responded with arousal when he touched her. She believes that what she has done feels wrong, but does not understand why her body reacted as though it was not.[59] Vuoso's semen on her face, scatological evidence of the rape, becomes the visible rem(a)inder of her emotions and her actions; so to see herself in the mirror would be to constitute her subjectivity based on these emotions and these actions. Her reflection would belie the confusion she felt and make truthful the lie of her consent and enjoyment. To wit, the presence of the mirror refracts all that has occurred in the past few scenes: it deflects the spotlight from the action of rape to the emotional aftermath. For Jasira, its presence marks her as a participant in the sex act, which is one reason why she wants to avoid looking in it. Her avoidance of it doesn't allow it to alter or distort her emotional reaction as it was in that moment or to give wholeness to a moment of fragmentation. Keeping in mind that "proximity and touch are never without risk, but the move to deny them [. . .] is bound to fail,"[60] avoiding the mirror prevents a privileging of sight over touch as the entry point to being or becoming in that moment. However racked with difficulty the touch, it still belongs to Jasira as a way to understand herself.

It is worth noting that this scene holds several mirrors that Jasira now mistrusts. The first is the literal mirror in the bathroom. The other mirrors are the *Playboy* images with which Jasira longs to identify. She gravitates toward the centerfold's discussions of sex as something they enjoy, and ejaculate as something they like to ingest or wear. Looking in the literal mirror would force Jasira to reconsider her relationship not only to Vuoso but to sex in general, a relationship built on her attraction to the *Playboy* models' articulation of sexual desire and fulfillment. The resulting misrecognition would engender a simplistic and incomplete narrative about her relationship to sex. The mirrors problematically articulate both wholeness and fragmentation, creating narratives that are neither accurate nor complex. So Jasira's desire to take a bath—to be touched and to touch herself—privileges her own embodiment rather than her image. It is not that Jasira seeks either wholeness or fragmentation but the primacy of her own emotive and phenomenological experience—whatever it may be.

In *Symptomatic*, the unnamed narrator's rejection of the mirror also performs dual work: one, questioning race as a visible, biological phenomenon and, two, thwarting a narrative about the narrator's subjectivity. In a subway car, the narrator locks eyes with another woman. As time passes, the narrator becomes more annoyed with the woman because it appears that the woman attempts to make contact with her. Establishing and maintaining eye contact in a subway car in New York tends toward the strange. One of the unwritten rules of subway car riders is that there is little contact between them except in rare cases. For the woman, the presence of the narrator becomes a rare case. What the narrator interprets is that the woman solicits her in a ploy for white racial solidarity. She says,

> Somebody was watching me. I was sure of it. I looked up into the faces on the subway car around me. A white girl. The only one here tonight. I stared back at her, irritated by the expression on her face, a slight searching smile, as if she thought we were comrades among all these dark bodies. That happened to me a lot. The one white person on board smiled at me as if to say, *Thank God you're here. We can help each other in case there is a riot.*[61]

The narrator grows indignant that the woman's ploy comes from fear of the "dark bodies" around her. The narrator never speaks to her, and, in fact, the woman disappears. From the narrator's vantage point, she remains aware of her body as one that could be read as white, but becomes incensed at the possibility that her body attracted someone who fears the "dark bodies" around her. The narrator understands herself as non-white, as she says the white girl is the "only one here tonight." Yet, her sarcasm about potential riots also suggests that she is sympathetic to, but knows she is not a part of, the group of potential rioters.

When Senna's narrator encounters the white girl in the subway, it isn't clear whether she has seen another young woman or herself. The narrator looks around as if expecting to see another person, but does not. Even if she has been looking at herself, the unnamed narrator does not comprehend the phantom white girl as a reflection of herself, but rather a reflection of other white girls she has encountered. Viewing this interaction as a mirror moment, I would argue that the narrator rejects not only the image of herself but the accompanying interpretation of that image as well. She does not perceive herself as white, nor does she view herself as afraid of the "dark bodies" on the subway car. In fact, her anger and frustration at the phantom white girl make it clear that the visual gives the lie to what she knows to be true about her own subjectivity. What solidifies the mirror's inaccuracy is the tactile. Touch operates as an unrealized, but extant, possibility between herself and the potential rioters. The narrator constructs her own disgust with the girl and her non-white subjectivity based on her understanding of the putative white girl's fear of being touched by the other subway passengers. On a New York subway car, where it is practically impossible to avoid touching others, the phantom white girl's fear assumes a kinship based on visibility and ignores the reality of her other senses.

Reading the scenes from *Symptomatic* and *Towelhead* alongside each other, it becomes clear that these mirrors give a false sense of wholeness and fragmentation. The images they provide cannot take the place of perceived experience as the images evict the protagonists from their own bodies, forcing them outside it by asking them to give primacy to the way others perceive their bodies and selves as subjective objects. For Jasira, her image would be predicated on Vuoso's view of her as an exoticized other and *Playboy*'s positioning of her as an erotic other. For the unnamed narrator, the image would corroborate that her race is legible and, with that, her adherence to racist and gendered scripts about white women and Black people. Of another mirror moment in *Symptomatic*, Michelle Elam notes that it is "less an example of the Lacanian mirror stage of identity formation than a bending of Du Boisian double consciousness."[62] I would add that for both protagonists, they can bend their being doubly conscious based on their tactilic experiences. These novels are set up to reject not just the mirror but what the mirror represents, either stable wholeness or permanent fragmentation, especially when those representations rely on the visual as the only maker of reality. Instead, the narratives suggest that the tactile and promise of touch has just as much of a hand, so to speak, in creating reality. Furthermore, these images attempt to confirm others' knowledge of the protagonists' bodies and reify the young women as solely subjective objects of exoticized desire and history. Reaching toward touch as a sense-making experience revises the available narratives. Touch repositions the young women as objective subjects, as agents.

Consider that these protagonists gravitate toward touch in moments of racialized and gendered anxiety. Invoking Faulkner, their touch "abrogates, cuts sharp and straight across the devious intricate channels of decorous ordering"[63] that govern our national narratives, specifically our implicit narratives about belonging and whiteness. These novels insist on the validity of the protagonists' embodiment, disrupting the implicit standard of whiteness as a prerequisite for social citizenship. For instance, Jasira's parents, Gail and Rifat, attempt to forbid her from visiting Thomas, her Black boyfriend (whom they believe is simply a friend). Given the backdrop of the imminent Gulf War, their commentary makes clear the repercussions of "boundaries of belonging and nonbelonging [that] are often entangled within U.S. imperialist projects in Arab countries and within Arab experiences of displacement, immigration and racialization to and within the United States."[64] Rifat attempts to explain to Jasira that she is white, citing that Arabs are legally white. Rifat equates Jasira's Arabness with being white because that is the box they check on forms.[65] Presumably, he refers to the census form that in 1990 allowed for Arab Americans to document themselves as white.[66] Rifat does not acknowledge his racism as such but instead couches it in terms that focus on his desire to protect Jasira from public opinion, saying that being friends with Thomas will ruin her reputation. For Rifat, Thomas's "blackness therefore signifies [. . .] an unavoidable marker of inferiority that not even [. . .] cultural affinity [. . .] or economic well-being can make up for."[67] Gail illuminates Rifat's rationale by pointing to her own experience with being called a "nigger-lover" while dating Rifat. By Gail's logic, Arab is considered Black and contact with more Blackness would hurt Jasira because of others' reactions. The result of the parents' comments is something of a sliding racial scale where Arab is somewhat Black and somewhat white. If Jasira chooses a Black partner, she becomes Black; and by not choosing a Black partner, she becomes or remains white. Both parents' explanations deny Jasira's Arab-looking body as they attempt to squeeze her into the Black/white binary. They each participate in a "gendered racialization [where] racial logics are flexible and mutable to accommodate imperialist power in different temporal and spatial contexts."[68]

In this case, Rifat and Gail's racial obsession articulates their anxiety around issues of citizenship and belonging. Specifically, the proximity to the Black body determines the extent of Jasira's racialization and, therefore, her ability to fully belong to the community in which she resides. Gail and Rifat advise Jasira not to see Thomas, but do not fully explain their rationale. Census forms and public opinion function as a metonym for larger national discourses. If Jasira can obey the unwritten social rules for Arab women's bodies, she can fully realize the promise of inclusion (a fact that Rifat makes clear when he says that Jasira's female friend's race does not matter). Despite their verbal meanderings, Jasira's own musings clarify the ways in which these ideas don't make sense given her own body's relationship to Blackness. She notes that schoolmates and Vuoso's son have called her a "sand-nigger," yet her parents don't want her to be called a "nigger-lover." Her tentative claim and identification with Blackness "expose[s] and negotiate[s] US racial hierarchies" differently than her parents because they suggest that her parents ought to "reformulate the positioning of Arab Americans within US racial hierarchies."[69] Though her questions aren't quite articulate, the confusion over her own racial classification lays bare that she understands her Arab identity as socially proximate to Black identity. She says, "I didn't understand how this would work, since the kids at school already called me a sand nigger. It seemed like that would make Thomas a nigger lover, too. Plus, I didn't even know if we loved each other."[70] What Jasira taps into about both the Black body and her parents' interpretation of her body is that the discourse ignores reality. In the case of her parents, this particular ignorance desires to capitalize on what they want to read as her whiteness. Jasira's confusion about her parents' ideas highlights Gail and Rifat's willful racism when she thinks of her sexual activity with Thomas: "I had gotten as close as you could to a black person and [. . .] nothing terrible had happened at all."[71] Her naïveté attempts to use touch as a way to mitigate her parents' objections to the sight of her with a young Black man. She views her touch as more important than their sight, and privileges her experience over theirs.

Reading Jasira's confusion alongside another scene in *Symptomatic*, what surfaces is a divestment in national narratives that construct whiteness as default standard. Senna's unnamed narrator dines with a coworker who holds a particular longing for the 1950s. Her presence disrupts the validity of the coworker's belief in the inherent excellence of white people. In this scene, the coworker drones on about quotas, saying,

> If only he had been born in a different skin, he might be editor in chief of the magazine by now. And [to her], he said, if you were born black, who knows where you'd be? [. . .] he [talked] about how he wished he had come of age in the 1950s. Didn't [she] wish that, too? Because that was the golden age for people like [them]. [She] didn't answer, just kept staring at [her]self. *This is what they see when they look at you.*[72]

This coworker's nostalgia neatly dovetails with the idea that "white power [. . .] reproduces itself regardless of intention, power dynamics, and goodwill and overwhelmingly because it is not seen as whiteness but as normal."[73] Implicit in the coworker's commentary is a belief in the inherent aberrance of an editor-in-chief of color. Moreover, the coworker's desire to have "come of age in the 1950s" longs for the culture of invisibility in corporate America and *de jure* segregation of Blacks. His dream is built on a foundation of oppression and a national narrative of exclusion. Yet the dramatic irony of knowing the narrator is Black creates a fly in the ointment of this coworker's fantasy. Her presence reminds readers that Blacks have always been a part of the national narrative, whether people choose to see them or not. Of course, here I deliberately seek to signify on Ralph Ellison (with whom

Senna creates intertextual affinity with her unnamed narrator), but I also point to the racial passing in this scene. Through the protagonist's silence about her race, *Symptomatic* "critique[s] a readerly model that encourages or allows readers to remain at bay even if it does not outline the terms of engagement."[74] In Danzy Senna's own words, the narrator's silence "forces the reader to experience the emotion" since "there's something about those absences in fiction that force you to respond in a way that the character's not."[75] Here the character eschews a response that discloses her racial affiliation and leaves the questions of racism, gender, and national belonging open for interrogation.

Frustrated responses to *Symptomatic* mark it as having "an implausible plot with little character development, and [. . .] while promising much in the area of mixed-race literature does not break new ground."[76] One reviewer described it as "tragic mulatto meets *Psycho* in Brooklyn."[77] Undergirding the frustrated responses and the reviewer's comment is the adherence to the script of tragedy, an idea that the tactile contests. Certainly, *Symptomatic* haunts readers with its gothic style, a thriller maze of doubles, halves, darkness, light, half-light, mirrors, and doppelgangers.[78] Yet viewing the racial gothic tale as solely an indicator of tragedy recapitulates that stereotype and, as Hortense Spillers reminds us, says more about the critic than the work itself. As Rebecca Walker so adroitly states, "the problem of the tragic mulatto is not that she is tragic, but that the presentation of her tragedy suggests no exit."[79] Circumscribing *Symptomatic* within the confines of a 'tragic mulatto' story leaves unexamined the narrative's suspicion of those who attempt to divest the mixed race subject of agency, including other mixed race people. As Hershini Bhana Young notes, *Symptomatic* "critiques overly optimistic cultural understandings of hybridity both as the source of community formation and as racial (non)identity" and "articulates the need for new models of community based on noncompulsory political identifications and strategies for redressing historical injustice."[80] I would add that this critique is achieved, not only through the deployment of racial gothic as a narrative strategy, but by privileging the body as a site where we literally and figuratively make sense of and to the world.[81] Greta/Vera, the narrator's would-be killer and mixed race doppelganger, chooses to access herself only through others' historically situated, racist and gendered narratives of desirability. She says, "I can become whoever the fuck people want me to be. [. . .] I can make a white man feel like he's with the most bodacious black girl alive, all earthy brown sugar and grits, and I can make a brother feel like he's got the whitest white girl beneath him."[82] Her fall off the building violently rejects the adherence to that changeling narrative. The final push, literally and metaphorically, is for an experience articulated through the body, not on it. The final scenes of the novel take place on the West Coast, and the unnamed narrator surrounds herself with a group of multiracial and queer friends. Those moments are haunted by Greta/Vera's presence, but they suggest the utility of a stasis in which the mixed race subject recasts herself on the frontier. Here, the mixed race subject becomes a participant rather than the result of a so-called progressive vision of the American imaginary.

Symptomatic's unnamed narrator has more agency in articulating a vision of herself as part of the American landscape where whiteness is not the center. Because of her naïveté, Jasira has no such agency. In fact, for all the novel does to create a national narrative of inclusion, it also undermines Arab American claims to a diverse American landscape. Steven Salaita notes, "*Towelhead* is not about Arabs or the Arab American community."[83] This is not Salaita's harshest critique of the novel (indeed, he has other well-argued objections), but the lack of Arab American community (unrealistic given the novel's setting in Houston, Texas) explains why the novel falters in its articulation of an inclusive America. There are no ethnic or gender enclaves to speak of (very unusual for Houston, Texas). Even the most generous reading of the novel must account for the incursion of white liberalism. After all, "focusing on whether or not a particular image is either good or bad does not necessarily address the complexity of representation. Rather it is important to examine the ideological work performed by images and story lines."[84] It is not my aim to suggest anything about how Erian ought to have written the novel. However, I do wish to point out what the barren cultural landscape of the novel permits. Jasira's white neighbors, Gil and Melina Hines, provide a safe haven for her from Vuoso and, later, shelter her from her abusive father while they are expecting their first child. Their assistance reasserts a well-meaning but benighted authorization of white privilege.[85] The lack of Arab American community allows the Hineses to assert their values as normal, privileging their ideas rather than providing a spectrum of culturally located values.

Moreover, the novel and the movie provide a common trope that the white people must "save brown women from brown men."[86] In film form, the movie narrative recapitulates the "fantasies of the colonizer and a logic that legitimizes colonialism" by showing "both 'good' and 'bad' Arabs [. . .] and for a white man to save the day."[87] Melina's altruism toward Jasira subsumes Jasira's claims to agency by placing them within this paradigm. What results is a narrative that appears more Byronic, white (wo)man's burden,[88] than multicultural celebration. The denouement of the novel leaves Melina and Gil as coparents with Rifat and Gail. The ending of the film allows Jasira to articulate control over her own body and pooh-pooh Rifat's response to Melina's delivery, saying that Rifat does not like bodies. In either case, viewers and readers see Jasira participate in a narrative that privileges white liberal notions of multiculturalism by virtue of the absence of Arab American articulations of a culturally relevant solution. Each ending shunts aside the question of how Jasira will navigate this landscape as an Arab American teen. As Lisa Suhair Majaj reminds us (and the *Towelhead* narrative bears this out, even if it does not point to a resolution): "Although ethnic identity may be a matter of individual choice for some European ethnic groups, [. . .] for Arab Americans—still subject to identity-based discrimination and to repercussions from political events in the Middle East—ethnicity cannot be understood in isolation from factors affecting the group at large."[89]

The unrealized potential of Erian's conclusion (and Alan Ball's) should not be interpreted as a complete failure on the narrative's part to create a complex conversation about the intricacy and intimacy of tactile experience. Rather, both endings open up the possibility to discuss what a vision of America might look like if mixed race subjectivity were imagined as an embodied reality. When read together, *Symptomatic* and *Towelhead* complicate what is visual and visible to disorder and reorder racialized and gendered stories. They prompt us to consider how we might articulate national belonging where whiteness is neither the center nor the goal. The next chapter examines national belonging more explicitly, analyzing how one articulates displacement and exile as an embodied experience.

NOTES

1. See Michelle Elam, *Souls of Mixed Folk: Race, Politics, and Aesthetics in the New Millennium* (Stanford, CA: Stanford UP, 2011). I am aware that Michelle Elam terms *Symptomatic* the "anti-bildungsroman" because Senna's narrator does "not come of age by coming into society. Rather [her] experiences critique the racial and economic basis by which individuals are incorporated" (127). My reading of the novel dovetails with Elam's conception of it, but I choose to use the label *bildungsroman* as shorthand.
2. Werner Sollors, *Neither Black nor White yet Both* (New York, NY: Oxford UP, 1997), 4.
3. Ibid., 4.
4. Rebecca Walker, "Introduction," *Mixed: An Anthology of Short Fiction on the Multiracial Experience*. Ed. Chandra Prasad (New York, NY: W. W. Norton & Company, 2006), 14.
5. Sarah Jones, "Your Revolution." *Russell Simmons Presents Def Poetry Jam: Season 1*, directed by Russell Simmons (2001; New York, NY: HBO Home Video, 2004) DVD. I invoke Sarah Jones's poem as a way to discuss the idea that sexual activity and desire cannot be an indication of larger societal harmony. Though her poem refers to hip hop culture specifically, her point (and mine) is that desire may be more indicative of the problematic fetishization of others' bodies in efforts to be socially and politically and culturally progressive.
6. See Elam, *The Souls of Mixed Folk*; Mary Beltrán and Camilla Fojas, eds. *Mixed Race Hollywood* (New York, NY: NYU Press, 2008). Elam explores the aesthetic and political concerns in mixed race literature, all of which question the notion that mixed race people are simply "the fashionable imprimaturs of modernity." Mary Beltrán and Camilla Fojas edited a collection of essays that point out the way the mixed race subject is forced to function as evidence of progress in a televisual space. The essays in that volume all point to the way the mixed race subject is constructed based on racial fantasy.
7. Elam, *Souls of Mixed Folk*, xiv.
8. Hortense Spillers, "Notes on an Alternative Model—Neither/Nor." *The Difference Within: Feminism and Critical Theory*. Ed. Elizabeth Meese and Alice Parker (Philadelphia, PA: John Benjamins Publishing Company, 1989), 166.

9. Sollors's extensive study *Neither Black nor White yet Both* examines black/white subjects in literature across Europe and the Americas. Michelle Elam's book examines contemporary literature by and about mixed race people.

10. Elam, *Souls of Mixed Folk*, 25.

11. See Evelyn Shakir, "Mother's Milk: Women in Arab-American Autobiography,"; Evelyn Shakir, "Arab Mothers, American Sons: Women in Arab-American Autobiographies"; Evelyn Shakir, "Pretending to Be Arab: Role Playing in Vance Bourjaily's 'The Fractional Man,' ". Shakir has an extensive discussion on Bourjaily and other writers in his generation, including William Peter Blatty, who wrote *Which Way to Mecca, Jack?* (1960); *The Exorcist* (1971); and *I'll Tell Them I Remember You* (1973).

12. J. Kadi, *Food for Our Grandmothers* (Cambridge, MA: South End Press, 1994), xvii.

13. Keith Feldman, "The (Il)legible Arab Body and the Fantasy of National Democracy," *MELUS*. 31.4 (2006): 34.

14. Walker, "Introduction," 17.

15. Salaita, *Anti-Arab Racism,* 5–6.

16. I have purposefully avoided writing that the narrator "looks white" or that her heritage is not visible on her skin. I find that these phrases give credence to the idea that race is supposed to be accurately determined by sight. My awkward phrasing is indicative of the paucity of language we have for refuting the idea that race is visible, given that it is often thought of as a visual phenomenon.

17. See Grosz, *Volatile Bodies*; Shildrick, *Dangerous Discourses*. Grosz notes this relationship in her text *Volatile Bodies* and Shildrick explains the implications of this reciprocity.

18. Shildrick, *Dangerous Discourses,* 31.

19. Grosz, *Volatile Bodies,* 14.

20. See Irigaray, *An Ethics of Sexual Difference*. Irigaray makes this point in her explication of Merleau-Ponty in her essay "The Invisible of the Flesh."

21. Irigaray qtd. in Martin Jay, *Downcast Eyes: The Denigration of Vision in Twentieth-Century French Thought* (Berkeley, CA: University of California Press, 1993), 493.

22. Irigaray, *An Ethics of Sexual Difference*, 162.

23. bell hooks, "The Oppositional Gaze: Black Female Spectators." *Black Looks: Race and Representation* (Boston, MA: South End Press, 1992), 115–131.

24. Feldman, "The (Il)Legible Arab Body," 40.

25. Danzy Senna, *Symptomatic* (New York, NY: Riverhead Books, 2004), 5.

26. Ibid., 6.

27. Danzy Senna, *Caucasia* (New York, NY: Riverhead Books, 1998), 408.

28. Aziz, *Scheherezade's Legacy,* xii.

29. Senna, *Symptomatic*, 35.

30. I am grateful to Susan Burch and Lori Harrison Kahan for their observations regarding this matter.

31. Therí A. Pickens, " 'It's a Jungle Out There': Disability and Blackness in *Monk*," *Disability Studies Quarterly*. 33.3 (2013). Last modified August 28, 2013. http://www.dsq-sds.org.

32. Merleau-Ponty, *Phenomenology of Perception*, 26.

33. Rosemarie Garland-Thomson, *Staring: How We Look* (New York, NY: Oxford University Press, 2009), Kindle Edition.

34. Senna, *Symptomatic*, 35.

35. Ibid., 44.

36. Walker, "Introduction," 17.

37. Grosz, *Volatile Bodies,* 98–99.

38. See Hershini Bhana Young, "Black 'Like Me': (Mis) Recognition, the Racial Gothic, and the Post-1967 Mixed-Race Movement in Danzy Senna's *Symptomatic*," *African American Review*. 42.2 (2008): 287–305. Hershini Bhana Young describes the unnamed narrator's relationship to her body, saying "the reader senses the protagonist's growing alienation from her own body, an alienation suggested by her inability to act [against racism]" (294). The alienation Young describes remains present as a symptom of the racial illness that pervades the text. However, it is important to note that the protagonist continues to reach toward touching and being in (phenomenologically experiencing) her own body as a way to redress the alienation forced by encounters with systemic and quotidian forms of racism.

39. Brenda Boudreau, "Letting the Body Speak: 'Becoming' White in *Caucasia*," *Modern Language Studies*. 32.1 (2002): 60.

40. Alicia Erian and Keya Mitra, "Defining Love, Enduring Brutality," *Gulf Coast: A Journal of Literature and Fine Arts*. 18.2 (2006): 241.

41. This holds true for the teen characters in a wide variety and significant volume of novels, including but not limited to Diana Abu Jaber's *Birds of Paradise* (2011), Randa Jarrar's *A Map of Home* (2008), Hisham Matar's *In the Country of Men* (2006) and *Anatomy of a Disappearance* (2011), Patricia Sarrafian Ward's *The Bullet Collection* (2003), and Mohja Kahf's *The Girl in the Tangerine Scarf* (2006).

42. Naber, *Arab America*, 5–6.

43. Alicia Erian, *Towelhead* (New York, NY: Simon & Schuster, 2008), 66.

44. See Maurice Merleau-Ponty, *The Visible and Invisible*; Luce Irigaray, *An Ethics of Sexual Difference*; Elizabeth Grosz, *Volatile Bodies*. Merleau-Ponty and Irigaray agree on the idea that sensory perception requires an engagement from multiple senses to register in the brain. Elizabeth Grosz explores this connection in her book chapter "Merleau-Ponty and Irigaray in the Flesh."

45. Erian, *Towelhead*, 18–19.

46. Salaita, *Anti-Arab Racism*, 123.

47. Erian, *Towelhead*, 110.

48. Shildrick, *Dangerous Discourses*, 28.

49. Ibid., 29.

50. Alan Ball, director, *Towelhead* (2008; Burbank, CA: Warner Home Video, 2008). DVD.

51. Erian, *Towelhead*, 241.

52. Ibid., 50.

53. Ibid., 50.

54. Judith Oster, "See(k)ing the Self: Mirrors and Mirroring in Bicultural Texts," *MELUS*. 23.4 (1998): 59.

55. Sobchack, *Carnal Thoughts*, 194.

56. Ibid., 179.

57. Erian, *Towelhead*, 232.

58. Ibid., 294.

59. Ibid., 245.

60. Shildrick, *Dangerous Discourses*, 35.

61. Senna, *Symptomatic*, 109, emphasis in text.

62. Elam, *Souls of Mixed Folk*, 154.

63. William Faulkner, *Absalom, Absalom!* (1936. Reprint, New York, NY: Library Classics of the United States, 1985), 115.

64. Abdulhadi, Alsultany, and Naber, *Arab American Feminisms*, xxvi.

65. Erian, *Towelhead*, 202.

66. See Helen Samhan, "Not Quite White: Race Classification and the Arab-American Experience," 209–26; Nadine Naber and Amaney Jamal, *Race and Arab Americans before and after 9/11*; Sawsan Abdulrahim, "Whiteness and the Arab Immigrant Experience." *Race and Arab Americans before and after 9/11*.

67. See Steven Salaita, *Modern Arab American Fiction: A Reader* (Syracuse, NY: Syracuse UP, 2011), 36.

68. Abdulhadi, Alsultany, and Naber, *Arab American Feminisms*, xxii.

69. Hartman, " 'this sweet/sweet music,' " 145.

70. Erian, *Towelhead*, 89.

71. Ibid., 202.

72. Senna, *Symptomatic*, 83 (emphasis in text).

73. Dyer, "The Matter of Whiteness," 12.

74. Elam, *Souls of Mixed Folk*, 158.

75. Rebecca L. Weber, "The Africana QA: Danzy Senna," *Rebecca L. Weber,* last modified July 6, 2004. www.rebeccalweber.com/danzy.html.

76. Young, "Black 'Like Me,' " 287.

77. Donna Seaman, "Symptomatic (Book)," *Booklist.* 100.15 (2004): 1349.

78. See Hershini Bhana Young, "Black 'Like Me.' "

79. Walker, "Introduction," 16.

80. Young, "Black 'Like Me,' " 288.

81. Sobchack, *Carnal Thoughts*, 2.

82. Senna, *Symptomatic*, 203.

83. Salaita, *Modern Arab American Fiction*, 126.

84. Alsultany, *Arabs and Muslims in the Media,* 13.

85. Dyer, "The Matter of Whiteness," 12.

86. See Gayatri Spivak, "Can the Subaltern Speak?" *Marxism and the Interpretation of Culture.* Eds. Cary Nelson and Lawrence Grossberg (Chicago: U of Illinois Press, 1988), 271–315.

87. Alsultany, *Arabs and Muslims in the Media,* 8.

88. See Mohja Kahf, "The Pity Committee and the Careful Reader." *Arab American Feminisms: Gender, Nation and Belonging.* Eds. Rabab Abdulhadi, Evelyn Alsultany and Nadine Naber (Syracuse, NY: Syracuse UP, 2011), 111–23.

89. Majaj, "Arab-American Ethnicity," 325.

3 Unfitting and Not Belonging
Feeling Embodied and Being Displaced in Rabih Alameddine's Fiction

In what follows, I examine the work of Rabih Alameddine, a Lebanese American author whose work has been hailed as provocative and postmodern for its rich exploration of Arab, Arab American, philosophical, queer, and transnational themes. He has also been lauded for his experimentation with the form of the novel.[1] Alameddine has published three novels—*Koolaids: The Art of War* (1998); *I, the Divine: A Novel in First Chapters* (2001) and *The Hakawati: A Story* (2008)—and a collection of short stories, *The Perv* (1999). Despite my discomfort with erecting an Arab American literary canon (for a variety of reasons), it is clear that Alameddine's work features prominently in any discussion of contemporary Arab American literature. He is arguably the most commercially successful author and, certainly, one of the most critically acclaimed.[2] Most secondary literature written about Alameddine's work tends to focus on the experience and implications of exile and displacement.[3] I should be clear that, for this author, exile takes on many forms. Some characters choose to leave Lebanon as a result of the Lebanese Civil War. Others are pushed away because of familial conflict, career, or sexuality—a set of narratives that correspond with what we usually term 'displacement.' In critical discussion, this displacement and exile takes center stage as a way to understand the fiction's critiques of Lebanon, the United States, or the condition of exile itself.

For the most part, these critical discussions are useful in that they foreground exile as one of the major themes of Alameddine's work. Nonetheless, they tend to focus on this larger thematic issue without reckoning with how that exile is felt in or enacted on the material body. Specifically, scenes that take place within hospitals imply that exile is not only tied to memory but also tied in multiple complex ways to illness. Alameddine's fiction crystallizes what Hammad's and Senna's titles, *Breaking Poems* and *Symptomatic,* respectively, imply about the interrelatedness of the somatic and the social. Yet, far from pathologizing exile, Alameddine's fiction holds up the hospital spaces and illness itself as a way to work through one's feelings of displacement. Alameddine's characters push back against the idea that normalcy or belonging is a state to which they should aspire, regardless of whether that norm or belonging is constituted in sexual, bodily, or mental terms. They are most at home in themselves when they are in a state of difference. In this way, Alameddine's characters work within the limitations of tactility or fragility in that they embrace those moments as liberatory. In mapping out a set of possibilities for understanding the relationship between being displaced and feeling embodied, I make sense of what potential exists in understanding oneself as non-normative.

I read Alameddine's fiction as conversant with the oft asked but seldom articulated question that W. E. B. Du Bois wrote in his seminal text *The Souls of Black Folk*: "How does it feel to be a problem?"[4] Here, I fixate on the phenomenological verb 'feel' as I explore how Alameddine's fiction crafts an answer to a question that has principally been thought of as a question of being (ontology). To be sure, Alameddine's fiction does not propose an answer distinct from Du Bois's own pithy 'peculiar,'[5] which signifies on the description of slavery as a peculiar institution.[6] Nor does Alameddine suggest an answer different from Moustafa Bayoumi, who writes in his book *How Does It Feel to Be a Problem?: Being Young and Arab in America* that being a problem is "frustrating."[7] Within his fiction, Alameddine's characters suggest that feeling like a problem remains uncomfortable, but it is preferable to the fiction of normalcy. The hospital scenes clarify that healing and belonging are neither desirable nor necessary.

The characters do not reject healing and belonging because they assume reconciliation, but rather because that reconciliation would only take place under terms specified by others. In short, these characters prefer double consciousness since striving for a singular conception of one's self would require a conciliatory attitude toward oppressive discourses. The thread of double consciousness runs through preceding chapters as Hammad, Senna, and Erian point toward the existence of this "two-ness [. . .] two souls, two thoughts, two unreconciled strivings; two warring ideals in one dark body, whose dogged strength alone keeps it from being torn asunder."[8] Alameddine's characters also experience what Edward Said terms 'contrapuntal consciousness,' a doubling of perspective based on being an exile.[9] Contrapuntal consciousness assumes the same tension and reciprocity as double consciousness in that both states require that the person exist in a state of consistent longing and disorientation. To avoid collapsing the two concepts neatly upon each other and effacing their difference, it is important to point out that double consciousness assumes a homeland within reach and contrapuntal consciousness assumes one that is forever out of reach. Yet each points to the way the outsider status is confirmed in social interaction. As Dickson D. Bruce, Jr., notes, Du Bois referred to multiple issues when describing double consciousness, including "the real power of white stereotypes in black life and thought and [. . .] the double consciousness created by the practical racism that excluded every Black American from the mainstream of the society, the double consciousness of being both an American and not an American."[10] At stake for Alameddine's characters is the practical racism that not only socially excludes but also legally creates and sanctions the hostile spaces in which these characters reside. These Arabs in America—being "not quite white"[11]—complicate and expand the twoness Du Bois articulates for Blacks. They not only open up the Black/white binary but also expand the definitions of practical racism and multiply the spaces for legally sanctioned hostility. I do not wish to figure into my comments an implicit narrative of progression (saying that Arabs are today where Blacks were at the beginning of the twentieth century). Instead, I wish to communicate the opposite: that both groups' struggles for social citizenship (and in differing legal battles) are concurrent and coextensive.

Given the impetus to deal with the feeling of Alameddine's fiction, I must address the way his fiction deals with Du Bois's implicit statement about strength. Du Bois writes of "two warring ideals in one dark body, whose dogged strength alone keeps it from being torn asunder."[12] The emphasis on the body's fragility here (and in works previously discussed) rejects the narrative of exceptional strength. As Michelle Elam notes, "the excruciating experience of 'twoness,' [. . .] is produced not by black pathology but by a national sickness that perversely weakens the nation itself through exclusion of some of its best citizenry."[13] Alameddine's fiction holds onto the gift of the second sight while repudiating the ableist notion that double consciousness requires that one be exceptionally strong in the face of oppression. The following hospital scenes imagine the articulation of double consciousness such that one can acknowledge the intense vulnerability and complexity of feeling like a problem. The delicacy that inheres in the human body allows Alameddine to depict a wide variety of relationships between being displaced while feeling embodied.

My readings in this chapter weave together two aspects of phenomenology that subtended the discussions in previous chapters. First, I accentuate that embodiment requires thinking of embodied experience as reversible and reciprocal. As one touches and sees, one must consider oneself as a subject who acts upon others (objective subjects) and understand that one is perceived as an object that is acted upon (subjective objects). Despite the simultaneity of this process, there are moments within Alameddine's fiction wherein his characters are unwilling or unable to participate in these interactions. As other scholars have pointed out, no body can ignore its grounding in the social and historical world, nor can it ignore the way that grounding is perceived by others.[14] As my analysis of the other authors has shown, one's perception of the body remains inextricably intertwined with discourses of gender, ethnicity, and sexuality.[15] (The phenomenological argot for 'perceived' is 'intended' or 'apprehended.' To avoid confusing repetition, I use the three interchangeably.) Second, I turn to what Sara Ahmed terms "queer phenomenology." That is, I examine how Alameddine's characters orient themselves toward objects and each other, asking how they force a redirection "toward different objects, those that are 'less proximate' or even those that deviate or are deviant."[16] Keeping in mind that the characters' consciousnesses (even if doubled) are always directed toward something, always intending an object, I focus on the way characters' perception is informed by their sense of the visual, tactile, and spatial. I should point out that the phenomenological emphasis on perceiving the world based mostly on our visual and tactile experiences needs to be troubled. Even though phenomenological theory embraces the difference present in human variance, it presupposes that everyone apprehends through visual or tactile cues. While I do not suggest a new mode of perception, I hope to give an inkling of how characters' engagement with the world through multiple senses fundamentally shapes their experiences of exile and embodiment.

As I conceptualize the relationship between being displaced and feeling embodied, I turn to three interrelated topics within Alameddine's fiction: the function of care, the definition of patient, and the multiple meanings of cure. I turn specifically to disability studies scholars here because their work on those concepts dovetails with Alameddine's fiction. Though there are significant differences between being sick and being disabled, I rely on this scholarship to discuss Alameddine's characters because all take on the characteristics of disabled bodies in that they "have proven to be more recalcitrant, reminding the medical and rehabilitation establishment of the limits of their authority in restoring the body to its 'normal' state."[17] First, I explore the function of 'care.' The characters shun some of the etymological baggage of the word, which implies trouble, grief, and sorrow.[18] As a noun, 'care' currently describes a burdened state of mind arising from fear, doubt, or concern, and, in its verb form, 'care' indicates the act of being concerned.[19] In addition to this lineage of denotation, acts of care and caretaking assume a feminized status. Ventriloquizing Evelyn Nakano-Glenn and Eva Feder Kittay, disability studies scholar Nirmala Erevelles points out that "by virtue of one's gendered status (as wife, mother, daughter), it is generally accepted that one necessarily has to take on the role of caregiver."[20] This role understands caring to be all-encompassing—"labor, an attitude, and a virtue"[21]—while it is thought of as degrading and "implicitly situate[s] disabled care recipients as the oppressive partner in [these] relationship[s]."[22] In Alameddine's hospitals, caretaking foregrounds an anxiety about this putative burden, spotlighting the tension between the necessity of caretaking, the praise received for doing it, and the unwillingness to do so. Alameddine's characters trouble the presumed relationship between care and caregiver, disavowing care as a virtue or rendering it useless or selfish. Their points of view align with Margrit Shildrick, whose ideas are worth quoting at length:

> A lot of what is justified as caring behaviour tends towards limiting the autonomy of those with disabilities. Taking responsibility for another, even claiming empathy, is rarely straightforward, but potentially masks an unwillingness to engage person to person. And at the other end of the spectrum, in the worst cases the vulnerability elicited in those who would see themselves as 'normal' can invoke a *dis*engagement expressed as real violence.[23]

The second recurring topic within this chapter is the definition of a patient. As we are aware, 'patient' is both noun and adjective. In Alameddine's fiction, the interplay between these two parts of speech implies that the patient be patient. In other words, being a patient requires that one's very being demonstrate the adjectival meaning of the word, 'to bear hardship' and 'to endure.' Being a patient also suggests that one is not an agent since "people living with chronic/terminal illnesses [. . .] suffer from similar social effects of being designated as uncontrollably pathological."[24] This definition assumes a particular kind of subservient attitude from the patient as well as a fundamentally inert state of being. Therefore, to be patient is to be an objective subject who wishes to be a subjective object, acted upon but with a curtailed agency of one's own. Paul Longmore discusses the difference between how people with disabilities see themselves and how the medical establishment stigmatizes them. He cites that "the opinions of disabled and nondisabled people sharply diverge"[25] because the medical model presumes the superiority of the medical professional and requires that patients' opinions be subordinated.[26] In the doctor/patient relationship, "the patient is expected to yield up the most intimate secrets of the body as succinctly as possible and submit them for the physician's perusal so as to garner a coherent diagnosis from the corporeal complexity observed."[27] Alameddine's patients question the validity of what these exchanges assume about patients, asking whether it is ever possible for one's body to be inert or acted upon without exerting some agency of its own. Certainly, upending the definition of patient also challenges the role of care and caretaking as fundamentally virtuous and inherently useful. In so doing, they also challenge the authority granted to those who understand them as patients. They advocate for bodily authority as equal to or greater than medical authority.

Third and finally, I examine the idea of what it means to be cured. As I mentioned before, these characters do not find the state of so-called normalcy or belonging curative. If the cure for exile is return or if the cure for illness is wellness, they seem to prefer illness and exile because return and wellness do not offer rest or peace. As Jennifer James states, "disability scholarship has shown that the goals of ontological restoration are all too frequently bound to ideological objectives that are little related to a disabled person's needs."[28] Cure tends to be a state that allows for one to move continuously forward without deliberate acts of remembering or attempts to foreclose the recourse to memory completely. James highlights the way disability challenges that notion in her discussion of the way injured veterans' wounds were "lingering memorials to the epic disaster of the war" and the desire to reduce their visibility sanctioned the denial of "human culpability in [their] making."[29] As Syrine Hout has written, Alameddine's works explicitly engage with memory and cure as imbricated concepts: "[m]ore significant than what is remembered of the past—be it collective or personal— is how and why it is recalled."[30] In consonance with these ideas, cure forecloses the possibility of looking back, discounts the power of memory.

In short, Alameddine's characters deliberately shun or shy away from the putatively curative because it diminishes the retrospective. Moreover, cure implies that one can be fixed, an idea that tends to dovetail with the acceptance of medical authority. In these works, cure can come in the form of delusion, discomfort, dystopia, or death—all of which sanction one's bodily authority.

As with any writing that maps out possibilities, the routes are "alive, many-layered, multi-dimensional, open-ended, and braided"[31] while traversing the relationships between care, patients, and cure. I ordered the texts based on the idea that each builds on the one that precedes it. This is not to say that they could not be ordered differently or that my particular order argues for a narrative of progression *vis-à-vis* Alameddine's work. In the discussion of *The Perv* and *I, the Divine*, I analyze the responsibility of caring and the troubled definition of cure. Alameddine experiments formally in all his work, but I bring it into sharp relief in my analysis of *Koolaids: The Art of War* and *The Hakawati: A Story*, with a discussion of how care, patients (pun intended), and cure are shaped by Alameddine's formal concern with sentimentality. The second set of texts builds on the first by complicating the seemingly straightforward ideas present. Moving into and out of these fictive works mirrors some of the characters' experiences in that we are never quite settled in one place. Such movement exposes the relationship between being unsettled and feeling so in one's material body.

In the titular story of Alameddine's short fiction collection, *The Perv*, the unnamed narrator understands the hospital as a fundamentally disruptive space and attempts to disorient the narrative so that the hospital is no longer central to it. The narrator splices his own story with letters between a middle-aged man and a teenage boy. As the letters progress toward being more explicitly sexual, the narrator weaves in his objections to what he presumes will be the readers' reactions. So, the true pervert—the reader or the narrator—of the story is never revealed.[32] It becomes clearer that the narrator has an unknown illness that requires constant medical attention and he amuses himself by pretending to be teenage boys in correspondence with middle-aged, pedophilic men. He later discloses, "Remembering is the disease [he] suffers from."[33] He describes his symptoms as fundamentally disorienting—fever, confusion, headache, numbness, diarrhea. For the unnamed narrator, his hospital stays reorder his world. In response, he attempts to depose the hospital with the imaginative world of the letters.

Even though the letters provide an alternate world for the narrator, they offer little in the way of orienting the narrative. Rather, they become desultory as more than half the content consists of lies. So, despite the narrator's best effort, his time spent in care grounds the narrative. After each letter, he comments from his home or hospital room. He addresses the reader directly about his time in the hospital, saying, "Minor surgery is when they perform it on someone else. You open me up and it is not minor. Four weeks away from the world. [. . .] Four weeks in a sterile hospital room."[34] Here, the trajectory of the story is similar to other life writing in that the illness is viewed as an interruption, a moment that halts the action of one's life temporarily before it is overcome and one moves on.[35] This surgery interrupts his lives—fantasy and reality—and he has to re-orient himself around his stay in the hospital or the recuperative activities at home. In this moment, the hospital space acts as a centrifuge for the rest of his life, even if temporarily. All other details, including his rich fantasy world, become subordinate to his hospital stay. In that moment, he must return to this putative interruption, such that the hospital stay is no longer a pause or a moment, but the central action of the story.

Though the narrator never adjusts to this new center, his resistance to it pinpoints the limitations that result from being the recipient of care. Given that the hospital assumes the focal point is the patient, the corollary is that the focal point for the patient must be the illness. In insisting that the hospital stay is a disruption, the narrator makes clear that his focus is not his illness, but rather the letters and exchanges that we read. Such a shift attempts again to move the focus away from the hospital and place it on the fantasy life woven by the narrator. This shift indicates that he would rather not focus on being the recipient of care, insisting that his life cannot be bound up by being a patient. Nevertheless, the narrator must return to the hospital and his need for care since his fantasy life cannot ground him more than the needs of his own body. Eventually, we learn that the narrator has not been out of his room for a year except for hospital visits. He says, "My world centers around this container."[36] Care becomes something he is obligated to receive regardless of his want. Since the antecedent of "container" is not clear in the story, his statement collapses all possible "container[s]," including his body, his home, and the hospital room. In his frustration, care and these containers become harbingers of disease and constrain his movements.

As an antidote to his physical tether, the narrator visualizes himself as someone else, at someplace else. According to one scholar, "Alameddine's infecting [sic] some of the lead characters [in *The Perv*] with the AIDS virus [sic] introduces a further alienating factor that complicates and broadens the spectrum of exilic existence."[37] I would argue that it isn't clear whether the protagonist in "The Perv" has AIDS, but the illness does force him to re-create his world. His imaginative letters provide an ironic escape for the limits imposed by his illness. Instead of curing him, the hospital precipitates his pretending and feeds what he terms his real disease: "Remembering is the disease I suffer from. It breaks my soul. It destroys my body."[38] If we take seriously his statement that remembering is the ailment, then the cure of imagination only partially solves the problem. He hints that his memories are of his own childhood as a gay child during Lebanon's civil war years. In his letters, he has to rely on these memories to create his teenage personas. His fantasy and memory remain side by side. The new world, full as it is of color, vigor, and movement, stands in stark contrast to the sterile, controlled, and bland environs of the hospital. Despite his cure not getting rid of his disease, it offers a useful, if ironic, antidote. Rather than perceive what is around him, he opts out of that perception and focuses on an imaginative one. When he creates a new environment, he no longer has to engage with the hospital or his home or his body and can minimize the role each is supposed to play.

The interplay between the narrator's physical space and its imaginative counterpart, cause and cure, rests on an intertwining of memory, illness, and exile. His description of memory as painful and disorienting, due to its somatic manifestations and emotive consequences, echoes Salman Rushdie's understanding of memory as a fundamental and dangerous component of exile.[39] Here, the memory turns dangerous because it becomes a miasma that the narrator chooses to transform through his imagination. He creates what Rushdie would term a third space, an imaginary homeland, in his letters to middle-aged men. Though he attempts to, in Edward Said's words, "compensat[e] for disorienting loss by creating a new world to rule," the narrator cannot untangle his own memory from his creative impulse, or his illness, or his feelings of displacement.[40] The hospital space, withal its itinerant anxieties, pain, and disorientation, blends with his imaginary world. The result is a powerful, revolving centrifuge with memory, illness, and exile at its center. This becomes more evident at the end of the story when the narrator confesses, "I can't go on anymore with this," but begins another correspondence, saying, "Joshua is a really nice boy. He is a fourteen-year-old Jew from Baku. He has been in this country for three years."[41] Clearly, this center must continue revolving in order to hold since the temporary, imaginative escape only fuels his illness and the resulting disorientation.

Since the narrator's imagination cannot fully heal him, it vexes the curative function of the hospital. With his illness, as he describes it, he cannot be a patient patient for there is no medicinal knowledge that proves useful. Instead, he reassembles his world by means of fantasy and eschews the supposed healing capacity of that space, inverting the commonly understood purpose of the hospital from being curative to being destructive. By itself, the hospital only reminds him of the bodily manifestation of his memory. As a precipice for his imagination, it promises at least a temporary cure.

In *I, the Divine*, the protagonist, Sarah Nour al-Din, attempts to write her memoir, but cannot write beyond the first chapter, be it preface, introduction, fiction, or epistle. The resulting text is a series of first chapters that make a coherent narrative about Sarah's life from prepubescent years in Lebanon to middle age in her chosen homes within the U.S. Sarah's older sister Lamia functions as a kind of violent doppelganger, pushing Sarah's detachment to extremes. Lamia kills several patients while on duty as their nurse because they irritate her by asking for assistance. Sarah tells Lamia's story over the course of several thwarted first chapters, eventually allowing Lamia's unsent forty-year correspondence with their mother to represent Lamia's own voice. Whereas the narrator in "The Perv" attempts to change his perception by finding an imaginative respite, Lamia in *I, the Divine* finds a respite by choosing to not be perceived by others. Much as in "The Perv," Lamia's story line problematizes the idea that the hospital is a healing space, but in *I, the Divine*, Lamia is the agent of destruction, not the hospital. Her murders not only indicate the hospital's dysfunction but also highlight the problematic understanding of care as a 'virtuous burden' by pushing it to disturbing extremes. Given her profession as a nurse, Lamia's behavior challenges the curative as it is realized within the duties of care. Her relationship with Sarah (as sister) and her relationship to Sarah (as narrative foil) exaggerates and comments on the relationship between being displaced and feeling embodied.

Lamia's actions perturb two of the foundational aspects of the relationship between caregivers and patients: first, that care is an activity one wants to do, and, second, that there is a clear demarcation between patients and caregivers.[42] Within one of the earlier first chapters, Sarah describes Lamia's depression as part of the familial landscape. True, Lamia's murders seem to be driven by a number of factors, among them her past life, her missing relationship with her mother, her estranged relationship with her husband, and her predilection for being alone (which Sarah labels the family's curse of loneliness). Nonetheless, I contend that each of these reasons point to a single issue: namely, Lamia's desire to be left alone or, in phenomenological terms, not to be perceived as a subjective object. In addition, both Lamia's letters and Sarah's writing hint at a more porous border between patient and nurse. Lamia's own writing evinces her need for psychological support and lack of desire to take care of most others. Her desires are particularly acute given that much of her narrative takes place in Lebanon during the civil war. The causal link between war, illness, and disability is well documented.[43] Lamia's duties, and therefore her frustration, would have been more onerous during this time. Lamia's character, a murderous female nurse, challenges the assumed feminized virtuous burden of caretaking. Her actions give primacy to the burdensome aspect, taking it to an extreme solipsistic conclusion.

Lamia's desire to not be intended manifests itself early in childhood. Within family interactions, Sarah recounts that Lamia refuses participation in storytelling and card games. Both activities require visual and oral communication wherein a person is required to perceive and be perceiving. Given Lamia's predilection, she would rather avoid all contact in which she becomes someone's object of intention, which moves her away from having to apprehend someone else except on her own terms. Unfortunately for her, the logistics of caretaking require that patients be interactive. One particular patient, whose need for morphine and constant care insists that she be his intended subjective object, forces her to reciprocate, so she kills him. Considering her actions in terms of the previous chapter's discussion of touch, her resistance to caretaking highlights the necessary reciprocity between touched/touching: namely, that "to touch another is in some sense always to compromise control, for even where the intent is outward—whether aggressive or palliatory—we are also touched in return."[44] Her other killings perform the same function: destroying the patients' need and reorienting her toward herself. The fact that her murders generate publicity seems to contradict her desire, but her notoriety is merely a by-product of her actions, not part of her initial goal.

Eventually, her solipsism reaches a logical, if disturbing, conclusion. In one scene after Lamia has been sedated for killing her patients, Sarah and her other sister, Amal, stand over a supine Lamia, talking. It must be noted that Sarah and Amal, in going into Lamia's room, perform the duties of care that Lamia refused to do, adhering to the normative behavioral codes for women. The conversation quickly drifts away from Lamia's situation to Amal's extramarital affair. What facilitates this shift is the presence of Lamia's supine and corpse-like appearance. Sarah narrates,

> In a darkened room, the heavy curtains drawn, Lamia lay on her bed, looking almost dead. A fairy tale came to mind, Sleeping Beauty, except Lamia was no beauty. She looked peaceful, a hint of a smile creased her lips. Someone had brushed her black hair, which surrounded her head on the pillow like a halo. The presentation was discomforting.[45]

Sarah and Amal's physical positioning *vis-à-vis* Lamia engenders the funereal quality, placing Lamia in a vulnerable position while Sarah and Amal assume a position of power. By staring down at her, they re-create the bodily positioning of a funeral, where the living stand while the dead cannot. The darkness also casts a literal shadow over Lamia's body as the curtains block out the warmth and light.

Despite Sarah's commentary, Amal and Sarah's discussion of Lamia is cursory and they quickly segue into a conversation about Amal's extramarital affair. When Sarah protests, Amal retorts, "It's not like she's listening."[46] Lamia's inert body makes this swift transition possible. In contrast, in the hospital's waiting room where the rest of the family is gathered, Lamia is not physically present but dominates the conversation. It is only after Amal and Sarah have stood over her that they can discuss other topics. Though Lamia "remain[s] unconscious throughout [their] hysterical giggling,"[47] her supine and quiet presence allows them to discuss themselves. Phenomenologically, Amal and Sarah do perceive Lamia and her surroundings. They look at her, see the darkness of the room, feel the coolness from lack of light, perceive her lack of movement, and understand themselves as physically above her. Nonetheless, Lamia does not remain their intended object and they are not oriented toward her for long. Much like an inanimate object, she can be mentally bypassed because she cannot intend them back. Prior to this, Lamia's desire to not be an intended object pushed her to sequester herself away from the rest of the family, yet by virtue of her being able to apprehend others she still remained a subjective object. Here, she becomes as unintended as she wanted to be.

Even if Lamia were awake, her participation in a conversation about Amal's sex life would be limited because of the sexual dysfunction in Lamia's marriage. (Her husband brings home a blowup doll and does not explain why.) The sisters' standing position solidifies their ability to ignore her and their power over her. As Rosemarie Garland-Thomson intimates in "Feminist Disability Studies," the standing position tends to be thought of as more powerful than the seated or supine.[48] Their discussion also reinforces their power via heterosexual privilege. In discussing Amal's doubled receipt of heterosexual desire (from both her husband and her lover), the sisters confirm Lamia's status as unintended by them, her current husband, and her husband from her past life (he was more sexually interested in her daughter). Their discussion of Amal's sex life queers Lamia based on her nonnormative marital relationships and their presence queers Lamia because they perform the gender-conforming caring behavior that Lamia resists.

Taking my cue from Steven Salaita, who considers Lamia a narrative foil for Sarah, I want to explore briefly how Lamia's character amplifies Sarah's difficulty belonging.[49] It is important to note that Sarah's understanding of her own belonging is peculiar to her feelings of displacement *vis-à-vis* her sexuality and national identity.[50] After Sarah leaves Lebanon for the United States, she struggles to understand herself in both places, eventually moving toward an acceptance of a permanent transnational identity. With Lamia (who does not leave Lebanon), the inability to belong takes on a transcendent quality. Unlike Sarah, she is not displaced from a particular nation-state, but instead from her existence. Lamia is a "talker," or a reincarnated soul according to Druze religion. Lamia's letters to her mother describe her intimate knowledge of her past life, her visit to her previous family, and her anger regarding her death.[51] Lamia's struggle to belong on earth *qua* Lamia parallels Sarah's struggle to belong within the United States or Lebanon. Whereas Sarah's failed relationships suggest difficulty with intending others, Lamia magnifies that difficulty by severing relationships so that she doesn't have to intend others. Lamia describes Sarah as a "sexmachine" who "swallows life out of her men."[52] Lamia not only describes Sarah's relationship with her ex-husbands and ex-paramours but this description also dovetails with Sarah's brief stint as a volunteer with HIV/AIDS patients. Sarah attempts to comfort the ill and the dying, but they die before she arrives. Unlike Lamia, Sarah wants to apprehend others, but is thwarted.

In addition to being an analogy for Sarah's displacement, Lamia's narrative also proffers commentary based on its incorporation of illness. In consonance with what Syrine Hout labels an intolerance for nostalgia in *The Perv*, Lamia's storyline pathologizes the nostalgia that attempts to recuperate a lost past.[53] Sarah's primary longing is for her mother and the cohesive family unit that she remembers before her mother was sent back to America. In contrast, Lamia's nostalgia is for her past life, a life where she felt valued and loved, if only by her children. Lamia's narrative seems to suggest that nostalgia is, as Rushdie hints, dangerous and, at its worst, homicidal.

This train of thought partly echoes the relationship between memory and illness in "The Perv," as it suggests that looking to memory can only provide a modicum of comfort. Yet it complicates the relationship between memory, exile, and illness because a one-to-one correlation between illness and memory assumes pain and loss inherent in memories, particularly those memories attached to experiences of displacement. If that were true here, Sarah's displacement would become more than the scaffolding that architects Sarah's life; it would make Sarah's life itself the experience of a long illness. In light of Lamia's narrative, Sarah's final first chapter becomes pivotal to understanding how discomfort can be curative. She asks,

> How can I expect readers to know who I am if I do not tell them about my family, my friends, the relationships in my life? Who am I if not where I sit in the world, where I fit in the lives of people dear to me? I have to explain how the individual participated in the larger organism, to show how I fit into this larger whole.[54]

The fact is that Sarah does not completely fit and in so (not) doing, she fits perfectly. Here, Sarah's series of questions functions much like Lamia's supine, funereal pose in the hospital. Both scenes ironize what it means to be stable and at peace.

In mapping out the relationship between embodiment and displacement, illness, as one particular instantiation of embodiment, provides a lens through which to understand the exilic condition. In "The Perv," illness functions as a metaphor for exile itself; and in *I, the Divine*, it is a commentary on displacement. For those characters, being a patient patient becomes difficult as they eschew common notions of cure. Instead of being a space for healing and rest, the hospital transforms into a destructive atmosphere and the care that would be assistive, corrosive. *Koolaids: The Art of War* complicates these ideas in several significant ways. Because this novel is concerned with HIV/AIDS, being a patient becomes necessary, though difficult, given that, within the early days of the epidemic, cure felt impossible. Rather than fight back by attempting to change one's perception, as with "The Perv," these characters fight back with the instrument of perception itself: their bodies. Their material bodies contest the validity of medical knowledge by upholding bodily knowledge as equal or superior. Care and caretaking figure prominently in this novel, carving out healing spaces in opposition to the pervasive, pernicious (and often medicalized) discourses about gay men during early years of the HIV/AIDS epidemic.[55] Without discounting the unique formal structures of "The Perv" and *I, the Divine*, I spotlight *Koolaids*'s formal concern with the sentimental narrative as that shapes the novel's engagement with illness and death.

Koolaids chronicles the lives of several friends whose lives have been changed by the early years of the HIV/AIDS epidemic in San Francisco and New York. It also depicts several families whose lives have been transformed by the Lebanese Civil War. The novel has a pastiche structure, so the narrator is not always clear and the text moves between past and present. The novel includes several genres, such as drama, letters, fantasy, emails, and Associated Press articles. Though the structure can be difficult to follow, common threads cohere, like the characters' narratives or stories repeated from different points of view. In part it is the text's construction that holds some of the sentimentality at bay. As Alameddine does in other works, he avoids creating a linear narrative and, as a result, disrupts the movement toward individualizing the narrative about HIV/AIDS and becoming enraptured by an individual and anecdotal story. Lennard Davis notes that narrating the sentimental is inherently bourgeois and individual.[56] *Koolaids* avoids that link by displacing the focus from one individual to a large and heterogeneous group.

Koolaids participates in the first-person-plural injunction of early HIV/AIDS activism. During the 1980s, activists harnessed the power of a critical mass such that 'we' questioned the invocation of individual stories to discuss HIV/AIDS and chided the public for its investment in simplistic narratives. *Koolaids* extends this critique by avoiding narratives that romanticize death and focusing on the living body and its function. Alameddine invokes the sentimental narrative only for a short moment, but he stops just short of allowing the characters to emote in a manner germane to the literature of sensibility. In that genre, characters are praised for their virtue and their relation to the sublime, usually underscored by or expressed through tears. Within sentimental narratives about HIV/AIDS, the person with the illness is either erased for the purpose of highlighting a usually uxorial, sororal, or maternal narrative; or the person becomes highly individualized such that the collective experience disappears.[57] In both instances, the sentimental focuses on the individual at the expense of "social and economic conditions that make [the] celebration possible."[58] Such a focus sanitizes the narratives about HIV/AIDS by obfuscating material reality and the bodily decay that accompanied the ill and the dying. Katrien De Moor hails *Koolaids* for its counter-discourse to *Philadelphia,* saying, "Alameddine's anti-sentimental strategy exposes how movies like *Philadelphia* chiefly elicit pity, thus providing a sham 'comfort' to the mainstream viewer."[59] The novel attempts to avoid the overindulgence of emotion characteristic of sentimentalism, yet harnesses the emotive and political power engendered by illness and death. Given the urgent politics at stake with the HIV/AIDS epidemic (and the Lebanese Civil War), the text eschews those reactions since they grant temporary cathartic release and provide little incentive to focus on preventive and proactive measures.

Mohammad, arguably the main character, narrates the last days of Kurt, an acquaintance who becomes a friend. In these scenes, the moments of perception slow down the narration and produce a temporal quality akin to real time in that each detail ticks off minutes and seconds. When Kurt discusses death as a trip, his euphemism seems to beckon sentimentality and symbolism, but he thwarts it when others attempt to confirm that the trip indeed is a sentimentalized version of death. One friend probes, "What kind of trip are you taking, Kurt?"[60] and Kurt ignores him. When the same friend asks whether he wants anything for his trip, Kurt asks for Coca-Cola via needleless syringe. The desire for Coke not only demonstrates that his sense of taste has not dissipated but also places the narrative squarely in the moment of taste and tactility instead of moving it toward the great beyond. Another friend talks to Kurt about "crossing to the other side, turning into a being of light, [and] getting rid of his earthly body."[61] This dissuades Kurt, who says that she "changed [his] mind"[62] since her ethereal comments make it unappealing. They remove Kurt from the sensory and concrete nature of the world, rendering him and the trip symbolic or transcendent.

As these friends wait for "something deep and meaningful [to] occur," they seem to miss a point that Hammad's poetry would corroborate: namely, Kurt's breathing is already "deep and meaningful." In contrast, Mohammad focuses on the mundane aspects of Kurt's living. Kurt coughs, wheezes, breathes, and talks.[63] In one instance, he preys on their sense of impending death by saying "I wish," pausing for dramatic effect, and singing the Oscar Mayer jingle.[64] Kurt's words and desire for Coke illume the absurdity of waiting for the dying moment that brings exemplary sagacity or transcendental experience. It is the consumption of the Coke, the mundane activities, and the singing that are significant. As an example, the moments in which Kurt remembers his childhood are relegated to a single paragraph within the four-page vignette. His recitations of childhood—moments of finishing supposedly unfinished business—become less important than the rote aspects of living.

When Kurt determines the flow of conversation, he, like the narrator in "The Perv," has power and agency over his own story. Others in *Koolaids* have similar control, since the patients or their friends narrate the scenes in the hospital. As a default function of these points of view, the narrative privileges the patient's body and troubles the caretakers' authority. Here, "the imagined authority of medical discourse seem[s] powerless when confronted with the human body unwilling to yield its secrets by constantly transforming itself after every medical intervention, thereby confounding predictability and wresting itself from medical control."[65] For instance, another peripheral character, Tim, defies hospital orders toward the end of his life. The narrator describes the machines as "forcing themselves upon him" and baldly states, "It was rape."[66] Darkly punning on the sexualized violation, the narrator says, "later his lungs actually exploded."[67] Doctors, Tim's parents, and other caretakers, as a vaguely defined and menacing 'they,' enforce their medical authority and rapaciously penetrate Tim's lungs with the machines. The narrator takes for granted that the lungs were not cooperating with the ventilator and air was not being exchanged, but rather pushed into the lungs. In this scenario, Tim's body has the ultimate authority as it refuses to participate in being a patient or receiving care. His lungs defy the mechanical breath and reject the life 'they' ordered.

Similar to Alameddine's other work, this novel questions the absolute (and inherently kind) nature of medical authority. Since *Koolaids* ekes out a space for the patient to have a voice in opposition to medical personnel, the implication is that the medical establishment does more harm than good. Tim's treatment violates his body, despite the desire to keep him alive. The doctors and those who trusted in them did not defer to Tim's body as an authority. Medical professionals, even as a complicated, amorphous group, become the shadows on the patients' authority because the medical professionals' opinions are constantly present. In Tim's story, his lungs must speak over and against others' ideas and orders. Consequently, bodily authority and medical authority remain in conversation, even if in tension. Whereas in "The Perv," the narrator foregrounds medical professionals' ideas to refute them, in *Koolaids*, the interplay between bodily assertions and the doctors' orders highlights that there is a consistent though uneven exchange.

These moments spotlight the inaccuracy of how we define patients, particularly as it relates to the notion of long-suffering. The unnamed narrator of "The Perv," Lamia, Tim, and Kurt trouble the definition of a patient. When the definition applies to one who is undergoing medical treatment, these characters challenge the adjectival definition of 'patient' as inaccurate and useless since these patients refuse to suppress their own agency. It is not the treatment but the patient's agency that sustains him or her. In fact, Mohammad narrates that Kurt's treatment had stopped working long before he drinks the Coke. Tim defies the expected inertia and pliability associated with patients' bodies. When Tim's body rejects the treatment, it exerts its own influence. Although Kurt and Tim's agency does not keep them alive, it buoys them as others attempt to usurp their power.

Since these fictions question the very idea of being a patient, they invite scrutiny regarding the relationship between doctors and patients, specifically the dynamics of how and when doctors intend patients. This relationship assumes doctors' absolute authority and upholds the notion that doctors care about their patients as part of a moral impulse unfettered by stigmatizing and paternalistic narratives. In one regard, the doctor and patient relationship relies on a patient who remains theoretically disembodied because she or he has no power over his or her own body. Here, the patient cannot participate in this relationship beyond being an object. When these texts physically remove the doctors from the room, they upend the common conception of doctors' authority and knowledge. Because doctors are absent (or, in some cases, wrong), the patients fully realize their identities as objective subjects based on their ability to intend their doctors even in absentia. It could be argued that the doctors maintain authority in the room and still objectify the patient even when they are physically absent because their orders are still followed. Tim is still on a ventilator and the narrator in "The Perv" still has a surgery. Yet in Tim's case, the body does not (perhaps cannot) follow the order and, in the "The Perv," the narrator refuses to accept medical authority. In short, doctors' power is rendered impotent when it comes into contact with these patients' bodies. Here, medical authority must interact with the authority that emanates from having bodily-centered knowledge. As a result, sentimentality fails because it too relies on the patient's theoretical disembodiment, as sentimental characters do not truly inhabit their bodies. As with Tom Hanks in *Philadelphia*, sentimentalized bodies are objects to be discussed, modified, medicated, and acted upon, rather than sentient, moving entities that help the person inside give the world meaning. When the doctor can no longer lay claim to the patient's body, his or her virtuous burden is moot and the patient's body (living or dead) cannot be used in service of the sublime, nor can the patient's body simply be an object.

In narratives about death, sentimentality occupies a vexed position. In *Koolaids*, Mohammad appears in a recurring scene in which the four horsemen of the apocalypse approach him and try to take him to his death. In four of the five repetitions, three of the horsemen are in agreement with taking Mohammad and the other horseman (usually portrayed as Jesus Christ) rejects him. In the fifth repetition and final scene of the novel, the fourth horseman takes on the persona of Mohammad's close friend Scott, and Mohammad dies. This recurring scene weaves Mohammad's disembodied transcendental experience with his embodied reality because Mohammad remains in his hospital bed as he views what may or may not be a fantasy. Regardless of whether the horsemen are real, Mohammad consistently returns to the bodily experience of being in a hospital bed. In the first scene, he says, "the hospital bed hurts my back."[68] In the second scene, he complains, "My eyes hurt. They hurt from the inside. A constant throbbing."[69] In the third, he says, "I would give anything for a good night's sleep."[70] In the fourth, he connects his material experience with the metaphorical, saying, "I still have no feeling in my fingers. I can't touch home."[71] In the final scene, he ends the novel, stating, "I die."[72] Each of the experiences highlights the sensory via the neurological: pain, insomnia, sensation loss, and cessation of brain function. In emphasizing these kinds of experiences, where the brain fires electrical pulses to the nerves, Mohammad moves the scene away from the sentimentalized understanding of moving into the great beyond, and classifies it as a neurological event or, in the case of the first four scenes, a thwarted neurological event.

Given that Mohammad is dying of complications related to AIDS (hinting at toxoplasmosis), the transition between the four horsemen and the neurological sensations could be interpreted in two ways. First, this could depict AIDS dementia where the intermingling of Mohammad's fantasy life and his bodily sensations indicate a gradual movement toward death. Second, this could be Mohammad's vacillation between dreams and reality—unrelated to AIDS dementia—wherein he tries to make sense of his own dying. For both interpretations, I turn to the politicized phrase 'dying from AIDS.' During the early years of the HIV/AIDS epidemic, the main understanding of AIDS patients was limited to images of emaciated men and children in hospital beds. As the fight for research funding and awareness gained momentum, the image changed to one where healthy-looking people 'lived with HIV or AIDS.' The movement between these two images, the emaciated hospital patient on the one hand and the active, healthy-looking patient on the other, leaves no middle ground. Whereas the sickly hospital patient plays into common ideas regarding illness, the active patient eclipses the bodily reality associated with having HIV or AIDS. Mohammad's scenes offer a portion of middle ground: Mohammad's fantasy points toward a sentimental, if unorthodox, experience as he is being ushered away while the return to a bodily reality grounds his understanding of a movement toward death in his sensory experiences. He has to feel the pain from his back or eyes, or not feel sensation in his fingers. Even his statement "I die" appears redundant given that the fourth rider "leads [them] away."[73] However, his declaration underscores the fact that his body is a part of this moment. The ending of the novel and his life underlines the sentimental nature of dying as coupled with the bodily reality thereof.

Syrine Hout's work on *Koolaids* classifies it as a Lebanese exilic novel,[74] referring to the phrase "In Lebanon, I fit but I don't belong. In America, I belong but do not fit."[75] I wish to point out how the characters' understanding of their exilic or displaced condition rests on their material realities. In one of the four horsemen scenes, the loss of sensation in his fingers precedes his understanding of an inability to "touch home."[76] Here, the metaphorical and the attendant dissatisfaction precede the loss of sensation in his fingers. Of course, emotions or feelings of displacement do not automatically correspond to physical sensation or perceived experience. However, bodily references suggest that thinking of exile solely in emotive terms is insufficient. As for the sentimental, Kurt, Mohammad, and others become dissatisfied as the reliance on it makes a moment too saccharine, effaces their agency, and downplays a physical reality.[77] As Andreas Pflitsch argues, "Home and homelessness are always ambivalent in the work of Alameddine [because] he does not provide simple solutions, but shows the unavoidable complexity of the topic."[78] Part of this 'unavoidable complexity' is that, for these characters, the physicality of exile extends beyond simply being in a different country than one's country of origin. Recalling the illness of "The Perv," Lamia's violence, and Mohammad's fingers, these novels suggest that exile or displacement is an experience manifested in the very bodies of the exilic or displaced.

Yet exile is not simply embodied, so it is imperative to consider the instances when illness becomes an analogous experience to exile. If exile uncovers limitations within geopolitics, illness parallels that experience, foregrounding the limitations of the physical body. Though *Koolaids* attempts to avoid the sentimental, there are scenes that toe the line. There, the sentimental leverages the critique of simplistic narratives regarding HIV/ AIDS. In one scene between Scott and Mohammad, Mohammad encounters the physical and material effects of illness, the re-orienting of his world as well as sadness and grief, all of which make it difficult to turn completely away from sentiment. Scott and Mohammad discuss Scott's changed appearance because of his Kaposi's sarcoma (KS) lesions. In this passage, which does not extend past one page, Scott looks at himself in the mirror. Mohammad has already told us that "the most beautiful boy in the world was gone, the swan into the ugly duckling. The KS was feeding on Scott's face. Omophagia."[79] Despite the definitive nature of what Mohammad narrates, his conversation with Scott is tentative. He asks whether Scott is okay and hesitates in his speech. After Scott responds, "I always wondered what it felt like to be a blueberry muffin,"[80] the scene ends. Certainly, the humor "counter[s] illness indignities."[81] In addition, the vignette's brevity keeps it from being sentimental, and so does the appeal to memory. Recalling that Mohammad resorts to memory often, this story gains as much importance as others that are less bittersweet and more violent.

Though this scene remains critical of sentimentality, it relies on it to participate in the vexed mourning that pervades the text. That is, Scott's subjectivity relies on Mohammad's mourning. Mourning constitutes an inescapable component of the novel as it demonstrates the physical destruction of AIDS. As Douglas Crimp notes of art that mourns, particularly art during the AIDS epidemic, the championing of activist art dismisses the integral nature of loss and mourning. It is possible to "[draw] too rigid a distinction between the two kinds of art about AIDS, that the feelings of loss and despair expressed in the one kind of art would become necessary in activist art as well."[82] *Koolaids*, then, as activist art, questions the investment in narratives that only mourn, though it cannot avoid those moments, however brief. In terms of an engagement with sentimentality, caretaking in *I, the Divine* mirrors the conversations about death and mourning in *Koolaids*. Sarah volunteers to take care of HIV/AIDS patients and they die before she arrives. Even when Sarah does form a relationship with an AIDS patient, he mistreats her and tirades against Mexicans, creating a three-dimensional character who cannot, despite his peripheral position in the novel, be reduced to a victim. *Koolaids*'s chronicle of the epidemic's early years also performs the same kind of ambivalence present in looking at AIDS activist videos or art projects. Inasmuch as the video footage, the AIDS quilt, and the giant condom on the Place de la Concorde worked for their particular time and space, examining the art in retrospect reveals that the art oversimplified the activists' lives.[83] Likewise, to understand Scott solely in terms of his domestic life with Mohammad or Sarah's patient solely in terms of AIDS would dismiss them as fully realized characters. It would be dangerous not to "confront the daily emotional toll that AIDS inevitably takes."[84] Because so many characters die between its pages, *Koolaids* confronts grief while simultaneously showcasing frustration at poor funding for AIDS research, public stigma, and scant government support.

The Hakawati complicates the multiple interpretations heretofore available in Alameddine's fiction regarding the relationships between embodiment and displacement. For "The Perv," illness metaphorizes displacement so much that the deleterious effects are written on the body of the subject. In *I, the Divine*, Lamia's storyline comments on the condition of exile, suggesting that displacement proffers an ironic stability. For the characters of *Koolaids*, exile is only one form of displacement and illness another. The two become parallel narratives that cannot be summarized in emotive terms. *Koolaids* also suggests that neither embodied experience nor displacement can be detached from the politics that creates it. Whereas the previous texts allow for illness to be a productive lens through which to understand displacement, *The Hakawati: A Story* upends that proposition. When illness becomes one's impetus for reflection, these characters reinscribe the problematic narratives attached to medical authority and care. Consequently, *The Hakawati* implies exile, and illness can work to uphold systems that usurp bodily authority. Like *Koolaids*, the novel's structure and preoccupation with sentimentality shapes the engagement with these ideas.

Similar to "The Perv," *The Hakawati* (meaning 'storyteller' in colloquial Lebanese Arabic) juxtaposes the fantastic with the hospital. The protagonist, Osama al-Kharrat, returns to Lebanon to visit his ailing father, Farid, in the hospital. Prompted by his visit to both his boyhood home and the hospital, he remembers his childhood, specifically memories of events and stories narrated to him by others like his Uncle Jihad and his grandfather. Interspersed throughout the novel are fantastic stories of jinn, deities, and epic battles. Osama and his sister, Lina, view the hospital room as a hospice since their father's condition is terminal. Though the space carries the foreboding of death, Farid does not die within the novel. Instead, the final scene depicts Osama asking others to listen to his storytelling. Other critics have noted *The Hakawati*'s structural similarity to *1001 Nights* and both texts' emphasis on storytelling as a way to stave off death.[85]

The similarities to *1001 Nights*, the juxtaposition of fantastic stories with realism, allows for the hospital space to be bathetic as well as dispassionate, disturbing as well as inviting. In one scene, the family gathers to celebrate *Eid al Adha*, the Festival of Sacrifice, in Farid's hospital room. Though other scenes privilege the near-empty, silent, recuperative space common to Western conceptions of hospitals, here the hospital room becomes a place where people can gather *en masse*. As with any space with an open invitation, this series of scenes (they are spliced by other stories) allows for the family to continuously enter, eat, and drink together. In response to a comment that there is "so much food," Aunt Samia replies "so much of us" because "there's more family coming."[86] The space continuously fills up, emphasizing the abundance of bodies and, by implication, life and vigor. Having the *Adha* feast in the hospital also adds an element of celebration where there is generally a more morose atmosphere. Whereas the celebratory atmosphere of these scenes disrupts the clinical nature of the hospital, the narration complicates the authority upon which the clinical atmosphere rests. Within these spaces, the patient typically becomes a muted object about which caretakers speak. Consider the earlier discussion of the virtuous burden. *The Hakawati*'s illustration of the patient defies the same norms, again relying on the patient's agency to do so. In some instances, the father, Farid, speaks to assert his agency, and in other moments, he can assert it without speaking.[87] When Osama describes what is clinically wrong with Farid, the hospital room shrinks to focus on his father's experience and perspective even though first-person narration implicates Osama as the authority. Osama literally looks down on his father or looks laterally at Farid's hospital bed. Osama's authority gets undermined by his tone of detachment and inability to describe his father's wants or needs. Other characters' physicality grants them a degree of authority over Farid as well, but they cannot truly speak for him either. At one point, Osama's niece asks Farid questions, telling him to squeeze her hand in response. She takes on the role of translating these squeezes into responses. Though she receives responses from him, she still concludes not only that he is not awake but also that it is "better that way."[88] Keeping in mind the injunctions, elsewhere in the novel, that one should "never trust the teller. [. . .] Trust the tale,"[89] the novel itself also undercuts the niece's assumed authority. The tale, his fingers, tell one story, and the niece, the teller, another. The hospital becomes disruptive since the caregivers upset the expectation that they would be able to speak for the patient.

Thinking through the spatial set-up of *The Hakawati*, there is a distinction between Osama's literal point of view and Farid's silence. In reading Osama while he watches Farid, the novel maintains focus on Farid. At times, Osama's whereabouts with regard to Farid's hospital bed aren't quite clear in that he sometimes looks down, or over, or to his side. Given that prepositions are supposed to articulate a "specific relational and spatial structure,"[90] it is worth noting that these prepositional phrases give little information regarding physical proximity or height. They do not ground Osama's position specifically, and by default Farid becomes the center as all visual points converge upon him. This provides a counterbalance to the inherent lack of clarity in others' perspectives of Farid, and centralizes Farid's experience by making the novel revolve around his physical location. He is everyone's intended objective subject. If Osama is looking down at the father, he assumes a kind of power; if he is at his side, there is a presumption of care. Regardless of Osama's position, his power is tenuous and his care minimal since Osama's position remains relative to Farid's. Farid cannot be simply the object of the narrative, but an objective subject and, therefore, a participant in shaping it.

Farid's hospital stay also opens up the possibilities for contextualizing the validity of others' literal and figurative perspectives. If exile is about negotiating one's time in the homeland and the host space, these hospital scenes re-examine the authority granted to the stories one tells about homeland and exilic space. All of these stories are told from the space of Osama's homeland (Lebanon), rather than his host country (America). Because Osama's stories are shaped by memory and the *hakawati* assumes creative license, Osama holds a vexed authority over the story since he is both the principal narrator and the least trustworthy. He is not the only source of information, but all stories are filtered through him. The reader and the listener remain under the *hakawati*'s influence even if they retain the option of deciding whether to believe. All that we know of Osama's exile, Farid's illness, and the family's memories is told from the point of view of one person—who tells us not to trust him. We must "never trust the teller. [. . .] Trust the tale."[91]

Osama's feelings of displacement and his experience as an exile force him to probe his memories, a journey made more provocative because of Farid's illness. Osama's ability to process his displacement and Farid's healing become contingent on each other. Farid becomes an object with whom Osama relates in order to understand his own subjectivity. For example, Osama tries to see his father but cannot. He says, "I forced myself to look at him, to see him as he was. The image of a younger version kept superimposing itself upon his face."[92] Recall that only the act of seeing is perception. All other acts that attempt to make sense of that initial sight are association, judgment, memory, or paying attention. These go beyond the immediacy of apprehension to interpretation.[93] When Osama reverts to memory, he desires to make sense of what he visually perceives. His action is intentional as he does intend to perceive his father, but the superimposition of a memory onto reality thwarts his attempt.[94] This memory should be comforting as it displaces the older Farid with a younger, presumably healthier version, but it provides little solace since it only emphasizes Farid's current condition. The foray into memory yields no particular insight since Osama cannot divorce either his memory or his perception of Farid from Farid as father. As with Alameddine's other works, memory becomes dangerous territory, difficult to navigate and comprehend. The hospital converts to a space where recuperation is constituted by evanescence, not permanence. Osama cannot recover from his memory any more than Farid can from his illness. This scene suggests that memory can be not only inaccurate and blurry but also useless for understanding the past. The exile's memory is no longer trustworthy, no longer capable of providing healing, making exile itself vertiginous or what Edward Said calls "a jealous state."[95]

Osama's inability to separate his father's authority from Osama's present understanding bears implications for the power dynamic between caregiver and recipient. Since their past parent/child relationship and their current relationship exist simultaneously within the novel, it becomes clear that the power to heal and to care is not already determined by their roles, nor is it mutual. It can be transformed and exchanged. At the conclusion, the intricacies of their relationship become more pronounced as Osama is asked to speak directly to Farid. It appears that Farid is nearing death and Lina says, "He is not responding to anything."[96] She asks Osama to "just tell him you're here."[97] This scene has all the characteristics of a sentimental moment: Lina is crying. Osama is speechless. Much like the scene between

Mohammad and Scott in *Koolaids*, this moment harnesses the emotive power of grief. Yet regardless of the sentimentality and attempt to honor Farid, this moment is also rebellious. For the bulk of the story, Osama recounts his father's disdain for stories and Farid's strict order that Osama not listen to or retell the grandfather's stories. Despite Farid's clear stance, Osama says, "Your father told me that story. [. . .] Do you want me to tell you?"[98] He rebels against his father's wishes by narrating his grandfather's origin story. What adds insult to injury is that the novel forms a feedback loop, which suggests this rebellion continues *ad infinitum*. Both the first and last word of *The Hakawati* is "Listen." The repeated injunction loops the narration, and the novel becomes cyclical where Osama tells his stories as well as the grandfather's stories continuously. Subsequently, Osama's rebellion and the power oscillating between himself and his father is the story of the novel, the story of Osama's exile, and the only avenue that allows Osama to work through his exile.

It is only after Osama can recognize (potential) loss that he can negotiate his own feelings in relation to it. The final scene with his father and the scenes of Uncle Jihad's death suggest that Osama must have authority to explore his feelings *vis-à-vis* exile. As with *Koolaids*, little saves the characters from a confrontation with death. For instance, Uncle Jihad's final moments are like Kurt's final days and Mohammad's encounters with the four horsemen in that the depiction of Uncle Jihad's death focuses on bodily function. Osama describes finding his uncle's body while Jihad, Farid, and Osama are on a trip: "Uncle Jihad sat on the toilet, his pajama pants around his ankles, his head slumped, his eyes staring at a spot on the carpet. The bathroom smelled of shit."[99] Though Osama and Farid cry, the focus of the prose remains on the meticulous acts of cleaning and moving Jihad's body, calling Mohammad's mother, getting rid of Farid's mistress, and calming Farid down. The detailed recitation of Osama's actions recalls the slow, ticking minutiae of Kurt's last days. Just like the vignettes in *Koolaids*, the passage of finding Uncle Jihad does not take up much physical space in the book. There is a swift movement from cleaning Jihad's soiled bottom (and its smell) to the memory of a story Jihad told Osama. To emphasize the scatological swiftly shifts the focus from overarching, emotional narratives to mundane, task-oriented details. A detail-oriented focus also grants Osama agency as he cleans his uncle and buttresses his narrative agency about his time in America. Here, the power within the story echoes the power over the story, implying that working through exile requires that one usurp narrative agency. Furthermore, Osama's ability to explore his exile is contingent upon his father's failing health and Uncle Jihad's failed health, suggesting that the exploration of exile, at least in this novel, depends on illness or death.

The relationship between embodiment and displacement illuminates how the two remain contingent on each other, assuming multiple forms throughout these fictive works. The hospital space, specifically the patient's room, upsets facile understandings and easy analogies about illness and exile. One cannot understand the narrator of "The Perv" without understanding his illness or *I, the Divine*'s Sarah without Lamia. *Koolaids* is not possible without the interaction between the displacement caused by the Lebanese Civil War or the experiences of embodiment germane to the early days of the HIV/AIDS epidemic. The very structure of the novel sutures these two stories together as uneasy analogies. Within *Hakawati*, illness and exile circulate in a feedback loop catalyzed by power. Even though a hospital stay can re-center one's life or prepare one for death, cure is not as easy as leaving or dying, care is not as simple as being present, and authority is not solely in the hands of the medical professional. Sentiment, or the affect that might tether these ideas together, ruptures as well. It creates too simplistic a picture of death and disease. However politically charged it can be, the sentimental eviscerates characters, denying them the bodily experiences germane to living. Here, the complex relationship between feeling embodied and being displaced makes clear that characters not only feel personally fulfilled as non-normative, but also the peculiar, frustrating experience of being a problem moors their critiques of what displaced them in the first place.

In this chapter, I explored how Alameddine's fiction comments on narratives about the relationship between embodiment and the imbricated concepts of belonging and the nation-state. In the next chapter, I explore how the nation creates a narrative about embodiment and demarcates which bodies make acceptable activists. Certainly, the previous chapters have pushed at the limits of embodied critique by highlighting the body's ephemerality. The next chapter explicitly analyzes under what conditions embodied experience reaches limits when engaged in social and political critique.

NOTES

1. See Rabih Alameddine, last modified August 2013. http://www.rabihalameddine.com. Much of the commercial praise for Alameddine's work can be found on his website.
2. For more discussion on Alameddine's place in Arab American fiction, see Salaita, *Modern Arab American Fiction*.
3. See Syrine C. Hout, "Memory, Home, and Exile in Contemporary Anglophone Lebanese Fiction," *Critique*. 46.3 (2005): 219–33; Syrine C. Hout, "Of Fathers and the Fatherland in the post-1995 Lebanese Exilic Novel," *World Literature Today: A Literary Quarterly of the University of Oklahoma*. 75.2 (Spring 2001): 285–93; Syrine C. Hout, "The Last Migration: The First Contemporary Example of Lebanese Diasporic Literature." *Arab Voices in the Diaspora*. Ed. Layla Al-Maleh (New York, NY: Rodopi, 2009); Syrine C. Hout, "The Predicament of In-Betweenness in the Contemporary Lebanese Exilic Novel in English." *Literature and Nation in the Middle East*. Ed. Yasir Suleiman and Ibrahim Muhawi (Edinburgh: Edinburgh University Press, 2006); Syrine C. Hout, "The Tears of Trauma: Memories of Home, War, and Exile in Rabih Alameddine's *I, the Divine*," *World Literature Today: A Literary Quarterly of the University of Oklahoma*. 82.5 (2008): 59–62; Aleksandar Hermon, "Changing the Subject," *PEN America: A Journal for Writers and*

Readers. 9 (2008): 19–28; Cristina Garrigós, "The Dynamics of Intercultural Dislocation Hybridity in Rabih Alameddine's *I, the Divine.*" *Arab Voices in the Diaspora*; Carol Fadda-Conrey, "Transnational Diaspora and the Search for Home in Rabih Alameddine's *I, the Divine: A Novel in First Chapters.*" *Arab Voices in the Diaspora.*

4. W.E.B. Du Bois, *The Souls of Black Folk* (New York, NY: W. W. Norton & Company, 1999), 9.
5. Du Bois, *Souls of Black Folk*, 10.
6. I am not the first person to note the relationship between Du Bois's use of the word 'peculiar' and the description of slavery as a peculiar institution. See Moustafa Bayoumi, *How Does It Feel to Be a Problem?: Being Young and Arab in America* (New York, NY: Penguin Books, 2008).
7. Bayoumi, *How Does It Feel to Be a Problem*, 6.
8. Du Bois, *Souls of Black Folk*, 11.
9. Edward Said, *Reflections on Exile and Other Essays* (Cambridge, MA: Harvard University Press, 2002), 186.
10. Dickson D. Bruce, Jr., "W.E.B. Du Bois and the Idea of Double Consciousness." *W.E.B. Du Bois: The Souls of Black Folk*. Eds. Henry Louis Gates, Jr., and Terri Hume Oliver (New York, NY: W. W. Norton & Company, 1999), 238.
11. Samhan, "Not Quite White," 209.
12. Du Bois, *Souls of Black Folk*, 11.
13. Elam, *Souls of Mixed Folk*, 130.
14. Gayle Salamon, " 'The Place Where Life Hides Away': Merleau-Ponty, Fanon, and the Location of Bodily Being," *Differences: A Journal of Feminist Cultural Studies* 17.2 (2006), 97.
15. Grosz, *Volatile Bodies*, x–xi.
16. Sara Ahmed, *Queer Phenomenology* (Durham, NC: Duke UP, 2006), 3.
17. Erevelles, *Disability and Difference*, 2.
18. I am grateful to Dr. Ruth Lexton for this observation.
19. "Care." *Oxford English Dictionary,* last modified August 2013, http://www.oed.com.
20. Erevelles, *Disability and Difference*, 174.
21. Eva Feder Kittay, "When Caring Is Just and Justice is Caring: Justice and Mental Retardation," *Public Culture*. 13.3 (2001), 560.
22. Erevelles, *Disability and Difference*, 175.
23. Shildrick, *Dangerous Discourses*, 21.
24. Erevelles, *Disability and Difference*, 3.
25. Paul Longmore, *Why I Burned My Book and Other Essays on Disability* (Philadelphia, PA: Temple UP, 2003), 208.
26. See Tom Shakespeare and Nicholas Watson, "The Social Model of Disability: An Outmoded Ideology?" *Research in Social Science and Disability*. 2 (2002): 9–28. Centre for Disability Studies—Disability Archive. Retrieved 6 April 2010. http://disability-studies.leeds.ac.uk/library; Lennard Davis, *The Disability Studies Reader*. 4th ed. (New York, NY: Routledge, 2013). Many other scholars have taken up the issue of the medical model explaining the way that outlook assumes a norm and a standard that disabled people do not meet. The medical model also subordinates embodied knowledge to putatively objective scientific knowledge.
27. Erevelles, *Disability and Difference*, 10.
28. Jennifer James, "Gwendolyn Brooks, World War II, and the Politics of Rehabilitation." *Feminist Disability Studies*. Ed. Kim Q. Hall (Bloomington, IN: Indiana UP, 2011), 137–38.
29. Ibid.
30. Hout, "Tears of Trauma," 60.
31. Kadi, *Food for Our Grandmothers*, xiv.

32. Though it is outside the purview of this chapter, the lack of clarity regarding "the perv" opens this story up to a queer reading in which the narrator attempts to queer the reader by suggesting that the readers have a non-normative sexuality. He positions himself as saving the world from these men and states that it is the readers' imagination that makes the interaction 'perverted.'
33. Rabih Alameddine, *The Perv* (New York, NY: Picador, 1999), 54.
34. Ibid., 20.
35. G. Thomas Couser, *Recovering Bodies: Illness, Disability and Life Writing* (Madison, WI: U of Wisconsin Press, 1997), 5.
36. Alameddine, *The Perv*, 24.
37. Hout, "Memory, Home, and Exile," 221.
38. Alameddine, *The Perv*, 54.
39. Salman Rushdie, *Imaginary Homelands* (New York, NY: Penguin Books, 1992), 10.
40. Said, *Reflections on Exile*, 181.
41. Alameddine, *The Perv*, 61.
42. There is much to be said about Lamia's patients and their forthright claim to her attention even though she deprives them of it. For the purposes of scope, I have limited the discussion to Lamia.
43. Erevelles, *Disability and Difference,* 18.
44. Shildrick, *Dangerous Discourses,* 23.
45. Alameddine, *I, the Divine,* (New York, NY: W.W. Norton & Company, 2001), 131.
46. Ibid., 132.
47. Ibid., 134.
48. See Rosemarie Garland-Thomson, "Feminist Disability Studies," *Signs: Journal of Women in Culture and Society.* 30.2 (2005): 1557–87. I draw from Rosemarie Garland-Thomson's allusion to sit-point theory in disability studies, which asks us to consider the way that stance determines power vis-à-vis the disabled. In Lamia's case, the sisters draw their power from her being supine.
49. Salaita, *Modern Arab American Fiction*, 52.
50. In *Modern Arab American Fiction*, Salaita contends that Sarah's rape is the traumatic experience that keeps her from moving beyond first chapters (52). See Salaita. Syrine Hout, in "Tears of Trauma," situates the novel within the genre of trauma fiction and makes a similar claim (60–61). See Hout.
51. The Lebanese Civil War forces Lamia to search for her other family members as the constant barrage of fighter planes makes noise anxiogenic. For Lamia, the patients' noise parallels that of the fighter planes and causes her to silence them.
52. Alameddine, *I, the Divine*, 155–56.
53. Hout, "Memory, Home and Exile," 223.
54. Alameddine, *I, the Divine,* 308.
55. See Lynne Rogers, "Hypocrisy and Homosexuality in the Middle East: Selim Nassib's *Oum* and Rabih Alameddine's *Koolaids,*" *Journal of Commonwealth and Postcolonial Studies.* 10.1 (2003): 145–63; Dervla Shanahan, "Reading Queer A/theology into Rabih Alameddine's *Koolaids,*" *Feminist Theology.* 19.2 (2011): 129–42. Rogers discusses Rabih Alameddine's approach to rendering gay identity as distinct in the Arab literature tradition. Shanahan also provides an apt reading of the queer cosmology Alameddine creates as a way to sustain his critiques within *Koolaids*.
56. Davis, *Enforcing Normalcy*, 3–4.
57. See G. Thomas Couser, *Recovering Bodies*; Sharon Oard Warner, "The Way We Write Now: The Reality of AIDS in Contemporary Short Fiction," *Studies in Short Fiction.* 30 (1993): 491–500.
58. Erevelles, *Disability and Difference* 14.

59. Katrien De Moor, "Diseased Pariahs and Difficult Patients," *Cultural Studies*. 19.6 (2005): 744.
60. Rabih Alameddine, *Koolaids: The Art of War* (New York, NY: Picador, 1998), 160.
61. Ibid., 161.
62. Ibid., 161.
63. Ibid., 160–61.
64. Ibid., 162.
65. Erevelles, *Disability and Difference,* 12.
66. Alameddine, *Koolaids,* 67.
67. Ibid., 67.
68. Ibid., 1.
69. Ibid., 53.
70. Ibid., 98.
71. Ibid., 166.
72. Ibid., 245.
73. Ibid., 245.
74. Syrine Hout has written at least five articles on Rabih Alameddine's work that classify him as an exilic Lebanese novelist. Four of these articles discuss *Koolaids* explicitly in these terms.
75. Rabih Alameddine, *Koolaids,* 40.
76. Ibid., 166.
77. De Moor makes this argument about sentimentality in *Koolaids*, citing that the novel eschews the sentimentality usually prevalent in HIV/AIDS narratives to push the audience out of their default reactions. See De Moor.
78. Andreas Pflitsch, "To Fit or Not to Fit. Rabih Alameddine's Novels *Koolaids* and *I, the Divine*." *ArabAmericas: Literary Entanglements of the American Hemisphere and the Arab World*. Eds. Ottmar Ette and Friederike Pannewick (Madrid: Iberoamericana, 2006), 279.
79. Alameddine, *Koolaids,* 57.
80. Ibid., 57.
81. De Moor, "Diseased Pariahs and Difficult Patients," 734.
82. Douglas Crimp, *Mourning and Melancholia* (Cambridge, MA: MIT Press, 2002), 262.
83. Here I refer to specific activist acts by the AIDS Coalition to Unleash Power (ACT UP), which I will discuss in more detail in chapter 4.
84. Crimp, *Mourning*, 264.
85. This marks a possible structural similarity to *Koolaids* as well. One could interpret Mohammad's stories as a way to stave off death. See Salaita, *Modern Arab American Fiction*, 53.
86. Rabih Alameddine, *The Hakawati: A Story* (New York, NY: Anchor Books, 2008), 125.
87. Though Farid asserts agency in speaking, that agency does not showcase the phenomenological as it relies on words rather than Farid's senses or others' sensory experience of him.
88. Alameddine, *Hakawati*, 219.
89. Ibid., 206.
90. Sobchack, *Carnal Thoughts,* 5.
91. Alameddine, *Hakawati,* 206.
92. Ibid., 271.
93. See Merleau-Ponty, *Phenomenology of Perception*.
94. In phenomenology, the act of seeing is perception. All other acts that attempt to make sense of that perception are moments of association, judgment, memory, or paying attention. These other acts go beyond the immediacy of perception

and beyond the reach of a phenomenology of the body and embodied experience. See Merleau-Ponty, *Phenomenology of Perception.*

95. Said, *Reflections on Exile,* 178.
96. Alameddine, *Hakawati,* 508.
97. Ibid., 508.
98. Ibid., 513.
99. Ibid., 291.

4 Beyond 1991
Magic Johnson and the Limits of HIV/AIDS Activism

To detail the aims of this discussion, I will return to the analysis of the previous chapter briefly. In it, I explore how Rabih Alameddine's fictional characters answer the question "How does it feel to be a problem?" Their answers correspond to W.E.B. Du Bois's answer ("peculiar") and Moustafa Bayoumi's response ("frustrating"). Yet they eschew the might implied by Du Bois's articulation of "dogged strength." For Alameddine's characters, to be an embodied problem requires that one find comfort in dismissing the fictions of normalcy and belonging. In Du Bois's terms, the second sight is a gift that allows these characters to understand that the foundations of inclusion are tenuous within the American imaginary. As a result, one of the questions that undergirds the previous discussion is the following: how does one create oneself as a subject when one has consistently been viewed as an object? More to the point of this book: how does one create subjectivity by harnessing the illegible body's diegetic capacity?

Earvin "Magic" Johnson's national narrative about HIV/AIDS speaks directly to these questions. As a sports star, he was understood as a subjective object based on his athletic prowess. As an HIV/AIDS activist, he had to construct himself as an objective subject based primarily on his vulnerable and ill body. After more than two decades since he contracted HIV, we have to wonder how that transformation occurred and the mechanisms by which it was (not) sustained. To be sure, Johnson's intervention into HIV/AIDS discourse was a game changer, to use a sports metaphor. He entered into public consciousness as HIV+ during his prime as a basketball star, upending the distinction assumed in HIV/AIDS discourse between gay and straight, Black and white, guilty and innocent, and (to a lesser extent) men and women. As a result, Johnson was able to speak directly to younger audiences and Blacks who erroneously believed that HIV/AIDS did not affect them. Yet as we progress in time, Johnson's ability (and some would argue his desire) to speak to those audiences about HIV/AIDS has deteriorated significantly. For a time, Johnson's personal story about his own embodiment was socially and politically significant. What happened? By way of partial answer, I offer that Johnson was not able to construct an autobiographical self in real time that would have sustained him over time. His waned relevance to the current HIV/AIDS movement (other than his presence as a part of its history) directly correlates to the limitations of the able Black body in time.

Johnson's narrative foregrounds the reciprocity of being embodied in the world—seeing and being seen, touching and being touched—as well as the way one's body is anchored by the confines of time, space, and sociopolitical milieu. As a sports star, Johnson was understood mostly as a subjective object. Most intended him or perceived him for the purpose of watching his body in motion. In other words, the public remained oriented toward him as an object against which they defined themselves. When he announced his HIV+ status, he changed the terms of this engagement as he emphasized his own ability to give the world meaning. In the remainder of this chapter, I do not intend to discount what I have already noted is the simultaneity of being both subjective object and objective subject, but rather highlight the conflict between them. For Johnson's narrative, part of the conflict stems from the general public's understanding of what healthy looks like and the reality of what it feels like. To be clear, Johnson's ability to somatize health—however fraught the definition and image of putative health—is at the crux of his ability to engage in political discourse. In other words, "the tension between health as therapeutic intervention and as a vehicle for social change is not a matter of putting politics into or keeping it out of health care."[1] Indeed, the conception of who is healthy and who is not is already a political issue.

My analysis of Johnson's Black body in time, space, and culture dovetails with two interrelated ideas about how culture works in phenomenological terms: namely, that "social mediation shapes not only our *knowledge* of our bodies but our *feelings in* them as well,"[2] and the converse of that statement, which is that social mediation shapes our knowledge of others' bodies and our feelings toward them. I keep with Charles Johnson's assertion that the Black (male) body is intended based on an assortment of racialized narratives, "epidermalized" in his words, and reduced to being merely a body.[3] I read Earvin "Magic" Johnson's narrative as conversant with the narratives about Black male bodies. Examining Johnson's story over time, I write with the scholastic impulse to expand the reduction inherent in parts of his narrative and add much needed breadth to the epidermalization he encountered in public spaces. I mine a rich archive of biographies, autobiographies, news media, and popular culture to understand how Johnson's anchoring in the social world influenced his activism. I should be clear in that I do not seek to demonstrate knowledge of Johnson's interiority (as that is not accessible in the same way as a fictional character) but rather to focus on the way his body in public spaces evinces the rich interplay between his body as object and him as subject in a narrative with racialized, gendered, abled, and sexualized overtones.

I trace the tenuous positions that Johnson's body has occupied and the way his manipulation of it was both necessitated and circumscribed by HIV/AIDS activism. In the first section of this chapter, I begin by laying out the cultural circumstances of the 1980s and early 1990s that made John-son's narrative possible. I find that activism prior to Johnson, specifically that of ACT UP, spectacularized the body and made HIV/AIDS aware-ness hinge on images of the body. Second, I turn to Johnson's mobilization of his own body and embodied experience immediately after his public announcement in 1991. I point to the ways that Johnson intervenes in the competing discourses about HIV/AIDS, sexuality, basketball, and Black success. He had to rely on and undercut his visually objectified body, which remained in the public imagination. In hindsight, it appears that Johnson attempted to harness the power of multiple narratives simultaneously, but was only able to captivate his intended audiences briefly. Johnson's cameo in Michael Jackson's "Remember the Time" and his basketball career place the focus on his healthy appearance and disrupt the concept of what health could look like given his HIV status. As an author, Johnson attempted to educate others about HIV/AIDS, relying on the fact that people were perplexed by his ability to stay healthy. *My Life* (1992) and *What YOU Can Do to Avoid AIDS* (1992) both stress the importance of not relying on one's appearance to judge whether one has HIV/AIDS. In reading John-son as a cultural figure, it becomes clear that the narratives by him can-not be divorced from the narratives about him. For example, news articles like those in *Ebony*, *Sports Illustrated*, *Newsweek*, *Playboy*, *Time,* and the *New York Daily News* capitalized on Johnson's athletic body to educate others about HIV/AIDS or to report Johnson's story. Third, I turn to the early twenty-first century for the way two incidents in popular culture, namely *Comedy Central's Roast of Flavor Flav* and an incident involv-ing Minnesotan radio disc jockeys, evince the difficulty of being "Magic" while having HIV.

In 1981, physicians in New York and California began to notice that some of their gay male patients had illnesses that would normally be fought off except in cases where the patient had a weakened immune system. These opportunistic infections, like Kaposi's sarcoma (KS), or *Pneumocystis cari-nii* pneumonia (PCP), became symptoms of what we now know as acquired immunodeficiency syndrome, or AIDS.[4] The fight to secure funding for AIDS research, change public opinion, and save lives has been fraught with difficulty caused by two factors: the stigma associated with AIDS and AIDS patients, due in part to the fact that physicians first discovered KS and PCP among gay men; and the conservative social and political climate that shunned open discussion about AIDS. Approximately thirty years later, many Americans believe that AIDS is no longer a threat despite the fact that as of 2010, Black men represent almost one-third of all new HIV infections in the United States. Though Blacks are only fourteen percent of the total population in the United States, they account for almost half (forty-four percent) of all new HIV infections.[5] Conservative social politics and the stigma attached to LGBTQI identity continue to add to the pervasive belief that HIV/AIDS is not a serious issue. Given the prevalence of highly active antiretroviral therapy (HAART) and other AIDS drug cocktails, it is not a surprise that some believe that AIDS is treatable (if not curable). Certainly, the belief that the crisis has abated should be partly attributed to scientific breakthroughs. However, this belief also owes its existence to a complex web of social interactions that emanates from the way people conceptualize the healthy material body as mostly image or object.

Given the abjection HIV/AIDS patients often faced and the ignorance about the disease, the AIDS Coalition to Unleash Power (ACT UP) formed in 1987 to protest many issues, including stigma and the high cost of AIDS medication. Activists' civil disobedience relied on the visibility of their bodies, marked as gay and possibly infected with AIDS, to command public attention and demand that the government provide funding for AIDS research and make medication available. Certainly, their activism grabbed the attention of the world. They infiltrated television shows, shut down the U.S. Food and Drug Administration (FDA) and, in one display of moxie, put a giant prophylactic on the Place de la Concorde in France.[6] Not only did these actions garner attention (and even infamy), they also, in the spirit of the organization, unleashed power because the result of their actions was increased funding, available medications, and awareness of AIDS as a serious health threat.

However, public discourse in the late 1980s and early 1990s remained fixed in three ways. First, people continued to believe that HIV/AIDS affected only white gay men, despite the change in nomenclature from gay related immune disease (GRID) to HIV/AIDS. Originally, the Centers for Disease Control (CDC) had labeled HIV/AIDS as gay related immune disease based on their knowledge that the disease weakened the immune system and was found predominantly in gay men. The CDC also later apologized for its use of the "4H" risk group terminology, which included homosexuals, hemophiliacs, heroin addicts, and Haitians. The 4H risk group terminology came about when scientists learned more about the transmission of HIV/AIDS. In addition to revealing homophobia and xenophobic racism, these two events signaled that scientists were trying harder to find the origins of the disease and its methods of transmission. The belief that the disease affected only gay white men was also not abated by the deaths of public figures like Rock Hudson in 1985, Liberace in 1987, Robert Mapplethorpe in 1989, Keith Haring in 1990, and Freddie Mercury in 1991.[7] Second, the general public continued to believe that HIV/AIDS was a death sentence. ACT UP's slogan "SILENCE = DEATH" corroborated this in some way, but also (and more important for this conversation) the dominant images of AIDS patients were those of emaciated individuals with KS lesions and persistent coughs. Such images did little to evoke more than pity with regard to people with HIV/AIDS. Third, there was little attention paid to the distinction between HIV and AIDS. It is for this reason that Johnson became such an important figure, as his announcement of HIV-positivity forced the larger public to make the distinction between the two.

In these instances of fixed public discourse, it was the image of the body—in activism and in dying repose—that captivated the public and dictated how it responded to and discussed AIDS in the 1980s. Shadowing this discourse was the idea that the body existed between two poles of healthy and not healthy. Healthy meant that the body was active, unscarred, and, perhaps, beautiful. Unhealthy seemed to be equal to being emaciated and static. Both of these conceptions of the body relied much on the image of a healthy body and ignored the reality that one can be or feel sick without evincing visible symptoms. Activism of the late 1980s and early 1990s did little to complicate these ideas. Instead, activism focused on changing the language, foregrounding the blurry discursive lines between "living with HIV/AIDS," "dying from AIDS," and "dead from AIDS." To "live with HIV/AIDS" meant to complete daily tasks as one did prior to diagnosis, and usually this was accompanied by a normalized appearance. Media coverage of ACT UP and advertisements for pharmaceuticals made this rhetoric and image more common, but it was not common in the early years of the epidemic.[8] As mentioned before, to "die from HIV/AIDS" was a phrase commonly used to describe all who had HIV/AIDS regardless of their bodily experiences. Activists tried to change the terms of the debate because "dying from HIV/AIDS" implied a hopelessness that was, in some cases, misrepresentative of the patients' experience. In other cases, many of which were shown in the media, people were dying because they had AIDS. Photographs of AIDS patients were also misleading, as they tended to show them in isolation, in hospitals, and in frail condition.[9] Not only did this further corroborate that anyone with AIDS was emaciated or debilitated, but it also misrepresented the way the syndrome works. No one dies from AIDS. People die from AIDS-related complications. People's obituaries also omitted that they died from these complications, which had the effect of erasing the disease in death.[10] It need also be said that the solitary nature of these depictions also erased some people's inclusion in vibrant communities during their illness. Activists fought over these terms because they believed that changing the public discourse might translate to more support for research and better health care. In the late 1990s and early 2000s, advertisements for HIV/AIDS medication featuring Johnson would further complicate the perception of the relationship between HIV/AIDS and death. The interplay between the virile, active bodies of ACT UP members and ill patients normally shown in the media created a schism between the images of health frequently aired and the putative reality thereof, even though the reality was also heavily mediated by television.

On November 7, 1991, Earvin "Magic" Johnson dramatically shifted the conversations about HIV/AIDS. His athletic Black body upended notions of what HIV/AIDS could look like and who could have it. HIV/AIDS was no longer "their" (read: whites', gays', sinners') problem, but was now "our" (read: Blacks', heterosexuals', innocents') problem. He announced that he would retire from the National Basketball Association (NBA) and his stellar career as a Los Angeles Laker because he had tested positive for HIV, the virus that causes AIDS. Johnson was embraced, however problematically, as an AIDS icon and began the work of AIDS activism. Johnson's impact on HIV/AIDS activism was due in significant part to his palatability to white audiences "as the ambassador of basketball with the unforgettable smile."[11] As Cathy Cohen, Douglas Crimp, and Christopher M. Bell have pointed out, Johnson's status as an icon is predicated on the erasure of Black gay men, lesbian women, and IV-drug users with HIV/AIDS.[12] I concur with their ideas, and add that part of what made (and makes) Johnson a difficult figure regarding his activism is the vexing influence of his athletic and suddenly ill, but not debilitated, body. Images of Johnson relied on the public's perception of people with HIV/AIDS as emaciated, sickly, and unhappily alone.

In the early 1990s, Johnson's engagement with HIV/AIDS activism and his role as the supposed new face of HIV attempted to disrupt some of the common cultural narratives about the body with HIV/AIDS. Not only did it shatter the idea that all HIV/AIDS patients were emaciated and sickly, it also allowed for a different, sympathetic face and persona to be associated with the disease. Prior to Johnson's announcement, Ryan White, a young white hemophiliac, gained attention when he was barred entry to school because he had AIDS in 1985. White and his family became AIDS activists because his youth, presumed heterosexuality, and whiteness allowed him some distance from those people considered immoral AIDS patients, like gay men and IV-drug users, even though White himself eschewed the label 'innocent.' The perception of his innocence was crystallized in the lyrics used in Michael Jackson's 1993 ode to him after he died from AIDS-related complications, "Gone Too Soon," in which Jackson croons about White's ability to inspire and the fleeting nature of his life.[13] In short, White's body brought with it the contours of white and heterosexual privilege regarding HIV/AIDS: the assumption of innocence and the belief in his inherent value. Those privileges received state sanction in August 1990 when the United States passed the Ryan White Comprehensive AIDS Resources Emergency Act in posthumous recognition of White. The act, which federally funded programs for low-income and uninsured people with AIDS, placed a government stamp on HIV/AIDS as an issue of national importance. Nonetheless, naming it after Ryan White shunted aside the significant others it affected and placed a white face on the legislation in perpetuity, codifying into law the erasure of people of color, LGBTQI people, women, and those whose identities include two or more of those categories. President Barack Obama extended the act for the fourth time in 2009.[14]

Despite Ryan White's own disavowal of terms like 'innocent' or 'guilty' and his desire to place premium focus on HIV/AIDS, his legacy was that of an innocent victim.[15] As a figure, Johnson inherited some of this legacy, especially because of his palatability to white audiences, but he also had to reckon with what others considered his moral failings, and rumors regarding his sexuality. The rhetoric of guilt and innocence persisted because "societies need to have one illness which becomes identified with evil, and attaches blame to its 'victims.'"[16] Despite the fact that Johnson's body had long been spectacularized in the same way as the ACT UP activists'—as virile, fit, and athletic—it was the moral failing already attached to his body as a Black male basketball player that made this rhetoric of guilt and innocence a constant presence. Johnson had to navigate the way others perceived him and his new role as HIV/AIDS spokesperson. In the former, he remained an object to be desired, distanced from, or watched. In the latter, he was an agent for change. Given that Johnson existed as both simultaneously, he became a conundrum in the public eye.

In an effort to educate others about HIV/AIDS, Johnson showcased his own embodied experience and put himself on display. He directly engaged the fear others had about the disease by grappling with the rumors that circulated about HIV/AIDS. As Cathy Cohen points out in *Boundaries of Blackness*, the federal government erred in putting too little emphasis on the demographics affected and publicly misrepresenting AIDS in communities of color. As a result, there was confusion regarding how it was contracted, how it was spread, and who might have it.[17] As Evelyn Hammonds notes, "As late as 1990, many Black women still did not perceive themselves to be at risk from the disease. There were few media representations of them in public health prevention materials."[18] At this time, public institutions like the Centers for Disease Control, World Health Organization, the U.S. Surgeon General's office, National Institutes of Health, and the U.S. Health Services and Resources Administration attended to rumors by attempting to dispel myths about HIV/AIDS and promoting awareness with conferences, funding for education, and printed material.[19] Johnson's public appearances addressed the rumors about how he contracted HIV (some speculated gay sex) and what one with HIV/AIDS looks like (some speculated that HIV/AIDS patients could not appear healthy).[20]

Rumor is often difficult to discuss because it is unsubstantiated and therefore rendered illegitimate. However, rumor does become a part of the public discourse in a way that has a specific strange effect on celebrities. Since celebrity discourse consists of a "collection of images, ideas, representations, artistic and informational data, advertisements, clues and conversations, that in the end do not amount to any integral knowledge that could be claimed as 'authentic,'"[21] rumor becomes an integral part of understanding the official discourse by and about celebrities. For example, Jason King points out the way that rumors about Luther Vandross's sexuality and possible AIDS diagnosis became part of the official narrative when Vandross sued a British tabloid and discussed his dieting habits. In Vandross's effort to counteract rumor, his official statements incorporated the rumor into his own narrative. King argues that these rumors helped Black queer communities disrupt the pervasive heteronormative discourse surrounding Vandross and allowed these communities to recuperate Vandross as a Black queer icon. When the rumor demanded entry to public discourse, it forced others to reckon with the idea that Vandross's masculinity was not as fixed as previously thought. Johnson's attempt to respond to rumors about his sexuality and HIV/AIDS itself function similarly to Vandross's rumor mill in that both public speculation and public repudiation of rumor become part of the official discourse about Johnson and HIV/AIDS. Johnson's public display of his body transforms the conversation about what constitutes an ill body even if, like the rumors about Vandross's sexuality, the rumors about Johnson and HIV/AIDS resist erasure.

I turn to Johnson's appearance in Michael Jackson's "Remember the Time" video in March 1992 since it creates a counter-discourse about the somatic appearance of illness.[22] In keeping with phenomenological thick description, I describe the video at length since its narrative and staging participates in shaping these ideas. As with many Michael Jackson videos after *Thriller*, "Remember the Time" is a short film featuring several star protagonists. Here, Jackson is accompanied not only by Johnson but also by supermodel Iman and actor Eddie Murphy. In the beginning, sand whirls around an hourglass and morphs into some of the most recognizable Egyptian pieces of art and architecture, including the Sphinx of Giza and a bust of Nefertiti. It transitions into a scene featuring a pharaoh (Eddie Murphy) and his bored and jealous queen (Iman). At the behest of the pharaoh, a court attendant (Johnson) announces two entertainers, both of whom the queen sends to their deaths. Next, a person in a robe enters (presumably Jackson) who throws down black sand and magically disappears within it, only to reemerge from the now golden mass to the opening beat of the song. In what follows, Jackson is chased by the pharaoh's guards through a *souq* (marketplace), dances with veiled women, and kisses the queen. The video culminates with Jackson's dance number during the breakdown of the song and ends when Jackson dissolves into sand again, much to the frustration of the guards.

To understand this music video as a cultural text requires reading it alongside the rumors at play about Johnson, Jackson, and Murphy. I do not wish to give credence to these rumors but rather suggest that the way they work within a larger narrative becomes meta-textual for the video. The three men perform sexualized roles that rely on heteronormativity and obliquely suggest the rumors are not true. First, many suspected Johnson was gay because of his announcement of his HIV status. Given that HIV/AIDS was often associated with white gay men, some were unable to reconcile Johnson's heterosexuality with his diagnosis. Second, Michael Jackson's sexuality had long been speculated upon because of his assiduous attention to his monkey, Bubbles, and his nebulous romantic relationship with actress Brooke Shields.[23] Third, Eddie Murphy had been romantically linked to a friend, singer Johnny Gill. Johnson's role as a court attendant places him as an arbiter between Iman and Murphy, suggesting he be read as part of the heteronormative love triangle narrative that features Murphy and Jackson as virile men in combat over a beautiful woman. Johnson's facilitation of Jackson's ability to woo Iman ironizes Johnson's role on the basketball court as someone famous for assists. Yet, the difficulty of dispelling rumors is that no amount of denial assists any of the men in affirming their heterosexuality. For instance, the campiness of the video might suggest a queer space wherein all the participants exaggerate heterosexuality as part of the performance. In any of the possible interpretations, the video functions as part of the archive King describes in which heterosexuality and queerness remain side by side as part of a collection of data.

For Johnson, the video becomes a public service announcement about the indiscriminate nature of HIV/AIDS. His visible body along with the knowledge of his HIV+ status allows him to insist on his heterosexuality (with varying results), embody risk, and perform wellness. Johnson affirms his health in terms of the visual codes attributed to having HIV/AIDS: he is neither emaciated nor isolated nor covered with KS lesions. His shirtless appearance marks him as virile since he is still lean, muscular, and sexually desirable (*chacun à son goût*). Despite this virility and desirability, his position as court attendant (read: eunuch) along with the knowledge of his HIV status neuters his sexuality.[24] He exudes sexiness but also embodies the consequences of promiscuous sex. Viewers have to be ever mindful of the Johnson they see before them and the reality of his positive status, his body as an image and an object. Though Johnson's presence attempts to affirm heterosexuality and desirability, it also and perhaps more stringently affirms the danger of both. This ostensible public service announcement relies on a delicate balance between the public's expectation that he will appear sick and his message that anyone can live with HIV. He must rely on the vexed nature of his being an off-limits sex symbol. Given that many women found Johnson attractive while he was in the NBA (perhaps because of his money and fame), part of his ability to sell safe sex to men rests on his ability to still be attractive to women. The potency of his activism depends upon his embodiment of the risk associated with carrying a desirable but lethal erection.

As a result, Johnson does not and cannot perform his heterosexuality in the same way as Michael Jackson or Eddie Murphy. He must embody the "look but don't touch" nature of the video. For much of the video, the dancing couples do not touch, and when they do it is shadowed, creating a *mise-en-scène* that highlights illicit sexual rendezvous. The pharaoh and his queen also do not touch each other and, when Michael Jackson kisses Iman, the moment remains ensconced in shadow. The dancing echoes this premise as well, since the dancers perform in heterosexual couplings that move in geometric and staccato fashion. Certainly, part of the rationale behind the dancing is to capture the appearance of hieroglyphics in choreography. However, the dancing resonates a bit differently when read alongside Johnson's appearance. *Ebony* magazine provided instructions for a "post-Magic" era of dating in which it counseled people to avoid risky behavior and rehashed the debate of whether to engage in sex before marriage at all.[25] The pairs in the video highlight the tension of the couples in the magazine's pages (both the images and the imaginary couples to whom the text is directed) whose chaste touches anticipate or desire sexual congress. They dance near each other, hardly touching, and the geometric, stylized movements do not leave much room for a heightened sexuality. Furthermore, many of the dancers remain expressionless. Yet toward the end of the video, some of the dancers begin to wind their torsos in a more sexualized fashion. In one pair, the woman bends over backward as the man leans over her, though they never touch and their winding movements remain restricted. In this way, the video affirms Johnson's stance *vis-à-vis* HIV/AIDS: that one must be ever mindful of risk.

In 1992, Johnson published his educational text, *What YOU Can Do to Avoid AIDS*. He writes explicitly against rumor, mobilizing his own embodied experience as a point of departure. The *Los Angeles Times* reviewer urged parents who are uncomfortable discussing the topic with their children to buy the book because it might be the "gift of life."[26] It was heralded by the American Medical Association as a book that "could help save lives."[27] During the year of its release, AIDS became the number one cause of death for men between the ages of twenty-five and forty-four.[28] Despite the fact that this was not Johnson's target demographic, it is notable that his image (as healthy and virile and smiling, emblazoned on the cover of his book) helped in educating others about the facts of HIV/AIDS. The title elides the distinction between HIV and AIDS in order to make the point that the former could lead to the latter. Despite the fact that sero-conversion is not inevitable, the title panders the fear that it is, even though the content says otherwise. Much like his appearance in Jackson's video, Johnson's healthy appearance allows him to shift the conversation to bodily reality. *What YOU Can Do to Avoid AIDS* places a premium on body parts, bodily functions, and bodies engaged in sexual activity rather than the narratives that govern them. Johnson teams up with groups like American Federation for AIDS Research (AmFAR), Gay Men's Health Crisis (GMHC), and shelters for runaway teens,[29] all of which serve the so-called guilty victims of HIV/AIDS: gay men, indigent people, and single mothers, among others. Implicitly, he makes the case that he represents those Black, male, straight bodies who had been invisibilized in HIV/AIDS discourse. The endorsements suggest an interconnectedness and unity based on the processes and exchanges of the human body thus far ignored or unrecognized by media and scientific discourse in their discussions of transmission. Given that AmFAR and GMHC started because of the stigma associated with HIV/AIDS during the 1980s, Johnson's alliance with them, though it does not dissolve the divide between a putatively virtuous "us" and immoral "them," makes explicit the nature of HIV/AIDS as a pandemic that affects everyone.

Specifically, Johnson's book focuses on the processes of the human body and changes the topic of conversation from stigma and rumor to prevention and infection. He has a disclaimer about his use of language, warning readers that his words may be explicit: "You're going to read some very frank things about sex in this book. Sometimes I use words you'll hear more often in the locker room than the classroom. I do so because it's important that every reader—especially young people—understand exactly what I'm talking about."[30] Following his desire to be direct, the text contains short, simple sentences and cross-section images of the penis, mouth, and vagina to explain HIV/AIDS transmission. In the coming years, Johnson's text would not be considered explicit, but in 1992, he thought that mention of body parts and actions—especially when aimed at a teenage audience—was taboo. He refers to body parts and actions with their colloquial names in parentheses. For instance, he uses "balls" for testicles, "comes" for ejaculates (he does not use the colloquial spelling "cums"), "rimming" for describing anilingus, and "getting hard" for having an erection. Here, the main focus is on concrete preventative action like buying, using, and properly disposing of condoms or dental dams, and increasing sexual pleasure without increasing risk. The rationale behind such a focus is two dictums that Johnson highlights in bold: first, "You don't get AIDS because of who you are—you get it because of what you do";[31] second, "Remember, you can't tell who has HIV by looking at them. [. . .] You have the power to choose to be safe."[32] These pithy sayings align with the main thrust of the book, which is what one can *do* to avoid AIDS. His focus on action and the reminder that people may not appear sick point out that HIV/AIDS is everyone's concern because everyone has a body that can contract HIV/AIDS.

In the mid-to-late 1990s, Johnson's presence became somewhat illegible because of the discord between his putatively healthy-looking body and the multiple and conflicting articulations of his embodiment. Specifically, Johnson's new role as an HIV/AIDS activist was incompatible with the role he played on court. To illustrate this point, it will be useful to briefly sketch Johnson's career in the NBA with an eye toward how others understood his body in motion prior to 1991. His basketball career testifies to the excitement Johnson generated both as a sports star and, later, as an activist. In 1976, the American Basketball Association (ABA), known for the three-point shot and enthusiastic players, merged with the National Basketball Association (NBA) to create one national franchise. Despite the prominence of stars like Kareem Abdul-Jabbar, Dr. J, and Wilt Chamberlain, the franchise gained a substantial financial boost when two potential NBA stars garnered national attention during the 1978 NCAA basketball championships: Larry Bird and Earvin Johnson.[33] The Boston Celtics and Los Angeles Lakers' rivalry had been long standing, but these two stars made it the story of legends. When the NBA could pit Johnson against Bird, they had a story that read like a modern-day clash of the titans. It is not possible to think of Johnson's career without thinking about his relationship to Larry Bird, especially because the discourse about Johnson's career relies on his opposition to Bird: Black vs. white, west vs. east, flamboyant vs. calm.

These oppositions would later surface after HIV/AIDS replaced Bird as his major rival.

Without discounting the other facets of the Johnson/Bird rivalry, I want to focus on the racialized personality distinctions since these carried implications for how people thought of Johnson's and Bird's off-court personas. Larry Bird was billed as the "hick from French Lick" (a reference to Bird's Illinois hometown) and understood as the more serious (and abrasive) competitor. Johnson was pegged as the flashy "showtime" Laker based on his enthusiasm and camaraderie. While Johnson trotted up and down the court whooping and giving high fives, Bird maintained an even and, at times, blank face. Johnson's sociability led people to believe that the label "Magic" was quite apt, and that there was an intangible quality in Johnson that made others around him better.[34] This intangible quality speaks to a very specific (though not exclusive) talent. Johnson has an aptitude for assists, the act of passing the ball to another player before that player makes a shot. In addition to his talent for assists, Johnson also demonstrated an accompanying skill for guiding the pace of the game, thereby maximizing control over the other team's possible plays. He was also able to assess the spatial dynamics of the court, which permitted him to anticipate and disrupt opposing players' movements. Johnson galvanized other players by creating opportunities for them to score points. His particular flair for the no-look pass and adept ball handling (unusual for someone of his size) also earned him and the rest of the Laker franchise the reputation for being glitzy, Hollywood showtime players.[35] When we think about the way Magic (and now I use this moniker deliberately) changed the understanding of HIV/AIDS, his reputation for assisting, enthusiasm (specifically the energetic smile), and razzle-dazzle play influenced the way his activism was understood. This was due, in no small part, to the fact that despite Magic's constant review of game tape and incessant practicing, few sportswriters discussed his skill as a calculated and crafted performance, but they retained and perpetuated the idea that Magic was magical.[36]

The rhetoric surrounding Magic, including that which is generated by Johnson himself based on his sports career, ultimately thwarted his activist efforts. When Johnson represents HIV/AIDS as an opponent, he places significant limitations on what he can do as a figure. His recasting of HIV/AIDS appeals to his fan base, but also works within heterosexist and moralizing paradigms from which Johnson had to later disentangle himself. Christopher M. Bell decries Johnson's influence over the discourse of HIV/AIDS activism for this reason. He argues that Johnson's persona, class, and body backfire as productive tools to bring AIDS education to the public. Magic's persona turns the us/them rhetoric into an "us/him" rhetoric and facilitates the erasure of gay men and of AIDS's potentially lethal nature. Bell cites two articles, "I'll Deal with It" and "It Can Happen to Anybody. Even Magic Johnson" in *Sports Illustrated* and *Time*, respectively, that presume the antecedent of "it" is AIDS, but neglect to mention it by name. What

Bell terms this "linguistic slight"[37] is just as virulent as President Ronald Reagan's silence with regard to the word 'AIDS.' In the case of Magic, HIV and, by extension, AIDS itself becomes a stand-in for an opposing team. I quote Bell at length:

> [I]t became clear that Magic was determined to "deal with it" strictly on (and literally with) his own terms. Statements such as this one are indicative of his decision not to align himself with other AIDS activists, proof of his determination to blaze his own path. [. . .] In blazing this path, Magic boasted the public's unyielding support, as evidenced in the tone of the *Time* magazine title. The "It Can Happen to Anybody. Even Magic Johnson" supposition reveals the mentality of late-1991 mainstream culture, that it is better or easier not to name the disease, to maintain the shroud of secrecy and silence surrounding the syndrome at all costs. This reckless mindset, the outright attempt to obfuscate the reality of AIDS, subsequently leading to additional infections and deaths, undermined the attempts by many activists to generate and sustain a collective dialogue about AIDS.[38]

The use of "it" in particular limits the ability to discuss HIV/AIDS openly because it forecloses honest discussion. In Bell's words, "Efforts to stimulate a discussion about a disease that do not take advantage of the obvious opportunities to name that disease seem destined to fail from the outset."[39] "It" maintains not only secrecy but also shame and stigma, and does not bridge the gap between the so-called innocent us and the so-called guilty them.

In addition, the use of 'it' problematizes the legibility of Johnson's athletic body. Not only are there temporal limits to a game, but there are also linguistic limits to positioning an illness as an opposing team. In a game, the clock must inevitably stop since the game has to end. No one knew how Johnson's game would end, but the expectation was not that it would last as long as it has. Certainly, few expected that Johnson would appear to triumph. With regard to the linguistic limits, the construction of a team makes Johnson a singular figure. He truly becomes Magic in the sense that he combats the viral host seemingly on his own. *Ebony*'s article "Magic Johnson's Full Court Press against AIDS," which was their cover story of April 1992, operates according to the same logic. The singularity also prohibits anyone else from joining the conversation. Both references to sports invoke Johnson's moving athletic presence with all the attendant discourses of super ability and magical quality. In so doing, Johnson becomes too wedded to his athletic body to inhabit what might be termed an ill subjectivity— one that positions his illness as a significant social identity regardless of his healthy appearance rather than subordinates his illness to his healthy appearance. I concur with Margrit Shildrick, who asserts, "To be named as differently embodied is already to occupy a place that is defined as exception to some putative norm, rather than to simply represent one position among a multiplicity of possibilities."[40] The problem with Magic is that he was already understood as exceptional because of his Black athletic body (even though that stereotype is rather commonplace). When he announced his HIV-positive status, he became exceptional again based on illness. In his and others' articulations of HIV/AIDS as 'it' or as an opposing team, the two exceptional Johnsons compete and cancel out the possibility of representing HIV/AIDS as a threat to larger communities.

In 1996, Johnson's wife, Earlitha "Cookie" Johnson, claimed in an interview that God healed Johnson.[41] She downplays the extent to which their wealth influences Johnson's treatment. When Nirmala Erevelles details the privilege of having health insurance during her husband's cancer treatments, she exposes the way class positioning grants access to treatments otherwise not available to those using Medicare or Medicaid. She explains how the currency of health insurance (made available by her and her husband's university jobs) bought her husband salvific medication that elongated his life by several years. In thinking through Johnson's wealth, analysis moves away from the tendency to conceive of class as a "social/cultural experience" and toward thinking of class as a "critical analytical category."[42] He has an illness he can afford to receive treatment for based on his career. In this way, Johnson was no different from an injured athlete forced into retirement (public responses notwithstanding). Neither Cookie Johnson nor the interviewer draws a correlation between Johnson's treatment and the couple's annual Mediterranean yacht vacations. In his coauthored volume with Larry Bird, Johnson dismisses the idea that his wealth gives him access to certain privileged medical treatment, saying, "I take the same meds as everyone else. I do what my doctors tell me to do, even though I feel great."[43] No matter how true Johnson's statement is now, two facts must be considered. In 1987, when antiretroviral drugs were introduced, they were cost prohibitive.[44] Though Johnson takes medication available to everyone, this does not indicate that everyone who has the need receives the medication. By virtue of having health insurance, steady income, and the luxury to take vacations to the Mediterranean, Johnson's income does influence his ability to maintain an HIV-positive status. Reading Johnson as wealthy places his singularity, athletic body, and outlook within a more understandable context. Johnson's wealth granted him an easement that confirmed his illegibility as an ill person to others.

Despite Johnson's use of his body to dispel rumor, he remained unreadable to many. I contend that Johnson's illegibility spotlights the anxieties that converge when others try to reimagine him as an objective subject. When Johnson opted to disclose his status and champion HIV/AIDS education, he differentiated between being the object of others' gazes as an athlete and controlling others' gazes as an activist and educator. Given his role as an author and spokesperson, he prioritized being an activist by exerting his own agency. The ghost of his athletic career haunted his abilities as an activist since his athleticism foregrounded the danger inherent in the reciprocal nature of being both objective subject and subjective object. To be sure, that reciprocity is not merely a closed loop between Johnson the subject and Johnson the object. Instead, that simultaneity makes clear the porous boundary between Johnson's body and others' bodies. Since one never touches without being touched, sees without being seen, or intends without being intended, Johnson's position as objective subject requires that others understand his body and the risk he embodies as more approximate than would have been comfortable. In short, to acknowledge him as a subject would mean that they too were implicated in his narrative about HIV/AIDS as potentially at risk. Furthermore, his Black male body pointed to those heretofore ignored in the fight against HIV/AIDS. Acknowledging him and his social grounding meant dealing with the significant confluence of race, gender, ability, and class that pervades the narratives about HIV/AIDS.

In the twenty-first century, two events clarify how the anxiety about Johnson's body resulted in a distancing from him (reimagining him as an object) and a culturally convenient amnesia about the historical context of Johnson's narrative. In 2007, comedy personalities and celebrities gathered to participate in the *Comedy Central Roast of Flavor Flav*.[45] A rapper-*cum*-reality-television star, Flavor Flav was once the hype man for Public Enemy, a politically conscious rap group famous during the 1980s, but Flavor Flav had his fall from grace after drug use and repeated incarcerations.[46] During the roast, comedienne Sommore told Flavor Flav that he looked like "what Magic Johnson is supposed to look like."[47] Her statement brings to the fore the disjuncture between what we now see of Johnson versus what we think we know about his seropositivity. Many of the jokes that night were about Flavor Flav's appearance—his height, dark complexion, weathered skin, and small build. Sommore's comments point to the understanding of HIV/AIDS as something that shrinks the body in size and ages the skin. Here, Sommore references Flavor Flav's past drug addiction and the HIV/AIDS diagnosis he presumably escaped. This moment showcases that people expected (and still expect?) Johnson's body to demonstrate his diagnosis. It bears emphasizing that Johnson's ability to somatize health also circumscribes his activism in the present moment. For a man aging with HIV, a long-term side effect of being on HAART drugs is lipoatrophy, or an emaciation of the face.[48] It is not my aim to speculate about whether Johnson has had lipoatrophy or surgery to correct it, but rather to point out that the girth of his face and the continuous familiarity of his trademark smile subscribe to common notions of health. Moreover, Sommore's joke comments on the classed nature of Johnson's experience with illness. In other words, Johnson should look like someone with HIV or AIDS, an assertion that further emphasizes the distinction between Johnson and other, less wealthy people with AIDS.[49] Sommore's comment also brings to light how Magic's vexed cultural cachet functions given the constraints of his bodily image. While Flavor Flav has had to suture a career together based on reality television shows and an embrace of his look as ugliness, Johnson has been able to avoid the oblivion reserved for celebrities whose primary careers are over. A year later, Katt Williams, another participant in the roast, bemoaned the racist overtone to the evening, saying that the writers of the show consistently referred to Flavor Flav as a "crispity crackily crunchity coon."[50] Williams does not overtly connect the racism with the obvious commentary on Flavor Flav's body, nor does he explicitly mention Sommore's comments, but he does point out the way Flavor Flav's complicity hinged on him being paid. Yet again, money curtails the conversations one can have about being embodied as Black or as ill.

In 2008, Minneapolis conservative radio show hosts Chris Baker and Langdon Perry accused Johnson of "fak[ing] AIDS for sympathy."[51] Though the disc jockeys later apologized, that sentiment evinces a more palpable shift from the public's shock at Johnson's diagnosis to a disbelief of it. The disc jockeys' commentary supports Bell's argument that Johnson's wealth and persona contributes to the way we understand him as a person with HIV. After all, Johnson has survived when no one thought he would and his ability to live longer comes partly from his early access to the best treatment possible. The DJs' commentary was anchored in the inability to perceive HIV/AIDS on Johnson's body since he still does not conform to the widely circulated images of emaciated and sickly patients. As for those with chronic illnesses and so-called invisible disabilities, Johnson's narrative was illegible to them because it did not adhere to the scripts made necessary by the putative invisibility. As Ellen Jean Samuels argues, "Narratives of people with 'hidden impairments' [. . .] are suffused with themes of coming out, passing, and the imperatives of identity."[52] In the twenty-first century, Johnson's life, girth, and clear skin (without KS lesions) appear to be acts of passing that engendered disbelief on the part of the radio DJs.

Sommore's and the Minnesotan DJs' disbelief "epidermalizes" Johnson by keeping him as a Black athletic body. Both comments ignore Johnson's social grounding in the 1990s as a Black man with HIV for comedic fodder. In an effort to understand how Johnson's anchoring in the social world influenced his activism, I find it instructive to examine the limitations placed on his Black athletic body in time. According to Anthony Foy, the Black athlete is limited in his ability to construct an autobiographical "I" in real time. He argues that the Black athlete's entrance into autobiography pulls from a long tradition of Black literary self-creation (dating to slave narratives), but the Black body in action thwarts the transformative potential of literary autobiography because that autobiography has already been performed in the athlete's body.[53] Similarly, Johnson's ability to construct an autobiographical "I" was limited based on his linguistic recourse to his sports career and the way others insisted on his ability at the expense of his illness. Inasmuch as Johnson harnesses his body to help construct a competing discourse to the narratives about HIV/AIDS, his body cannot sustain that discourse along with those about Black male athleticism and illness. There exists a wide gulf between his static self, as showcased in Michael Jackson's video and public photo opportunities, and his moving athletic self, as shown on the court and invoked elsewhere.

Those two narratives explode as antagonistic in an examination of Johnson's athletic Black body at rest. Johnson had several retirements: after his announcement in 1991, after the Cleveland Cavaliers game in 1992, and in 1996 after the Lakers lost to the Houston Rockets in the first round of the playoffs. After the first retirement, he played, not only in the All Star game, but also (and perhaps more famously) in the 1992 Barcelona Olympics alongside Michael Jordan, Charles Barkley, and Larry Bird as a part of the "Dream Team" of NBA players representing the United States. In addition to his announcement and the statements of doctors at the press conference in November 1991, his part as an NBA All Star and on the "Dream Team" forced people to learn about the difference between HIV and AIDS and the methods of contracting HIV. What's more, Johnson's vigorous athleticism and performance on the court demonstrated on the world's stage that he still could play. He was no longer a person dying from AIDS but one living with HIV. Such a powerful visual example revamped the understanding of what it meant to have HIV. However, the Cleveland Cavaliers game in 1992 illuminates the limitations of being Magic on the court. Karl Malone made clear his fear of being on the court with Magic in a November 1992 interview.[54] Such fears were crystallized when Johnson received a small cut during the Cavaliers game and the Lakers' physician fixed him up without gloves.[55] Johnson retired from the NBA after that because of the palpable nature of the players' fear and the public's. This short stint proved how tenuous the public's acceptance of him was at that time and how meager their understanding of HIV/AIDS. It was clear that Johnson's ability to be a good spokesman would need to be based on his body, but not his body in athletic motion.

Johnson's athletic body intrudes on his ability to be legible to the public he needs to read him most clearly. He becomes undecipherable based on the expectations placed upon his moving athletic body. Johnson places himself at rest, as opposed to at play on the court or temporarily at rest on the sidelines. He also violates the temporal mandate of the Black athletic body to work in the NBA because he was not at rest during time-outs, between games, or in the off-season. Another NBA player, Metta World Peace (né Ron Artest), illuminates the logic of this phenomenon. At a 2004 game in Michigan, Metta World Peace lay on the score table in protestation of a foul. After he inflamed hometown fans so much that one threw beer on him, he marched up into the crowd and punched a fan, precipitating a riot. In his supine position, Metta World Peace "refuse[d] the perpetual motion that is inveterately expected of the NBA athlete."[56] He became an enigma in his stillness because fans expected him to continue to move. Even when professional basketball players are resting on the sidelines, the expectation is that they will continue to be a part of the game. When Johnson places himself at rest by not playing any longer, he provokes the same kind of enigma as Metta World Peace. Though there is a distinct difference between Metta World Peace's actions and Johnson's, the logic still holds. Fans cannot understand him at rest because the expectation lingers that his Black body in the public sphere will perform specific athletic actions.

Part of the reason Johnson remains an enigma is because his rest is politically provocative based on its relationship to time. In Grant Farred's discussion of the basketball brawl, he argues that Metta World Peace refigures the understanding of his Black body in white public space by controlling the temporality of the NBA and suspending, through his inertia, the game clock.[57] As Sharon Holland notes, "The black subject is mired in space and the white subject represents the full expanse of time."[58] According to the narrative of Western progression, the same narrative that gives us post-racial rhetoric, whiteness is constructed as the arbiter of time and progress. That is, white understandings of race and racism determine whether we have reached racial harmony. In this ordering, Black subjects only take up space. They are the bodies to get beyond; they are what gets labeled "post." When Black subjects seek to control time, they challenge this ordering. They also truncate the narrative of progress, forcing one to engage with the way that story is predicated on an erasure of Black bodies. Given the heavily racialized understanding of Johnson (recall the narratives about him and Larry Bird), Johnson was shaped by the mainly white-owned industry that controlled time. When he steps off the court, he stands outside the parameters of this temporal control. Off the court with HIV, Johnson more explicitly occupies a racialized and politicized subjectivity that shapes its own time. Drawing on his configuration of HIV/AIDS as an opposing team, Johnson attempts to re-envision his relationship to temporality and politics. Such a reconfiguration becomes problematic for fans as they must adjust not only to his body at rest but also to his body as occupying a specific political position that reimagines time itself.

Yet it was only temporarily that Johnson could exist in the interstices between his athleticism and HIV-positive status. Several moments mark the shift from NBA star to AIDS icon to neither.[59] After he played an impressive second half of the 1995–1996 season, his wife announced his supposed healing.[60] In 1998, he opened several Starbucks stores and movie theaters. In 2002, pharmaceutical advertisements capitalized on his health. In 2007, Sommore used Magic's image to ridicule Flavor Flav during the *Comedy Central Roast*. In 2008, radio disc jockeys claimed Johnson faked AIDS. All of these incidents mark moments when he began to somatize health (according to a narrow understanding of healthy images) rather than risk. Given that media depictions of HIV/AIDS, particularly as inscribed on Black bodies in Africa, still include emaciated individuals, Johnson's weight gain eclipses his HIV-positive diagnosis. One could point out that Johnson exudes health in ways that are arbitrary yet compelling for the general public: he has a healthy marriage, makes a healthy living, and owns healthy businesses. This new Johnson image is not "Magic" in that Johnson has become the former NBA star and, now, entrepreneur. Much like Metta World Peace during the 2004–2005 NBA season, Johnson's stasis resulted in a loss of the cultural cachet that accompanied his basketball career, including his ability to discuss with great urgency the risk of HIV/AIDS. Johnson's 2009 publication, *When the Game Was Ours*, coauthored with Larry Bird and Jackie MacMullan, rhetorically refigures Magic's opponent as Larry Bird, recalling the days before HIV/AIDS. Though they discuss HIV/AIDS in the book, it is no longer Johnson's opponent. That is, Johnson had to submit to the death of his NBA career in order for his life to disabuse the public of their complacency *vis-à-vis* HIV/AIDS. However, the long-term effect of his dead NBA career juxtaposed with his healthy-looking (though not healthy) body is that Johnson sacrifices his efficiency as an activist given his survival, especially because his activism depended on the temporal proximity to his sports career.

Even more than Sommore's comment, the Minnesotan DJs' commentary evinces the convenient amnesia about the relationship between Johnson's activism and the cultural narratives in which he was invested. Johnson's stint as an activist was curtailed not just by his athletic Black body but also by the slippery social and cultural conservative politics of which he was a part. The sociopolitical climate of the late 1980s and early 1990s also presented significant challenges for discussing HIV/AIDS and its inscription on the human body. I have already delineated the hostile climate *vis-à-vis* HIV/AIDS, but it bears reiteration that the general public was fearful and even aggressive toward those with HIV/AIDS. As Cathy Cohen notes, it was Johnson's palatability to white audiences that enabled him to shift the conversation.[61] Nonetheless, Johnson faced another set of challenges when speaking directly to Black audiences. Namely, Black conservative cultural politics circumscribed him within a set of already scripted narratives about his sexuality and labor (on and off the court), demanding a sexualized, classed, and racialized performativity.[62]

In addition to the desire to counter the hysteria HIV/AIDS caused in the early 1990s, Black conservative politics also impelled Johnson's performance. HIV/AIDS was associated with people who were pariahs: IV-drug users and gay men. They were no more or less outcasts within Black communities, but Black conservative politics dictated a particular response to HIV/AIDS, which was not sympathy. In that sociopolitical climate, it was unknown whether Johnson's admission of having HIV would have made him a pariah or a sympathetic victim for two main reasons. First, he admitted to promiscuity. Despite the open secret about NBA players and the scores of women who follow them on the road, Black male promiscuity violated the politics of respectability. As a member of the Black elite, Johnson was expected to be a role model and not exhibit hypersexual or hyperviolent behavior. In Margrit Shildrick's words, "Given that intercorporeality of the sexual relation is in any case a potential point of disturbance to western normativities, the manifestation of corporeal difference in the context of sexuality appears especially anxiety provoking and threatening. In consequence, there is an extraordinary reluctance to acknowledge that disabled people have any sexuality at all, with the result that their sexual expression is highly regulated, if not invalidated or silenced completely."[63] Given its Victorian roots, Black politics of respectability has definitive Western origins and anxieties, especially regarding sexuality. Johnson had to police his sexual behavior as a public figure based on his Blackness. His admission of HIV-positive status would have signaled failure in this endeavor. Second (and this point draws on Shildrick's logic as well), the association of HIV/AIDS with gay men raised speculations that Johnson was hiding his sexual orientation from the public. He awkwardly quelled those rumors during his 1991 visit to *The Arsenio Hall Show* to the applause of a late-night television studio audience and the chagrin of gay men, particularly Black gay men. Johnson's remark that he was "far from homosexual" placed a distance between him and the putatively immoral sexual profligacy of gay men.[64] In order to emphasize his message that there is no "us" and no "them," he had to speak to the community constituted by "us" to the exclusion of many others. Johnson later had to acknowledge the gay community to which he was indebted for information, while distancing himself from it. When the radio DJs speculated that Johnson "faked AIDS for sympathy," they missed the point that it was not clear he would have received sympathy at all.[65]

Analyzing Johnson's narrative in retrospect reveals the difficulty of harnessing the body's diegetic capacity amid contradictory narratives about Blackness, athleticism, and subjectivity. The ironic twist in Johnson's national narrative is that the same cultural cachet he leveraged then makes him now an inadequate spokesperson. In terms of Black conservative cultural politics, Johnson's cultural cachet rested on his ability to perform labor with his body. Following from Booker T. Washington's Atlanta Exposition speech, Black conservatives have privileged manual labor and entrepreneurial enterprise, both of which are associated with Johnson because of basketball and his businesses.[66] Johnson's activism traded on this cultural mandate. He used his skills and traits—his smile, athleticism, and name—all of which are tied to his body and manipulation of it. He adhered to Black conservative dictums about valuable labor in service of his government, his community, and self-improvement. When viewed in this light, Cookie Johnson can claim healing "in the name of Jesus" and Johnson must rebuke his own promiscuity.[67] In addition to ideologically situating him in a Black conservative tradition and contemporary sociopolitical milieu, these rhetorical maneuvers also recast Johnson's body within acceptable parameters for being a role model. In other words, his promiscuous body had to be rescued from itself to be an acceptable example for others to follow. Given that these maneuvers rely on images and television footage of Johnson's body at work, Johnson's activism satisfied the requirements that impelled his performance. Nonetheless, Johnson's body remains unruly in that it manipulates conservative politics to invert some of the virulence of its own silence. That inversion was temporary, since Johnson's adherence to the rules meant that he eventually lost the platform to talk about HIV/AIDS and risk. Johnson's body eventually became part of the body politic constituted by the Black conservative "us."

His healthy marriage, healthy businesses, and healthy-looking (though not healthy) body ingratiated him to his audience so much that his message about risk was no longer viable. After all, if he was no longer at risk and he was part of the "us," then "we" would no longer be at risk either.

Currently, Johnson's performance as an activist remains curtailed by Black politics of respectability and their Victorian roots. The expectation was that Johnson's death would be the final moral lesson since he violated a set of cultural codes about sexual behavior. The radio DJs' commentary speaks to the fact that, after nearly two decades of being a Black basketball player at rest, Johnson's living body competes with what others thought would be his dead one. Johnson's ghost haunts his efficacy as an activist. Even though his body testifies to the powerful fact that HIV is not a death sentence, others still interpret his body based on their meager understanding of HIV/AIDS and attempt to impel his body to perform in such a way that coincides with their understanding. The narratives by and about Johnson reached their limits at his life, and his Black, male, athletic, material body in time. Inasmuch as Johnson's existence indicates that embodied experience does not necessarily coincide with the social and cultural meanings accrued to it, the material body (and people's limited imaginations in interpreting it) interposes itself as the ultimate boundary in addressing those meanings. Despite the popularity of Johnson's image as associated with safer sex, HIV/AIDS education, and AIDS prevention, Johnson's class status and current health allowed his living body to speak more powerfully than the ones who have died before him. In terms of HIV/AIDS activism, it appears that Johnson has used up his magic: the urgency he commanded as healthy-looking and fit in 1991 is not the same urgency he can command as healthy-looking and fit in the new millennium. Just like on the court, his body has its limits.

NOTES

1. Jenna Loyd, "Where Is Community Health? Racism, the Clinic, and the Bio-political State." *Rebirth of the Clinic: Places and Agents in Contemporary Health Care.* ed. Cindy Patton (Minneapolis, MN: U of Minnesota Press, 2010), 41.
2. Salamon, " 'The Place Where Life Hides Away'," 96, emphasis in text.
3. See Johnson, "A Phenomenology of the Black Body," 121–36.
4. See Brunilda Nazario, "History of HIV/AIDS Slideshow: A Pictorial Timeline of the AIDS Pandemic." *WebMD*, WebMD, LLC, last modified December 1, 2009. http://www.webmd.com. This is not to be confused with the virus that causes AIDS, human immunodeficiency virus (HIV). I do not use HIV/AIDS and AIDS interchangeably in this text. I use HIV/AIDS to discuss moments when the larger discourse includes them both. I use AIDS when I discuss AIDS as a syndrome or participate in discussions where AIDS was the primary focus.
5. Centers for Disease Control, "CDC Fact Sheet: New HIV Infections in the United States." *Centers for Disease Control.* Last modified 2012. www.cdc.gov.
6. See AIDS Coalition to Unleash Power, last modified August 2013, http://www.actupny.org.

7. Nazario, "History of HIV/AIDS Slideshow." It is widely believed that Freddie Mercury is of Persian descent, but he is not. In either case the American imagination especially given his pseudonym, read him as white, which necessitates his inclusion in this list. I am grateful to Leila Pazargadi for her insight regarding Freddie Mercury's heritage.

8. Douglas Crimp, *Mourning and Melancholia*; Gabrielle Griffith, *Representations of HIV and AIDS: Visibility Blue/s* (Manchester, UK: Manchester University Press, 2001). Douglas Crimp critiques the push for "positive images of people living with AIDS" (20) in two essays within his collection *Mourning and Melancholia*. He also points out the way that Magic Johnson became this so-called positive image, with homophobic results.

9. Douglas Crimp also has an extensive essay on the role of photography in the visual representation of HIV/AIDS. He concludes that these photographs and media images are not only unsettling but exploitive and misleading.

10. Couser, *Recovering Bodies*, 89–90.

11. Cathy Cohen, *Boundaries of Blackness: AIDS and the Breakdown of Black Politics* (Chicago, IL: U of Chicago Press, 1999), 167.

12. See Cohen, *Boundaries of Blackness: AIDS and the Breakdown of Black Politics*; Douglas Crimp, *Mourning and Melancholia*; Christopher M. Bell, "The Problem with Magic in/and Representing AIDS." *Culture and the State: Alternative Interventions*. Eds. J. Gifford and G. Zezulka-Mailloux. Vol. 4. Edmonton: CRC Studio Publishers. 7–23.

13. See Michael Jackson, "Gone Too Soon," *Dangerous*, Sony Records, 1993. CD. For reasons of copyright, I cannot reprint lyrics here but they are readily available.

14. See "Remarks by the President at Signing of the Ryan White HIV/AIDS Treatment Extension Act of 2009." *The White House*. 30 October 2009, last modified April 16, 2010. www.whitehouse.gov.

15. See Elton John, "Elton John's Letter to Ryan White, 20 Years after His Death from AIDS." *Washington Post*, last modified April 25, 2010. http://www.washingtonpost.com.

16. Susan Sontag, *Illness as Metaphor and AIDS and Its Metaphors* (New York, NY: Picador, 1978), 104.

17. See Cathy Cohen, *Boundaries of Blackness: AIDS and the Breakdown of Black Politics*, 78–118.

18. Evelyn Hammonds, "AIDS the Secret, Silent, Suffering Shame." *Still Brave: The Evolution of Black Women's Studies*. Eds. Stanlie M. James, Frances Smith Foster, and Beverly Guy-Sheftall (New York, NY: Feminist Press, 2009), 273.

19. See U.S. Department of Health and Human Services. "A Timeline of AIDS." Last modified 2013. www.aids.gov.

20. "Magic Johnson's full court press against AIDS." *Ebony*. 47.6 (1992): 108–11.

21. Jason King, "Any Love: Silence, Theft, and Rumor in the Work of Luther Vandross." *The Greatest Taboo: Homosexuality in Black Communities*. Ed. Delroy Constantine-Sims (Los Angeles, CA: Alyson Publications, 2000), 291.

22. *Dangerous: The Short Films*. Perf. Michael Jackson, Iman, Eddie Murphy, Earvin Johnson, Naomi Campbell. (1991; New York, NY: Epic Music Video, 1993). DVD.

23. See Couser, *Recovering Bodies*, 86. At that time, many people believed that AIDS originated on the continent of Africa with a bestiality sex act between a monkey and a man. People also viewed Michael Jackson's pet as eccentric and speculated that he and the monkey engaged in sex play.

24. If we are to read Michael Jackson's video as a version of an Orientalist painting, Johnson would have played the role of a eunuch. Such a role coincides

with his sexuality being considered dangerous, but rendered off-limits. I am grateful to Nasia Anam for this observation.

25. H. J. Massaquoi, "Ten New Dating Rules in the Post–Magic Johnson Era." *Ebony*. 47.4 (1992): 126–29.

26. Solomon, Charles. "*What YOU Can Do to Avoid AIDS* by Earvin "Magic" Johnson (Times Books: $3.99) and *The Complete Guide to Safer Sex* edited by Ted McIlvenna (Barricade Books: $6.95)." *Los Angeles Times*. 10 May 1992. www.latimes.com.

27. Sandra Crockett, " 'Magic's' Book on Avoiding AIDS Gives Blunt Advice." *The Baltimore Sun*. 27 April 1992. www.baltimoresun.com.

28. See U.S. Department of Health and Human Services. "A Timeline of AIDS."

29. Earvin "Magic" Johnson, *What YOU Can Do to Avoid AIDS* (New York, NY: Random House, 1992).

30. Ibid., xiii.

31. Ibid., 4.

32. Ibid., 71. One could attribute a "sic" to the use of the plural "them" after the singular "who," but Johnson's use of "them" opens up the space to include transgendered people who do not identify as either "him" or "her."

33. See Earvin "Magic" Johnson and Larry Bird with Jackie MacMullan, *When the Game Was Ours* (New York, NY: Houghton Mifflin Harcourt, 2009).

34. See James Haskins, "*Magic*": *A Biography of Earvin Johnson* (Hillside, NJ: Enslow Publishers, 1982). Johnson earned the nickname "Magic" in high school after a news reporter searched for and eventually found a name to describe his play.

35. See James Haskins, "*Magic*" *A Biography of Earvin Johnson*; "Basketball." *Ebony*. 47.10 (1992): 62–65; "Blacks in Sports." *Ebony*. 47.10 (1992): 26; Jack McCallum, "Laying Down the LA Law: Playing with Conviction on Their Home Court, the Magic Johnson–led Lakers Roared Back from a 17-Point Deficit to Beat the Boston Celtics." *Sports Illustrated*. 66.8 (1987): 20–23; Jack McCallum, "A New Face, but the Same Old Magic with Magic Johnson." *Sports Illustrated*. 70.22 (1989): 16–20; Bruce Newman, "Magic Faces the Music." *Sports Illustrated*. 62.19 (1985): 82–91; Jack McCallum, "Leaving a Huge Void." *Sports Illustrated*. 76.11 (1992): 20–24.

36. See Joshua L. Lukin, "Disability and Blackness," *The Disability Studies Reader*, 308–15; Douglas C. Baynton, "Disability and the Justification of Inequality in American History." *The Disability Studies Reader*, 17–33; Paul Beatty, *White Boy Shuffle* (New York, NY: Picador, 1996); Paul Beatty, *Tuff* (New York, NY: Anchor Books, 2000). The extent to which the black athletic body has been read as natural harkens back to narratives that rationalized slavery by asserting that blacks were better equipped for hard labor than whites or First Nation peoples. Paul Beatty takes up this idea in his fictional works, including *White Boy Shuffle* and *Tuff*.

37. Bell, "The Problem with Magic," 16.

38. Ibid.

39. Ibid.

40. Shildrick, *Dangerous Discourses*, 1.

41. Laura B. Randolph, "The Magic 'Miracle': 'The Lord Has Healed Earvin.' " *Ebony*. 52.6 (1997), 72.

42. Erevelles, *Disability and Difference*, 5.

43. Johnson and Bird, *When the Game Was Ours*, 294.

44. Congress had to approve $30 million in funding to states. This was foundational for the AIDS Drug Assistance Program, and later funding by the Ryan White Act. See U.S. Department of Health and Human Services. "A Timeline of AIDS."

45. *Comedy Central Roast of Flavor Flav.* Comedy Central. August 17, 2007.
46. A hype man is a person charged with getting the crowd excited before and during a performance. Usually they use call-and-response techniques. Flavor Flav is most famous for his exaggerated "Yeah boy" and "Flavor Flav."
47. *Comedy Central Roast of Flavor Flav.*
48. John Liesch and Cindy Patton, "Clinic or Spa? Facial Surgery in the Context of AIDS-Related Facial Wasting." *The Rebirth of the Clinic.* Ed. Cindy Patton (Minneapolis, MN: U of Minnesota Press, 2010), 1–16.
49. Kanye West makes explicit mention of Johnson's classed experience of illness in his song "Roses." For reasons of copyright, I cannot reprint the lyrics here, but they are readily available. See Kanye West, "Roses," *Late Registration.* Roc-A-Fella Records, 2005. CD.
50. Katt Williams, *It's Pimpin' Pimpin'.* Dir. Troy Miller. (Salient Media, 2008). DVD.
51. Associated Press. "Radio Station 'Regrets' Magic Johnson Remarks, Promises PSA." *ESPN,* last modified Oct 10, 2008. http://www.espn.com.
52. Ellen Jean Samuels, "My Body, My Closet: Invisible Disability and the Limits of Coming Out Discourse," *GLQ: A Journal of Lesbian and Gay Studies,* 9.1–2 (2003): 236.
53. Anthony Foy, "Joe Louis's Talking Fists: The Auto/Biopolitics of *My Life Story,*" *American Literary History.* 23.2 (2011): 312–13.
54. Johnson and Bird, *When the Game Was Ours,* 286.
55. Ibid., 288.
56. Grant Farred, "The Event of the Black Body at Rest: Mêlée in Motown," *Cultural Critique.* 66 (2007), 65.
57. Ibid., 68.
58. Holland, *Erotic Life of Racism,* 18.
59. I should be very clear that Johnson still performs some work on behalf of raising awareness about HIV/AIDS. He is not a pariah in this community, nor is he one in the NBA. Here I refer to his public persona, which is now entrepreneurial rather than athletic or political.
60. Johnson and Bird, *When the Game Was Ours,* 329.
61. Cohen, *Boundaries of Blackness,* 167.
62. In using the term "performativity," I do not intend to suggest that one can analogize narratives of racial belonging and gender. Instead, I would contend that racial identification is understood (in part) based on similar logics of performativity. Members of a racial group police inclusion and belonging to that group by judging behaviors to be appropriate (or not) to that racial group. This behavior is part of the foundation for popular texts like Touré's *Who's Afraid of Post-Blackness?.* Scholars have invoked Judith Butler's work (and through her, Michel Foucault) to discuss the performative aspects of race. See Judith Butler, *Bodies That Matter* (New York, NY: Routledge, 1993); Touré, *Who's Afraid of Post-Blackness?* (New York, NY: Atria Books, 2012); Michelle Elam, *The Souls of Mixed Folk*; Nadine Ehlers, *Racial Imperatives: Discipline, Performativity, and Struggles against Subjection* (Bloomington, IN: Indiana UP, 2012).
63. Shildrick, *Dangerous Discourses,* 11.
64. Bell, "The Problem with Magic," 14.
65. Associated Press, "Radio Station 'Regrets' Magic Johnson Remarks."
66. For a thorough history of black conservative politics, see Christopher Bracey, *Saviors or Sellouts: The Promise and Peril of Black Conservatism from Booker T. Washington to Condoleezza Rice* (Boston, MA: Beacon Press, 2008).
67. Randolph, "The 'Magic' Miracle," 72.

5 The Big C Meets the Big O
Pain and Pleasure in Breast Cancer Narratives

Good Morning America co-anchor Robin Roberts announced her breast cancer diagnosis on daytime television on July 31, 2007. She not only made her personal experience a public affair but she also narrativized it by adding an eighth chapter to her book, *From the Heart: Seven Rules to Live By*, and appeared on *Nightline*. Her public battle with illness intensified when she needed a bone marrow transplant in 2012. I turn briefly to Roberts's public battle with breast cancer as an indexical entrance to the discussion that follows. Roberts's narrative raises questions about the centrality of pain within a breast cancer narrative and what discursive or activist space pain can open.

In her first memoir, Roberts provides seven rules that she deems important to every life. Each chapter provides the rationale for each rule and a set of anecdotes from her life as a high school and collegiate athlete, ESPN sportscaster, and television personality. Her sports background comes through in her use of sports metaphors: from the rules themselves, "Position Yourself to Take the Shot," to key phrases like "keep your head in the game." Roberts uses these metaphors to galvanize and motivate. Much like the consequences of making HIV/AIDS an opposing team for Magic Johnson, these sports metaphors provide a source of familiar inspiration as they give hope to the putative underdog. Unlike Magic Johnson, Roberts chooses not to use the sports metaphor when discussing her breast cancer experience. Instead she opts for fast-paced language and shifts her focus from being deliberately motivational to being more instructive. In the additional eighth chapter that narrates her experience with breast cancer, "Make Your Mess Your Message," Roberts's language has a more staccato pace and her actions are immediate and quick. In other words, the lingering descriptions in her earlier prose are shortened; her focus shifts away from open discussions about mentality or keeping one's head in the game. Her staccato pace places a focus on her actions or, if you will, provides a highlight reel of her experience. This focus obfuscates the lived and felt physicality of Roberts's experience. To be fair, this is not a failing of Roberts's writing style but rather of the sports metaphor in this context. The so-called game of life or life with illness is more complex than innings, quarters, or rounds could ever be, so the sports metaphors would have to extend beyond strategy and mental agility to include the goings-on that are beyond the ostensible players' control. The limitations of language here raise similar questions to Magic Johnson's (and news media's) characterization of HIV/AIDS as "it." Specifically, how does one describe the portions of the story that remain outside the protagonist's control? What does one do with the fictions of social constructs like race, gender, and ability when dealing with the material realities those fictions create or control?

In some ways, Roberts's use of visual media attempts to capture this embodied experience, but her use of broadcast journalism falls into the same traps as her prose because there is no explicit discussion of her embodied reality in terms of race or ability. On October 8, 2008, Roberts appeared on an episode of ABC's *Nightline*, during which she told the story of her diagnosis and treatment. The broadcast included information from the second version of her book, *From the Heart: Eight Rules to Live By*, and previous *Good Morning America* episodes. The footage functions similarly to sports replays as it appears to be a highlight reel of Roberts's experience. It is not as staccato or fast-paced as a typical highlight reel, but it does not linger on Roberts's bodily experience of cancer. For example, much of the footage shows Roberts in the ABC studios or moving through her doctors' offices. Very little shows her in chemotherapy or in pain afterward. When the camera follows her through corridors, it appears as though she is walking through locker rooms. In particular, shots of her in the ABC studios and at the radiation treatment center are all medium shots that capture her from the hips up and follow her into a longer shot when she emerges at her intended destination. Medium and long shots depersonalize the object within the camera's view by placing more distance between the object and the camera lens. Moreover, Roberts's mobility underscores the rhetoric of the *Nightline* piece, "Living with Cancer," and Roberts's own statement that "the idea was to have surgery, and get rid of the tumor and get on with my life."[1] Much like the sports metaphors, these phrases and camera shots emphasize action and agency. They obscure other phenomenological parts of the experience, like the after-effects of chemotherapy (with the exception of balding) that Roberts does not depict in words or on screen. Though the visual medium of broadcast journalism allows viewers to see her raced and gendered ill body, it still fails to capture her embodied experience.

Roberts's narrative indexes the tendency of breast cancer narratives to efface the embodied experience of the disease. Breast cancer narratives tend to follow a comic plot formula and minimize the effects of chemotherapy and radiation.[2] Few narratives discuss physicality in detail, opting instead to focus on a discursive reconstruction of the narrator's life where cancer is an interruption. At the crux of these renderings is a narrator who is a whole subject, seeking to empower others based on her (now finished) experience.[3] As G. Thomas Couser notes, "Two focuses emerge: the personal (addressing the illness as an individual concern) and the political (addressing the disease as a women's health issue)."[4] Descriptions of bodily experience, and pain in particular, appear antithetical to this mission because such discussions presuppose a discursive disintegration that counteracts the wholeness and empowerment for which these texts strive.[5] The body becomes an object to the breast cancer patient, first during the experience of illness and the accompanying medicalizing discourse, and second during the narratives, when the body becomes a tool to be manipulated in service of the ultimate tale of overcoming.

Here, I make sense of how the bodily experience of breast cancer—particularly the physical pain—adds nuance to the understanding of breast cancer as a deeply political women's issue. In the two texts I explore in greater depth, Audre Lorde's *The Cancer Journals* and Evelyne Accad's *The Wounded Breast: Intimate Journeys through Cancer*, the authors' embodied experience takes center stage. Both authors' focus on their identities as intersectional challenges the dominant paradigm of breast cancer narratives: straight white middle-class women assuming universal feminine identity.[6] These memoirs, and even Robin Roberts's memoir, miss a point on which Audre Lorde insists: "Your silence will not protect you. But for every real word spoken [. . .] I had made contact with other women while we examined the words to fit a world in which we all believed, bridging our differences."[7] Evelyne Accad agrees, citing that the Arabic phrase for cancer is *"Al-marad illi ma btitssamma*: the disease not to be named,"[8] and she writes against this attempt to silence and suppress. They embrace the opportunity to discuss their experience from the perspective of their difference. In contrast, Roberts's memoir attempts to neutralize the idea that her race and gender would be a problem in her chapter "Never Play the Race, Gender or Any Other Card." She acknowledges that others take issue with these parts of her identity, but refuses to brook what she calls "get[ting] trapped in a victim mentality" in lieu of "focusing on your personal excellence."[9] As a result, Roberts's breast cancer narrative does not explore her experience from the perspective of her wealthy, Black womanhood. Certainly, Roberts's text performs a certain kind of discursive work in that it functions as a source of inspiration for others and, like many of the breast cancer narratives before it, warns women of the perils of breast cancer and empowers them by providing an ally. Yet the absence of a classed, racialized, and gendered perspective implies that women's empowerment is predicated on a silence about the intersection of their identities. There is a paradox at the heart of Roberts's representation of herself. The narrative suggests that breast cancer experiences are universal because they lie within the body while eliding the effects of social identities inscribed upon the body (e.g., health care disparities, racism in the medical and scientific communities, belief in women's hysteria). Lorde and Accad's attention to their own situated and specific identities avoids a discussion of breast cancer that adheres to what Kimberlé Crenshaw has already shown is a wrongheaded notion about the intersection between race and gender. They refuse to, in Crenshaw's words, "expound identity as 'woman' or 'person of color' as an either/or proposition [and they do not relegate] the identity of women of color to a location that resists telling."[10]

Moreover, Accad and Lorde usher their bodies into these discussions less as a tool to be manipulated (or overcome) and more as a partner in understanding oneself and redirecting the narrative of breast cancer. It is not my aim to suggest that Lorde and Accad succeed where Roberts (or others) fail, but rather to point to how their narratives strategize a discussion of embodied experience that unmakes the medical establishment. They both discuss their pain and pleasure as integral to their experiences. In some ways, pain resists phenomenological description. As Elaine Scarry articulates in *The Body in Pain: The Making and Unmaking of the World*, pain "may seem to have the remote character of some deep subterranean fact, belonging to an invisible geography that, however portentous, has no reality because it has not yet manifested itself on the visible surface of the earth."[11] To discuss physical pain is to attempt to create language while working against suspicion. That is, physical pain—by virtue of its invisibility and untouchability—exists as something that can be denied. To articulate one's physical pain is to work against the implied mutual, reciprocal relationship within phenomenology. What results is a simultaneous making and unmaking. The torture subject, who is Scarry's focus, is unmade by pain, whereas the torturer is made by virtue of inflicting pain. Accad and Lorde's descriptions of pain defy this relationship and reposition themselves as the tortured who unmake the torturers (read: medical establishment) while they remake themselves.

These authors also write against the linguistic limitations of representing pain as part of their "acknowledge[ment of] the therapeutic and pedagogical dimensions of narrating breast cancer."[12] The language to describe physical pain abets denial in that such pain resists language, resulting in a language about pain that persists in its unspeakability. Unlike other somatic and emotional states, pain takes no linguistic object: humans hunger for something or have ambivalence about something, but cannot explain pain in a similar fashion.[13] This resistance does not always enforce a silence about pain; in fact, everyone attempts to describe pain for themselves using figurative language (i.e., "it feels like a jackhammer is drilling into my head"). Martha Stoddard Holmes notes the difficulty in reconciling her embodied experience of pain with Scarry's description of it, noting that her body in pain proliferated language.[14] I would link Holmes's experience to Lorde's and Accad's in that the linguistic absence of referents does not result in automatic silence. Lorde and Accad attempt to describe pain using their proliferated language of approximation and, in the case of Accad, photography. Though their language and, to a certain extent, the photography remain mired in approximation, their decision to speak about the pain creates a kind of visibility integral to disrupting the common parlance regarding the experience of breast cancer.

I place these two authors in conversation based on the way their articulations of pain result in a call to activism. I agree that Accad is part of a cadre of breast cancer memoirists who are "Audre Lorde's postmillennial successors" and who "argue that breast cancer needs further feminist analysis and political scrutiny."[15] Certainly, activism is not unusual within breast cancer memoirs, as they tend to have some political message about early detection, environmental carcinogens, or health care legislation. However, Lorde and Accad's political messages include not only the aforementioned issues but also those issues that have remained a staple in their earlier work. Specifically, both women draw on the erotic as part of their call to activism. Lorde writes, "The erotic is a resource within each of us that lies in a deeply female and spiritual plane, firmly rooted in the power of our unexpressed or unrecognized feeling."[16] Accad echoes Lorde's idea that "in order to perpetuate itself, every oppression must corrupt or distort those various sources of power within the culture of the oppressed that can provide energy for change. For women, this has meant a suppression of the erotic as a considered source of power and information within our lives."[17] Accad writes, "Unless a sexual revolution is incorporated into political revolution, there will be no real transformation of social relations," following from her statement that "sexuality seems to have a revolutionary potential so strong that many political women and men are afraid of it."[18] They each agree that sexuality and the erotic are integral to fighting structures of oppression. Based on their earlier work as scholars and their narratives, I induce that Lorde and Accad advocate that embodied experience, including pain and sexual pleasure, be a part of breast cancer activism. In what follows, I examine how their breast cancer narratives mobilize pain to critique the medical establishment and enlist pleasure and the homosocial as healing mechanisms. I also sift through the implications of their critiques for the feminist stances they so urgently engage.

Evelyne Accad's book cover (Figure 5.1) literally positions pain at the forefront of her text. In it, she reclines with a serious expression, looking directly at the reader. The photo appears to be lit from above with a pinkish light, mirroring that of radiation therapy. Though the top of the book cuts across the woman's head, it is obvious that she is bald. At the center of the photograph is Accad's chest. Accad's stare toward the camera is not blank or lascivious, but forthright. To borrow from writer and disability rights activist Kenny Fries, Accad "stares back,"[19] reversing the gaze of the onlooker. Her forward stare, radiation marks, and missing breast emphasize the medical procedures that she has undergone and, at the very least, their physiological aftermath. In her photo, Accad does not lower her outward gaze, nor does she invite comfort. The photo appears to be a simple declarative statement: I am here.

Much unlike other photography taken of the ill and disabled, this particular photograph does not attempt "enfreakment."[20] In this portrait, she is not on display as an example of suffering or an "outsider admitted into culture

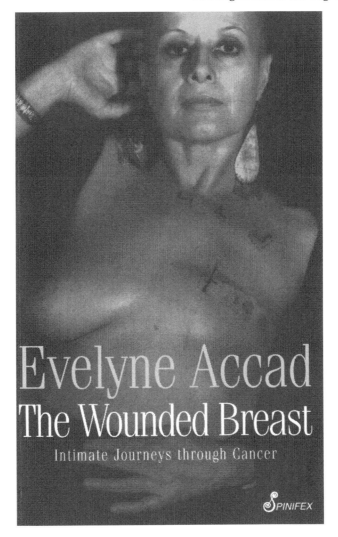

Figure 5.1 Evelyne Accad's *The Wounded Breast*

as [a symbol] of fear or pity" like previous portraits of disabled subjects.[21] In fact, Accad's direct gaze is disarming rather than alarming. Her portrait capitalizes on her body as a site to be pitied and feared: putting her bare chest on the cover invites staring. Yet the ability to read the photo exclusively with fear or pity is disarmed by her expression. Accad's photo disrupts "the perceived stability of normative expectations"[22] by invoking what Margrit Shildrick terms "dangerous discourse," that which "indicat[es] the depth of anxiety that engagement with disability elicits."[23] Accad's lips are in a straight line and one hand is deliberately positioned behind her head, both of which suggest that she is comfortable with her body. Were it not for the absent breast and the caption "the wounded breast," one might read her as being without pain. Her expression and her chest compete for attention and, as a result, create a vacillation between pain and painlessness, fear and fearlessness.

For a post-mastectomy woman to invite stares is not new. In 1993, a visual artist known as Matuschka invited readers to stare at her missing breast in the pages of the *New York Times Magazine*. Before then, she made a living from showing off her body as an exotic dancer and lingerie model. When a mastectomy forced her to reconsider her corporeality, she launched a photography campaign that featured her missing breast prominently by copying the format of Calvin Klein's Obsession perfume and Victoria's Secret advertisements. Matuschka's photographs received mixed reviews because few wanted to stare, but many were compelled to do so. As Rosemarie Garland-Thomson cogently argues, "She forces everyone to look hard, not so much at what we do not want to see, but at that which we are not supposed to stare. To see a wound where we expect a breast demands not just attention, but an explanation, a new reality."[24] No longer is the breast associated solely with maternity. That moment has passed and exists mostly in ruins or ecclesiastical settings.[25] In our current moment, the sexualized breasts must conform to or be regulated by a cultural expectation that they appear only in certain places, in certain shapes, and in matched pairs. Matuschka and Accad violate these expectations by inviting others to stare at a pair of breasts that defies the equation of two-ness with whole-ness. Both women force others to "look hard" and reexamine their expectations in light of wounded breasts.

Accad's photographer, Eva Enderlein, staged Accad's photo with the intent of getting Accad to stare back as people became awkward onlookers. Enderlein deliberately invokes Goya's image *La Maja Desnuda (The Nude Maja)*,[26] an image that once received a great deal of notoriety for its nudity. Enderlein's invocation of Goya's *Maja* relies on the expectation that others will be dismayed at having had their sexualized gaze ruptured by the presence of a scar in lieu of a breast.[27] Enderlein's staging of the cover photograph follows from Matuschka and others' precedent in breast cancer activism of calling attention to the breasts themselves. Like these earlier photos, Accad's cover invites the objectification of an ill or disabled subject. Since her face and her chest compete for attention, Accad's body in her photo becomes a site for interrogating the nature of pity and fear. Despite the increase in number and visibility of breast cancer narratives since the 1980s, breast cancer still invites those responses. When Accad's photo places a premium focus on her body, it insists that the viewer rethink his or her initial reaction as ineluctable and contemplate whether Accad's body corroborates a reaction of pity or fear. An initial reaction of either emotion seems to suggest that the viewers' response is to the possibility of breast cancer affecting them or someone they know. What they have interpreted is not Accad's body but their own or another's. Yet, Accad's body disturbs the certainty that she should be feared or pitied. Her chest prompts one set of responses based on the typical reactions to a missing breast, but her face suggests a different set of responses may be necessary. Here, the invocation of Goya's nude coquette (rough translation of *maja*) necessitates a different understanding of her chest since she assumes the pose of a pin-up girl. It becomes clear that the initial reaction to the chest is not actually a result of a reading of the chest but rather a set of assumptions about the chest. Rereading the chest requires a query regarding the validity of the viewer's initial response.

The cover of Lorde's *The Cancer Journals* does not present such a provocative image. On it, Lorde appears clothed and smiling with her head tilted toward the spine of the book. Despite the sartorial difference, both covers, because cancer is so often discussed through the metaphor of war, function as images of survivors, and, indeed, the existence of the personal narrative buttresses the idea that these books testify to their experiences.[28] The covers, as points of entry, rely somewhat on (if only to thwart) the dominant and problematic narratives of cancer as war: sympathy for the survivors, treatment of subjects as victims, and the sensationalism of images. In Susan Sontag's *Regarding the Pain of Others*, she meditates on the depictions of war and their implications for how we understand war, sympathy, and responsibility. To be fair, Sontag's work here examines images of military conflict; nonetheless, her meditations provide a useful framework for examining images of breast cancer as survivor images. Much of the rhetoric about cancer, as seen in Robin Roberts's *Nightline* appearance and the work of these two authors, is the rhetoric of war, and the photographs function accordingly. As Sontag argues, "All photographs wait to be explained or falsified by their captions."[29] Photographs become a weapon in the war against breast cancer. They can be used by either survivors or the medical establishment and, in the hands of propagandists, misused. Captions certainly have the authority to be unfaithful to their photographic companions. What occurs with the book covers of these authors is not downright unfaithfulness, but rather fidelity of a different sort.

Lorde's cover gains power based on its courting and querying of narratives outside itself—racial narratives and illness narratives—to remain faithful to the narrative of the text: one that deals with the conundrums and contradictions of those ideas. Lorde resists the stereotypical portrayals of Black women that uphold intertwined racial, gendered, classed, and abled ideologies. Images like Mammy or Jezebel positioned the Black woman's sexuality as linked specifically to her reproductive capacity, a womanhood that directly opposed the "cult of true womanhood" ideology in which these images were formed.[30] Lorde's cover and text recoil from these narratives because "even when the political and economic conditions that originally generated [these] controlling images disappear, such images prove remarkably tenacious because they not only keep Black women oppressed but are key in maintaining interlocking systems of race, class, and gender oppression."[31] On Lorde's original cover, she smiles and peers straight ahead with her head tilted toward the title on the left. She looks out from a blank backdrop, which makes her smiling presence more insistent. The head tilt toward the title, or caption, "The Cancer Journals," points to the resolution of a comic plot wherein Lorde is much better off than she was before. This caption allows for Lorde's happy image to provide a counterpoint to what would have been in the 1980s the fear-inducing idea of cancer. With this counterpoint, cancer becomes more complicated: it is no longer a death sentence, and even when it is, it does not guarantee that a person will be permanently silenced. This cover also delinks her Black breasts from sexuality and fertility and directly links them to illness, vulnerability, and (especially since 1992) death. Lorde's implicated breasts, like the body in her other work, "[become] a map of lived experience and a way of printing suffering as well as joy upon the flesh."[32]

Of Lorde's *Cancer Journals*, Elizabeth Alexander argues: "Because the history of the black female sexual body is fraught with lies and distortion, the story of those bodies as told by their inhabitors must take place on new, self-charted terrain with the marks of a traumatic history like a palimpsest."[33] This is equally as true for Arab American women's bodies since the Orientalist gaze exoticizes and endangers, dominates and demonizes. Accad's cover image undercuts the narratives (literally with a mark across the chest) that would dismiss her body based on its proximity to the image of the ultra-feminine Arab (American) female or, if she is understood as Arab, a putative exotic and ideal femininity with two breasts. Specifically, Accad's photo positions the subject's identity as it relates to the caption or, in this case, the book's author, title, and subtitle—Evelyne Accad, *The Wounded Breast: Intimate Journeys through Cancer*—as an explanation of what the image is supposed to represent: a specific person, a wound, an intimate journey, and cancer. The original French title, *Voyages en Cancer*, translates to 'A Journey in Cancer.' If a wounded breast or an absent breast compromises female identity, then the image thwarts this idea by insisting that a missing breast is equally feminine as a present breast or present set of breasts. It works against the common cultural narratives that position a woman's breasts as a cathected site of female sexuality. Note that the translation uses the word "wounded." "Wounded" as opposed to "missing" intimates that the breast is still present, just in another form. As Garland-Thomson argues, "a woman's understanding of herself may differ wildly from the message that her breasts convey [. . .], her breasts nevertheless announce the essence of her womanliness."[34] Here, the wounded breasts have the capacity to mark a woman as no longer woman, but the term "wounded" insists that the "essence of her womanliness" remains. What's more, the caption points to a plurality not present in the image itself. The plural noun 'journeys' repositions the woman as a representative. She becomes both an individual and an icon. As a result, the wound of the title is magnified and the pain of the wound multiplied by the plurality of jour-neys. Accad's image transforms into evidence of her survival of cancer and its resultant pain. The interaction of the caption and the photo delineate an ownership of a nuanced femininity: one that includes pain, cancer, and a missing breast.

These images can be undermined by the narratives created about them or taken out of context toward multiple ends (i.e., become pornography). In other words, staged images can create a mockery of the reality of suffer-ing and undermine it with performance, a gesture that ultimately works to dismiss the responsibility of the viewer. Accad's cover image challenges the viewer, suggesting that an image can create its own context and narrative. In this case, an image where a subject owns her pain challenges assumptions about pain itself. The seriousness of the woman's expression, unflinching, to be sure, implies that the portrait, the staged photo, is secondary to the reality of the missing breast. The breast cannot be ignored or dismissed; it is precisely the presumed discomfort with the missing breast and the subject's forward stare that turn what would be a spectacle into a meditation on the reality of the missing breast. What appears to be a performance—the large earrings, the hand at the back of the head—underlines the main subject of the photo: the focal point, the missing breast. In fact, the pose, the earrings, and the nude present breast demonstrate an acceptance of the lack as a reality. As a result, the image invites engagement with itself and its subject matter. Nonetheless, the woman's ownership of (her presumed) pain does not invite pity (though it cannot outright refuse it); instead, it prompts an interrogation of mastectomies, the experience of breast cancer, and the pain associated with both.[35]

Certainly, photographs provide a deviation from the verbal discourse that usually curtails the representation of pain. Both covers represent pain according to the logics of the photos, privileging a speaking body and ascrib-ing a certainty and immortality to pain and experience (however vexed) nor-mally unavailable in verbal discourse. Their photographs imprison a reality otherwise thought of as inaccessible by making it still, or they amplify scenes otherwise thought of as distant.[36] Given the understanding of cancer in the 1980s and the continued understanding of surgery as painful, the book covers confirm the certainty of pain for women with breast cancer. On Lorde's cover, her tilted head signals an interaction between her smiling presence and the experience of cancer. Without conflating cancer and pain, I emphasize how the two are intimate companions within the world of the photo as Lorde's tilted head reminds the viewer of the constant simultaneity of pain, cancer, and her voice. Much like Lorde's cover, Accad's body speaks for itself by marking the truth of her pain. Her missing breast, as evidenced by a surgical scar, underscores the reality of her pain, a fact emphasized by the caption, "The Wounded Breast." Despite the fact that her gaze prompts an interrogation of her experience of pain, the photograph does not allow a viewer to easily dismiss its existence.

The objections to photographs as a kind of *memento mori* are worth noting. What Karla F. C. Holloway terms the "troubled and ambivalent narrative"[37] regarding the disappeared and mourned Black body coincides with the erasure of the Arab body.[38] The communities' experiences with violence make suspicious any representation that attempts to anesthetize or desensitize one to the very real pain inscribed on Arab and Black bodies. Sontag views this as the danger with photos of any kind of suffering. Her ideas are worth quoting at length.

> To suffer is one thing; another thing is living with the photographed images of suffering, which does not necessarily strengthen conscience and the ability to be compassionate. It can also corrupt them. Once one has seen such images, one has started down the road of seeing more—and more. Images transfix. Images anesthetize. An event known through photographs certainly becomes more real than it would have been if one had never seen the photographs—think of the Vietnam War. (For a counter-example, think of the Gulag Archipelago, of which we have no photographs.) But after repeated exposure to images it also becomes less real.[39]

The danger for interpreting these covers would be if one who has not experienced cancer continues to look at them and finds that Lorde's and Accad's (or, for that matter, any woman's) suffering becomes "less real." For this kind of viewer, the images may hold the capacity to anesthetize one to the suffering within them. In some ways, this would thwart the efficacy of these images to create a discourse of pain, especially if the viewer's response ceases to be or never was one of compassion. In that case, these images would be much like the verbal discourse of pain—invalidated by uncertainty and resistant to depiction.

To my mind, two compelling arguments stymie Sontag's concern. First, her argument presumes that pity (Sontag uses the word 'compassion') is always a useful emotion that translates to action. As Joseph Shapiro's landmark historical study *No Pity: People with Disabilities Forging a New Civil Rights Movement* demonstrates, pity assumes a distanced stance, allowing the observer to be completely removed from that which is observed.[40] In phenomenological terms, the pitiable becomes solely an object to be viewed, moved, or ignored, not a subject who views, moves, or ignores others. With breast cancer, pity removes the impetus for action and solidifies the presence of fear. That fear of having cancer or of losing one's womanhood is buttressed by images of the ideal woman, which include a full head of hair and full breasts. Images of bald, post-mastectomy women still engender anxiety. In addition, Lorde's death functions as a reminder that recurrence is real. Not all gazes view these images with the same anxieties in mind, but the fact remains that these types of images of breast cancer patients continue to transfix and have not yet broached the realm of anesthetizing people. They still repel some viewers and shock others.[41] These reactions lie at the crux of the second argument that troubles Sontag's concern. Breast cancer is not a static historical event like the Vietnam War. Breast cancer has not happened. It is happening. These images are less a slice of time than they are an ongoing reality. As such, they lack the requisite temporal distance, which would provide a fecund place for viewers to be unmoved.[42]

The question remains, "What to do with such knowledge as photographs bring of faraway suffering?"[43] This question attempts to ascertain the value and impact of photographs without captions or narratives to explain them. After all, narratives have the potential to be manipulative, but photographs without them can be even more so because "compassion is an unstable emotion [that] needs to be translated into action, or it withers."[44] As I have stated before, I do not view Lorde's and Accad's covers as operating solely based on the generation of compassion, but also with some element of fear based on a possibility of or a reaction to pain. This fear requires translation as well. Pain continuously requires translation in order to be believed, and certainly to coerce someone into action. Otherwise, "it withers." For *Wounded Breast* and *Cancer Journals*, the narratives aid in translating these emotions to political action. The text itself buttresses the impact of the photograph, echoing it and, in some cases, magnifying it to move the viewer or reader past fear.

The texts' structures assist in translating these emotive responses, such as fear, into a political stance. Both memoirs showcase the writers' own movement through pain and from fear to overt political engagement. *The Wounded Breast* spans 528 pages and traverses four continents. The multiplicity of places and people Accad encounters with cancer underscores the disease as a minatory presence. The journal entries become a chronology of multiple instances of pain[45] and often feature her wrestling (alongside her friends' marginalia) to make sense of her experiences. In addition, her friends' marginalia, clinical observations from doctors, and personal letters allow Accad to participate in political and personal conversations about prevention, treatment, and cure.[46] Lorde's *Cancer Journals* is decidedly shorter and vacillates between essay and journal entry. She wrestles with what to do regarding her pain, saying that she does not want this to be "a record of grieving only."[47] Some critics make a distinction between her journal entries and "controlled exposition"[48] in the essays, noting that the former is more emotive. I do not find that distinction entirely accurate. Instead, the tension between the two—one that helps her create a book that does not only hold grieving—results more from the temporal distance between the journal and the essay, not necessarily emotional distance or difference.

At times, Accad confesses her own pain; at other times, she attempts to respond to the pain of others. She does not automatically jump from understanding pain to discussing the politics of the medical industry, but rather oscillates between the two. In her entry marked "31 March 1994," she discusses her body in relation to chemotherapy, saying, "I don't feel as if my body is a friend, the way I used to before I had the treatment."[49] In that same entry, she points out the necessity of speaking out against the cruelty of doctors and forming patient support groups. She writes about the political urgency in a friend's experience that prompts her to demand a new social politic. She recounts the story of her friend Alex, who was treated for a goiter until doctors realized it was a tumor. Here, she cannot engage politics based on her own experience despite her feeling that her body is not the same. Instead, she opts for narrating someone else's story as a frame for her own. The act of telling someone else's story permits politics by proxy, a way to engage the larger implications of her own experience with her friend's experience as a substitute for her own. It should be noted that this is a storytelling technique common to Arab American writing, which at times deliberately invokes the famous frame tale structure of *Alf Layla wa Layla* (*1001 Nights*).

Whereas her writing about her own experiences recycles her feelings of depression and prompts introspection (and some self-berating) about her decisions and motives, her writing about Alex's experience draws conclusions about his courage and describes a wide range of possible and understandable emotions. In some ways, she is kinder to Alex than she is to herself. Her engagement with his experience allows her to express her own need to "find help through participating in the support group."[50] She can also vent her frustrations with regard to the medical staff through her pride that "because Alex had the courage to speak out [. . .] the doctor started changing his ways."[51] Alex's experience brings to the fore Accad's own difficulty with feeling whole after medical treatment. His misdiagnosed tumor, resultant surgery, and arrogant doctors help to crystallize Accad's own feeling that her body is no longer a friend and that she "[has] conflicting feelings about her body."[52] Her praise of the support group allows her to form a political response to mistreatment at the hands of the medical establishment. A support group may not be considered radical politics, but it does respond to the feminist mantra that the personal is political, and, in keeping with other breast cancer narratives, a support group becomes part of a public mission to eradicate the disease. Accad's difficulty in expressing her own experience and her use of Alex to do so evinces that, on one hand, she understands the political urgency of supporting one another and telling each other's stories; on the other, she knows the weightiness and disorienting physical cost of experiencing pain and discomfort with one's own body. Her engagement with the story and advocacy of supportive politics suggests that the pain does not mitigate the necessity of action.

In addition to allowing room for Accad to chronicle her own pain and that of others, the vast scope of her memoir and the various stories it presents allows the text to corroborate itself and repeat itself. In some of the journal entries, Accad provides her own marginalia. For instance, when discussing a doctor's visit, she says, "I'm writing this account a year later, by reworking the notes I took during the consultation. At this moment, my dear friend Zohreh is undergoing chemotherapy for ovarian cancer. [. . .] We didn't know about her illness a year ago, and what else didn't we—don't we—know?"[53] These reflections, indicated by a change in font, build into the text a reflexivity that forecloses the possibility of ignoring cancer as a political issue. The question "What else didn't we—don't we—know?" seems ominous given that cancer affects not only her female friends— Zohreh, Séverine, Caryl—but also her male friends—Alex, her father, and her lover, Alban. Given the abundance of these stories from men and women, it appears that Accad has no choice but to work through her own pain and the experiences of others. Part of doing so includes figuring out an appropriate response. When she asks, "What else didn't we—don't we—know?," she has arrived at more questions than answers. Given that Accad's prologue voices that "we must make the facts known,"[54] it is clear that the text will progress toward a set of political responses.[55]

Moreover, Accad is not the only person attempting to understand her pain in *The Wounded Breast*; her friends' marginalia riddles the text, punctuating, confirming, and complicating Accad's words. Such a polyvocality offers responses to her experiences of pain, which allows her not only to give voice to the pain but also to counteract the discourse normally available with regard to it. The marginalia overshadows the linguistic conundrum usually present with descriptions of pain. Despite pain's lack of referent and its invisibility, the marginalia confirms pain's presence. At times, the commentators discuss pain directly. For example, Cindy asks about the lack of desire to look at reconstructed breasts or post-mastectomy scars: "I wonder why we're so afraid to see evidence of another person's pain."[56] Other times, they comment on other tangential issues, as when Madeleine condescendingly responds to Accad's questions about the prevalence of cancer, saying, "Here, Evelyne, I think you're overdoing it a bit. [. . .] There's no miracle cure—but I do understand your anguish and need to revolt."[57] In both comments, Madeleine and Cindy take for granted the fact of pain. As a result, the friends' comments are testimonials, witnesses to the reality of pain. This does not negate the fact that the descriptions of pain are still approximate, but it does create a certainty that it has occurred, despite a doubt inherent in Accad's language. Though pain destroys language and, in turn, the ability to sympathize and act on that pain, the opposite occurs in Accad's memoir. The marginalia—by virtue of the expressions of sympathy and pushes to action—assists in translating the pain into political urgency.

The voluminous nature of *Wounded Breast*, its length, breadth, and extensive commentary, works much like the interaction between the word 'journeys' and the cover photograph. Just as the plurality of 'journeys' amplifies the pain of the photo, the volume of the text amplifies the pain present in Accad's story. I have already stated that Accad's cover functions as evidence of pain. Likewise, Accad's book becomes evidentiary through its underscoring of the same. Consider again that pain destroys language and must create language out of suspicion. From this logic, pain can only be represented when it is confirmed as fact. The many and varied cancer experiences, the wide geographical coverage, and the self-reflexivity of the text (from Accad's marginalia as well as her friends') negate the need for suspicion because the many witnesses act as confirmation. Certainly, the need for an abundance of language points to pain's destructive (linguistic) force, but Accad has found a way to write pain into being by forcing an acknowledgment through sheer numbers. As with her entry regarding Alex, Accad's journals move between pain and politics by virtue of her friends' commentary.

Whereas Accad's text grapples with pain slowly and methodically, Lorde's text performs the very urgency it wishes to discuss. Lorde nestles her journal entries within larger essays, mixing personal reflection with a critical eye. At times, this structure can be disorienting, but it does not verge into being inconsistent or chaotic. The result is not just a meditation by an accomplished raconteur but self-reflexivity and introspection. G. Thomas Couser comments on Lorde's *Cancer Journals* and his ideas are worth quoting at length:

> [T]he book shifts back and forth between the proximate and the distant, between the emotional and the intellectual, as Lorde struggles to bring all her resources to bear on a new and frightening challenge. The strength of the book is in its inclusion of both her private responses—cries of pain and outrage—and her political analysis—seasoned, reasoned discourse.[58]

Certainly, Couser's analysis of her text is apt, but his statement gives the impression that Lorde's book is easily bifurcated into seasoned discourse and cries of outrage. This is not so. Her outrage is reasoned and her "seasoned discourse" is laden with (and, occasionally, propelled by) her outrage. The shift between the "proximate and the distant" is a temporal one, not an emotional one as Couser suggests. For instance, she says in one of her diary entries, "I don't want this to be a record of grieving only. I don't want this to be a record only of tears. I want it to be something I can use now or later."[59] By virtue of her use of metaphor and synecdoche, this diary entry remains more poetic than the text that surrounds it; however, the tone of defiance is not altogether more emotional than that which follows. Of her desires and duties, she says in the accompanying essay, "The need to look death in the face and not shrink from it, yet not ever to embrace it too easily, was a developmental and healing task for me that was constantly being sidelined by the more practical and immediate demands of hurting too much, and how do I live with myself one-breasted?"[60] Both the journal entry and the accompanying essay attempt to make sense of her healing and her pain in ways that serve others. She wrestles with the appropriate ethical response to her pain, but neither the diary entry nor the essay is more emotionally estranged from the experience than the other. In fact, if the essay is supposed to illuminate the so-called emotional journal entry with an intellectual response, it fails in this task. What it does instead is support the journal entry and buttress its concerns.

Both of the aforementioned passages evince a wrestling with the repercussions of her pain. Here, Lorde works quickly to translate her pain into something else, despite not quite knowing how to do so. This difficulty of translation and the desire to do so quickly illustrates the difficulty of discussing and reliving pain. Lorde's attempt to translate her pain is an attempt at giving her pain language and, true to Lorde's calling as a Black lesbian feminist poet, critical utility. In other words, though Lorde finds this pain uncomfortable, she does not find it useless. She finds utility in being honest about the painfulness of her experience, but also in urgently translating that pain to action. She meditates on pain primarily as an impetus to move toward awareness, discussion, and activism. If we recall that pain has no referent, Lorde's discursive response to the lack of referent is to be self-referential in that she links her pain to her intellectual and critical endeavors. Lorde's pain gains a referent because it gains a purpose. Locating a purpose means that she gives pain an objective even though, in terms of language, pain has no object: she hurts in order to do something or hurts for some purpose.

Thus far, I've discussed the ways in which Accad and Lorde use their narratives to testify to the fact of their pain and the necessity of a political response. Their more direct discussions of pain speak to the master narratives about cancer and treatment, specifically contravening medicalized narratives that insist on cure at the expense of patient care. The ambit of such a discourse on the medical establishment is that it makes permissible painful treatments and effaces patients' quality-of-life needs. In Susan Sontag's *Illness as Metaphor*, Sontag notes how cancer is often metaphorized as war within medical discourse. Lorde and Accad "reclaim these metaphors [of war] and, in doing so, reclaim both the social and physical significance of [their] changed bodies."[61] In each narrative, their discussions of pain as torturous highlight the disintegration of language and the inability of others—particularly doctors and medical personnel—to acknowledge the post-mastectomy woman's experience with pain. Whereas Accad focuses on the "poison, cut and burn" of chemotherapy, mastectomy, and radiation, respectively, as treatment, Lorde engages in a discussion about phantom pains and other physical effects of the mastectomy.[62] Their narratives dovetail with Scarry's theory that the collapse of language and the rendering of the tortured subject as invisible are two steps in a three-step process, the last of which is an insistence on the power of the regime that sanctions the torture. For Accad and Lorde, not only is the process torturous, but it also functions to solidify the power of the medical establishment.

Before discussing the invisibility of the tortured subject and the insistence on the regime's power, I turn to the women's collapse of language in their descriptions of pain. Accad's choice not to describe her physical pain in detail (though she comments extensively on it) proves that descriptions of pain tend to be approximate or rely on metaphor. This is why Lorde's elaborate descriptions of her phantom pain become especially powerful. Lorde's meditations bring the reader inside the body, emphasizing the fact of loss, the act of mourning, and the necessity of political responsibility. The language of approximation becomes an inroad to describing pain, a method that Lorde uses in her descriptions. Lorde writes:

> On the morning of the third day, the pain returned home bringing all of its kinfolk. Not that any single one of them was overwhelming, but just that all in concert, or even in small repertory groups, they were excruciating. There were constant ones and intermittent ones. There were short sharp and long dull and various combinations of the same ones. The muscles in my back and right shoulder began to screech as if they'd been pulled apart and now were coming back to life slowly and against their will. My chest wall was beginning to ache and burn and stab by turns. My breast which was no longer there would hurt as if it were being squeezed in a vise. That was perhaps the worst pain of all, because it would come with a full complement of horror that I was to be forever reminded of my loss by suffering in a part of me which was no longer there.[63]

In Lorde's words, we find specific linguistic maneuvers—approximations, temporal distinctions, and spatial distinctions. Lorde's words take advantage of this disintegration of language in that the approximations disorient rather than describe, confuse rather than clarify. The metaphors of family and music haunt her descriptions because she inverts the beauty and comfort generally associated with them. For instance, the different types of pain certainly do not conjure up the close-knit image alluded to with the term "kinfolk." Muscles also do not, as personified here, "screech." The mechanical term "screech" implies a cacophony wherein her muscles are performing, but in the wrong way. Her words point to a symphony gone awry. She says that the muscles work "in concert" or "in small repertory groups" to hurt her. This description of pain indicates the very inability to describe it, except by approximation or implication, and the excruciating prerequisite for such a loss of language. When juxtaposed with the laughing woman on the cover, this description of pain also highlights the multifaceted nature of dealing with cancer. In this moment, Lorde's book crystallizes the vacillation between feeling disempowered and feeling triumphant. She, like Accad, demonstrates that the image can work alongside the narrative, rather than simply be undercut by it.

In Accad's narrative, the descriptions of physical pain are not present at all; she opts for simple declarations that pain has occurred. Accad's straightforward and pithier remarks function similarly to Lorde's diary entry (though I would argue not as powerfully) in highlighting the inability to articulate pain. Coupled with the cover and her very detailed delineations of her treatment, Accad's more sparse description emphasizes the overwhelming nature of pain itself. Pain seems to surround the text, creating a discourse similar to Lorde's journals. Gaps of eloquence in Accad's memoir have a critical utility. Given the length of Accad's discussions of other issues, particularly those that are the result of pain, like changed sexual libido and function, strained patient-doctor relationships, and difficulty cultivating inner peace, this rhetorical reticence *vis-à-vis* physical pain underscores how much it robs one of language.[64]

Though Accad is silent about much of her physical pain and, to her friends, much of her psychological adjustment, she does not participate in the silencing of her own voice. What Accad experiences at the hands of family, strangers, medical personnel, and other healers bears striking similarity to a tortured subject. The tortured subject loses language just as the torturer doubles his language, thereby forcing silence on the tortured subject.[65] Here, language can be taken away to immobilize the victim and undermine the possibility of representation and, as a result, political action. For Accad, this occurs on several occasions. Within her doctors' offices, her doctors, specifically Dr. JE, deny her information or hide behind medical jargon, which usually results in her receiving poor care. Accad's sister, Adelaïde, calls cancer "Satanic" and admonishes Accad to repent in order to be healed.[66] Adelaïde's commentary usurps Accad's understanding of her illness, so that she is at a loss for how to describe her life except in religious terms in the journal entries that follow. In both cases, Accad has not only undergone physical pain but also theft at the level of language that removes her linguistic agency and places it in the hands of another. In her journal entries, Accad fights against these blanket narratives by questioning their validity in relation to her experience and as a way to recuperate her own voice. Of cancer and Satan, she writes, "Proselytizers often use individual or collective hardship to shamelessly exploit people who are in a position of weakness."[67] (It is worth noting that this direct correlation between Satan and cancer is not at all theologically accurate.) She expresses her irritation when Dr. JE "seems to be more interested in my intention to write about cancer than in answering my questions."[68] Her having written against them in a way that pinpoints their own agenda at the expense of her body echoes Lorde's truism "Your silence will not protect you."[69] Lorde contends that these types of silencing, these usurpations of one's own voice, force one to write in the first place. Their narratives point out that silences enable fear and reduce the possibility of political action.

In Accad's and Lorde's narratives, to understand language only in its disintegrated form or as usurped from the tortured person implies acceptance of the medical establishment's ideas about the authors' bodies and their embodied experience. When they write, they thwart the regime's ability to usurp their power by capitalizing on the difficulty of representing and discussing their pain. For both of them, their pain does not merely transform into the insignia of power, but it is their power. Their narratives reclaim agency and language as their own. To be specific, Accad draws on the discourse of the Holocaust ("never forget") and the necessity of survivors' stories in postwar Lebanon. The latter is the subject of one of her books, *Sexuality and War: Literary Masks of the Middle East*, and emphasizes her resistance against a "politics of invisibility"[70] *vis-à-vis* her experience. She draws on both the Holocaust and the space of Lebanon to create parallels between women transnationally and cross-culturally. This link becomes especially important given the way in which she arrays research and cancer narratives from across the United States, Europe, and the Arab world. Lorde's own transcontinental experiences in Germany, the United States, and the Virgin Islands emphasized the multiplicity and possibility within women's experiences. (Many of these transnational experiences as they relate to cancer are discussed in her final book, *A Burst of Light*.) Their journals reclaim language, not only on the basis of their subjectivity, but also on the basis of the subjectivities of others like them. Drawing links between various forms of oppression spotlights the seepage of injustice to which Suheir Hammad's poetry and interviews refer. In their view, the medical establishment's treatment of cancer is but one more insidious example of institutional power gone awry.

Wounded Breast and *Cancer Journals* act as discursive interruptions to the medical establishment's torture of each author's body and, indeed, as ways to cope with the pain of a lost breast. Yet there are other methods of coping present in the texts, each of which emphasizes the body's authority with regard to healing. More specifically, each text integrates homosocial bonds into the healing process. Their friendships are neither incidental nor accidental. Accad and Lorde rely on these friendships to understand their experiences with breast cancer and to privilege their sense of their bodies. During their wrestling with these experiences and in particular their pain, these homosocial bonds allow them to vacillate between fatigue and strength, feeling disenfranchised and feeling empowered. Because of this vacillation, both women's political action appears more necessary, more urgent. For instance, Accad narrates her difficulty with remaining inspired enough to fight for herself. Her friends' marginalia provides her the space to be fatigued. She notes that this contradicts the sentiments of Dr. Bernie Siegel, a medical professional (whom some might call a charlatan) who promotes people's ability to heal themselves and cultivate the inner peace that will help them defeat cancer. Accad's text discusses this issue directly, saying, "I want to develop this inner peace and overcome the disease. At the same time, though, I find it revolting to always project responsibility on to the patient without talking about the political and environmental factors that are so obviously involved."[71] Indeed, she wrestles with a desire for inner peace and the projection of responsibility onto herself throughout the text, often oscillating between the two poles and attempting to acknowledge the importance of both. She does not understand how or why one must undergo the loss of a breast during a mastectomy and the painful experiences of che-motherapy and radiation without paying attention to the reactions of one's own body. The text's polyvocality, made possible by her friends' inserted comments, points to reconciliation of having "inner peace" and fighting the system. For example, Accad's discussion of her doctors' poor bedside man-ner and the contradictions within the medical community (specifically those contradictions that result in poor patient care or uninformed consent) elicits remarks from her friends that support her political action and remind her to take care of herself. Her friends validate her understanding of her body and push her to acknowledge her sentient experience even while they advocate a political response to her mistreatment. Fusing the two acknowledges the importance of the journal entries themselves as acts that combat the silences that would be destructive.[72]

In Lorde's text, homosocial bonds receive credit for making healing pos-sible. She underscores the importance of her friendships: "I say the love of women healed me."[73] William Major states that cynics will find Lorde's ideas regarding women's love "mawkish,"[74] suggesting that Lorde's other-wise complex prose becomes inhibited and clichéd when discussing the love of women. Lorde embraces sentimentality in much the same way as Rabih Alameddine's characters, tentatively and, always, with a sobering eye. After all, Lorde's most disempowering moments are when she comes into contact with other women: a female volunteer introduces her to a pink prosthetic after her surgery and a nurse insists that she wear a prosthetic for the emo-tional safety of others. Though Lorde's narrative gains critical and political urgency from these encounters with women, it only makes her friendships more puissant in light of the other encounters with women. Lorde's ability to lean on these friendships represents the possibility of solidarity despite the presence of patriarchy and heterosexism that divides women from one another. To be more specific, Lorde's encounters with the nurse and the vol-unteer point to the virulence of patriarchy in maintaining women's silence regarding issues that affect their bodies. After all, both the volunteer and the nurse insist that Lorde disguise her post-mastectomy chest for the com-fort of others (including men and women), with the end result of silencing her experience. The volunteer makes the presumption that Lorde is hetero-sexual, attempting to soothe her anxieties by assuring her that men will still find her attractive. Lorde also mentions the friends that abandon her after her mastectomy, saying, "There were women who were like the aide in the hospital who had flirted so nicely with me until she heard my biopsy was positive."[75] In light of these experiences, Lorde's so-called mawkish senti-ment counters the treatment she receives from many other women. In recog-nizing the women who care for her, Lorde points to her homosocial bonds of friendship as a series of acts that save her from silencing her embodied experience.

In addition to the homosocial bonds of friendship, both Accad and Lorde tout the erotic as integral to healing. In so doing, they respond to the sterility, at best, and erotophobia,[76] at worst, of medical practice since voicing their sexual concerns opposes the general silence about breast cancer patients and sexuality. Accad's discussion focuses on the transformation of intimacy and only briefly discusses the physical pain of penetration, saying that her vagina has shrunken. She laments the loss of a vibrant sexual life with her lover, Alban, and points out that "[her] intimate relationship with Alban was a real letdown that [she] needed to express."[77] Nonetheless, she also describes the happiness she feels when they are physically intimate, even if they cannot, as she says, "'take the elevator', as [they] used to."[78] She and Alban remain sexual with one another, and this love and intimacy becomes a source from which she draws strength. During her travels, she is anxious to return to him and longs to comfort him when he is diagnosed with prostate cancer. The intimate space of their sexual relationship positions the erotic as an antidote to the silence surrounding sexuality and the rhetorical (and at times physical) sterilization of cancer patients by the medical establishment. Given that prostate cancer is the sexual cancer in men that is analogous to breast cancer, the frank discussion of sex works doubly against the medical establishment's silencing or dismissal of Alban's and Accad's experiences.

Lorde also privileges her relationship to the erotic as integral to her healing. She writes about her desire to masturbate in one of her journal entries, saying, "One day when I found I could finally masturbate again, [I made] love to myself for hours at a time."[79] As David Morris conjectures, Lorde's candor about her need for autoeroticism and other erotic experiences "enlists desire in aid of healing [and] honors a tradition respectful of dream, ritual, and a bodily presence that cannot be reduced to manageable concepts or meanings."[80] Lorde's erotic encounters disrupt the notion that she no longer has sexual desires. Her autoerotic experiences in particular posit that she still has a sexual desire for herself and still views her body sexually after her mastectomy. Lorde's attention to her body here echoes her attention to the erotic in other texts, like *Zami: A New Spelling of My Name*, wherein she details her sexual encounters.[81] In *Zami*, the erotic functions to validate her sexual experiences as a facet of her identity; in *Cancer Journals*, her attention to the erotic not only validates her sexuality but also works against the sterility of silence forced on her by cancer treatments. Lorde understands the body, and the erotic in particular, as an inroad to discussing multiple issues. To wit, she writes "Uses of the Erotic" approximately a year after having her first biopsy and a month prior to discovering a lump in her breast.[82] In *Zami*, she makes use of her bodily experiences—with abortion and with sex—to spark a conversation about health and embodied experience. Her autoerotic experiences in *Cancer Journals* point to a new conversation about sexuality: that it is not only integral to healing but also that it counters the medical discourse that would view a post-mastectomy body as desexualized and sterile. Drawing from my earlier discussion of the tactile, I would also add that Lorde's autoerotic experiences function much like those of Jasira in *Towelhead* in that she desires to remake herself in the wake of being unmade by others.

Accad's and Lorde's discussions of the orgasmic provide a powerful addition to their embodied understandings of healing. The orgasm requires that tension and relaxation be held simultaneously within the body. The vagina must be relaxed enough to permit blood flow to erogenous zones and, because of this blood flow, remain tense. With orgasm, the source of pleasure comes from "the explosive discharge of accumulated neuromuscular tensions."[83] With the neuropathic pain of mastectomy, tension is paramount and the source of pain is usually the misfiring of neurons.[84] The authors cannot control or ease pain in the way that they can facilitate and, in the case of Lorde, bring about multiple orgasms. The authors' attention to orgasm suggests that the erotic allows them to take back their own bodies from pain. First, they gain control of how tension can be used and how and when their neurons fire. Given that "the perception of pain is markedly blunted during sexual arousal,"[85] their control over this aspect of their lives diminishes the effect of pain on their bodies and, consequently, they thwart pain's ability to take away their language. When discussing orgasm, Accad relies on euphemism while Lorde describes her experience as making love to herself. In both instances, the authors understand their experiences as moments when they control their own bodies. Lorde's statement is also reflexive, pointing to the fact that she has agency and does this for (and to) herself. This is not just a physiological instance of having power over herself, but a linguistic one as well.

Lorde and Accad's desire to affirm their experiences coincides with their ethical position *vis-à-vis* breast cancer and silence. They mobilize their embodied experiences with pain and pleasure to pinpoint an ethos that ought to govern responsible preventative measures, humane treatment, and the search for a cure. In Lorde's oft-discussed "Breast Cancer: Power vs. Prosthesis," she enters her doctor's office, feeling confident of her style and flair without her breast, only to be told by a female nurse that Lorde's lack of prosthetic is "bad for the morale of the office."[86] This anecdote is flanked by critical contemplation of the understanding of a mastectomy as purely a cosmetic incident and a journal entry that buttresses Lorde's feelings with regard to the nurse's comment. Placing the contemplative essay in conversation with both the journal entry and the anecdote creates a multilayered story that fully demonstrates Lorde's point. Prosthetics mask the other issues surrounding breast cancer, most notably, but not limited to: a confrontation with one's own mortality, the criminalization of patients, dominant standards of beauty (which do not include Lorde anyway), fear of recurrence, and the presence of environmental carcinogens. The nurse's behavior demonstrates that she is not only concerned with the less relevant topic of aesthetics but also incapable of providing the kind of psychological support needed by the patients for whom she cares. The prosthetic not only disguises the reality of Lorde's embodied experience, but also privileges the norm of two white breasts because the prosthetic Lorde was given was pink. Lorde calls the prosthetic a "lie,"[87] making her desire for a march of post-mastectomy women on Capitol Hill particularly apropos.

Accad echoes this call in her text and affirms Lorde's decision. Accad finds Lorde's prose difficult to read because there is a great deal of suffering, but praises Lorde for her commitment to political action. Accad writes,

> Lorde thinks that women who've had a mastectomy should refuse to have their breast/s reconstructed, because if all the women who've been subjected to this mutilation were to march on Washington's Capitol Hill, bare breasted and asking for radical changes in the way the environment is being poisoned, as well as demanding more funding for cancer research, people would become more aware and changes would take place. She is so right![88]

Accad's agreement with Lorde echoes in other places when Accad discusses the environment and toxins. It also echoes in Accad's comments about Dr. Siegel, as she thinks that the insistence on cultivating inner peace obfuscates the material realities of pollution and bodily experience. Accad's belief that looking at bare-breasted, post-mastectomy women effects change dovetails with her cover photo. For both Accad and Lorde, it is precisely because the image of a post-mastectomy woman is difficult to look at that they must use it to mobilize. What both women would rely on during an Amazonian march are the social politics of exposing this image in particular. Matuschka's 1993 photos also generated negative responses from breast cancer survivors who were upset that people would know what they really looked like.[89] In a manner that dovetails with feminist disability studies scholarship, this mentality identifies how racialized and gendered normalcy "encourage the cultural conviction that disability can be extirpated."[90] Accad writes, "the whole tragedy is hidden under the veneer of normalization; if you seem normal, you're normal and everything's okay!"[91] The social understanding of breasts as sexual has not changed such that Lorde's cry for an army of one-breasted women becomes unnecessary. In fact, her rallying cry zeroes in on the fact that "when sex and disability are linked in contemporary American cultures, the conjunction is most often the occasion for marginalization or marveling."[92] These are the dangerous discourses to which Margrit Shildrick refers.[93] Still, the wounded or absent breast is associated with a wounded or absent womanhood, and, by covering it up, post-mastectomy women curtail their ability to be politically powerful.

I turn to famed feminist and disability studies critic Diane Price-Herndl because of her meditations on the ethical responses to breast cancer. She has taken Lorde to task for her decision, saying that Lorde's ideas are not the only feminist response to breast cancer and mastectomies. In her award-winning article, "Our Breasts, Our Selves: Identity, Community and Ethics in Breast Cancer Narratives," she makes the case that an ethical response within breast cancer narratives includes an acknowledgment of the politics at stake, a wariness of individualizing stories at the expense of a larger community of women, and a clear understanding that the self is mercurial and multifaceted. She finds that an emphasis on breast cancer as a cosmetic concern eclipses such responses:

> The focus on shopping, prostheses, and nourishing one's self is not necessarily contrary to feminist or ethical goals, of course. The ethical complications, for me, at least, arise from the fact that these essays rarely move out into that "well-informed 'army' of single-breasted women [. . .] ready to break with medical and social codes of normalization" (Major, 2002, 52) that Lorde imagined. There are few challenges here to either medical or social codes. This book promotes the idea of an individual self even as it establishes a community of women, yet that community is not outward looking but intensely privatized.[94]

Price-Herndl rightly takes four breast cancer narratives to task for focusing on the cosmetic at the expense of the political. She gives room for these reactions to be an individual's choice, but clearly articulates that the repercussions include a silence about causes and treatments of the disease. It is important to note that her critique that the cosmetic-oriented approach needs to push further to reach an ethical stance relies on Audre Lorde's disavowal of the prosthetic. The inward-looking and private community, then, works against any challenge to medical or social codes because those orientations are inherently outwardly focused. They deny the reciprocity of human existence and intention. The implication here is that the cosmetic approach rarely goes beyond a solipsistic understanding of coping with breast cancer and, by virtue of its being stalled there, remains unethical.

Yet, in another (earlier) essay, Price-Herndl challenges Lorde's complaints about the prosthetic and the cosmetic, arguing that post-humanist feminist thought renders these ideas somewhat obsolete. Price-Herndl contends that the cyborg assists women in thinking through their breast cancer experiences. The cyborg to which Herndl refers comes from Donna Haraway's seminal essay "A Cyborg Manifesto: Science, Technology and Socialist-Feminism in the Late Twentieth Century." According to Haraway, the cyborg (the word is an abbreviation of "cybernetic organism") is the antidote to discourses about race, gender, and sexuality that thwart political action. Haraway's cyborg consists of a human, machine, and animal hybrid, a mixture that intends to transgress ontological categories to prompt a critique of capitalism, which is considered the more virulent enemy. Price-Herndl thinks through the cyborg as an amalgamation of human and machine, engaging in a theoretical self-analysis to justify her own choice to undergo reconstructive surgery and to understand her choice in relation to her feminism. After chastising herself for making an anti-feminist decision *vis-à-vis* reconstruction, she notes, "I rethought what I meant by feminist theory and realized that feminist relations to the body are different now than they were twenty years ago for Lorde and that feminist relations to breast cancer are different."[95] Because the cyborg allows an understanding of oneself as already alien, the post-humanist feminist can and should embrace the prosthetic. Certainly, Price-Herndl correctly identifies the differences between Lorde's historical moment and her own (circa 1999). However, those differences do not extend to differences in aesthetic. It is not my intention to imply that Price-Herndl's stance is Pecksniffian, but feminists during the latter half of the twentieth century and the new millennium still have to contend with narratives that privilege two breasts. These narratives also privilege two very specific breasts: white, youthful, small or medium, and heterosexual. This ideal still does not include women similar to Audre Lorde or Evelyne Accad for that matter. Lorde describes herself as Black, with large breasts, well above the age of 25, and lesbian. Price-Herndl's commentary obfuscates the ways in which a desire for the ideal and an adherence to it dictates the necessity of political critique. While I do not find Price-Herndl's decision less than feminist (as feminism is about the availability of choice), it does appear to minimize the way that reconstructive surgery reaffirms the status quo she insists need be critiqued. Though Price-Herndl's choice, in her mind, becomes a way to embrace the post-human, her joint kinship with machines, and her cyborg identity, it does not explore the vacuum of political critique created by her "partiality for a normal appearance."[96] I would add that the partiality for a normal appearance entrenches Price-Herndl's white and abled privilege at the expense of her joint kinship with other women, including but not limited to breast cancer survivors of color.

Lorde's discussion of her choice not to wear a prosthetic directly challenges Price-Herndl's idea regarding the cyborg's utility in that Lorde refuses a prosthetic since it masks her experience of cancer. For her, the hybrid human/machine would not be the answer, because the machine, in this case the prosthesis, would erase the experience of the human. This is more than an idealist, humanist cry for the uniqueness of humanity. Lorde rejects the prosthesis because she is dissatisfied with the narrative it creates about the cohesion of humanity. This overarching narrative of cohesion elides the fact that the definition of the Western thinking subject was created in direct opposition to blacks (racism) and Arabs (Orientalism). Let me be clear: there are certainly moments in which a one-breasted woman may appear two-breasted even without a prosthetic and seem, therefore, part of this cohesive narrative. However, my point (and Lorde's) is that the deliberate masking of experience perpetuates silence about the experience of breast cancer. In other words, appearance can give the lie to one's experience, but one should not choose to give the lie to one's own experience with false or reconstructed breasts. From Lorde's point of view (and mine), the prosthesis is another attempt at a totalizing narrative that silences. The cyborg's merger between humans and machines ignores the extent to which the machine is forced onto a post-mastectomy body. In the case of the prosthesis, the machine is a mechanism of ostracism. After all, the original prosthesis presented to Lorde is flesh-colored, but not the color of her flesh. In fact, the only skin tone it matches is that of a white person's, specifically one whose flesh has pinkish undertones. Needless to say, this also leaves out other women of color and white women whose flesh has olive or golden undertones. The prosthetic also becomes a mechanism to create guilt and shame. The nurse's statement that her lack of prosthesis is bad for morale indicates that Lorde's acceptance of her own body disrupts the narrative of supposed normalcy created by prosthetics. In addition, the nurse's comments blame Lorde for not being a specific type of cancer survivor. Here, the prosthetic or, in cyborg terms, the machine emphasizes the gendered and racialized boundaries Price-Herndl's cyborg is supposed to critique.

It is worth noting that Price-Herndl does argue cogently that a mastectomy scar and a reconstructed breast would be the same for her in that both remind her of her missing breast. She confesses, "Prosthesis is technology, and it never lets me forget."[97] She understands that she will forever feel like a cyborg: not completely human, nor completely machine, but alien and ready to voice a political critique. In theory, Price-Herndl-as-cyborg does perform necessary political work. Nevertheless, Price-Herndl neglects a salient point: namely, "Reconstructive surgery and cosmetic surgery are two codings of essentially the same practice, namely that of surgically intervening into the shape of the body."[98] This intervention is at the heart of Lorde's comments regarding prosthesis and, by extension, reconstructive surgery: specifically, a woman's lack of prosthesis is not simply about how she conceives of her body, but how others understand her. Lorde understands prostheses as a barrier to forming support networks and asks where her Black, feminist, role models are.[99] Lorde privileges her body's power to speak for itself, as a focal point for generating political power and creating viable communities. As Price-Herndl rightly notes, women of color and poor women die more often of breast cancer–related complications and an ethical response would be to make visible their experience.

Moreover, Price-Herndl's positionality as a white woman illuminates that she would have more access to a so-called normal appearance. Inasmuch as a woman with reconstructed breasts can speak, as Price-Herndl bravely chooses to do, she still has a visible disconnect between her body and her voice. This disembodiment subtracts from the possibility of critique and reinscribes the body into a raced and gendered normalcy. There is a gendered difference between the way we understand reconstructive surgery as masculine (read: evidence of war) and cosmetic surgery as feminine (read: as obsessed with beauty).[100] These narratives converge in breast reconstruction, not only because it assumes a return to normalcy after a valiant battle (in keeping with the military metaphors), but also speaks to the insistence on a normal or more beautiful appearance. Based on the intersection of race and gender for Arab and Black women, neither group would have access to the narrative

Price-Herndl claims as her own. Considering the discourse of superhuman survival that surrounds Black womanhood and the normalization of war narratives for Arab women, breast reconstructive surgery would solidify their distance from femininity since it would confirm that they have survived yet another battle unscathed. Reconstructive surgery would become more evidence of war survival and, as a result, gender these women as masculine, since the narrative of war overtakes the emphasis on beauty. Moreover, breast reconstruction seeks a normalcy predicated on whiteness that was never available to Black and Arab women in the first place.

A reconstructed breast or a prosthesis positions the wearer to always create some modicum of doubt *vis-à-vis* her experience. With the experience of cancer, the body is essential to expressing the certainty of that pain and the necessity of political mobilization against the causes of that pain. As with Evelyne Accad's book cover and the Matuschka photo in the *New York Times Magazine*, the viewer cannot look away. For Accad and Lorde, there is no room for doubting their pain. Even when their language disintegrates, both women urge a meditation on their corporeal experience as an inroad to changing the medical system. They ratify the ways in which their recovery hinges upon their relationship to machines and surgical procedures, but they refuse to allow technology to silence their embodied experience.

NOTES

1. "Robin Roberts Personal Journey—Living with Breast Cancer." *Nightline*. New York, NY: ABC Studios, 2008. DVD.
2. For the purposes of my discussion, I refer to G. Thomas Couser's definition of a comic plot: "The master plot, then, of the breast cancer narrative, like that of autobiography generally, is a comic one; it ends 'happily,' with some significant recovery; the narrators are healed, if not cured. Without exception, then, the narrators are, or claim to be, better off at the end than at the beginning." See Couser, *Recovering Bodies*, 39.
3. Couser also states, "By definition women who write narratives of their breast cancer experience are survivors; they narrate their stories only when they are emotionally and physically well enough to undertake a sustained project" (39).
4. Couser, *Recovering Bodies*, 37.
5. It is also a possibility that such passages would not appeal to editors who may believe that discussions of pain make the memoirs less palatable.
6. Couser, *Recovering Bodies*, 38.
7. Audre Lorde, "The Transformation of Silence into Language and Action." *Sister Outsider* (Berkeley, CA: Ten Speed Press, 2007), 41.
8. Evelyne Accad, *The Wounded Breast: Intimate Journeys Through Cancer* (North Melbourne, Australia: Spinifex, 2001), 29.
9. Robin Roberts, *From the Heart: Eight Rules to Live By* (New York, NY: Hyperion, 2008), 65.
10. Kimberlé Crenshaw, "Mapping the Margins: Intersectionality, Identity Politics, and Violence against Women of Color," *Stanford Law Review*. 43.6 (1991): 1242.
11. Elaine Scarry, *The Body in Pain: The Making and Unmaking of the World* (New York, NY: Oxford University Press, 1987), 3.

12. Mary K. DeShazer, *Mammographies: The Cultural Discourses of Breast Cancer Narratives* (Ann Arbor, MI: U of Michigan Press, 2013), 44.

13. See Elaine Scarry, *The Body in Pain*; David Morris, *The Culture of Pain* (Berkeley, CA: U of California Press, 1993). Scarry points out later that psychological pain does have a referent, though it is difficult to describe and as such remains differentiated from physical pain within her (and my) discussions of pain. David Morris in his text *The Culture of Pain* has argued against such a distinction. His argument is that the understanding of pain (generally) has changed over the course of human history. He calls this idea the "Myth of the Two Pains," citing examples where psychological and physical pain overlap. He is correct in that the two cannot be easily parsed, but he neglects to deal with the linguistic differences in representation. My discussion of pain remains in the realm of the body, as the inability to describe physical pain is quite different from the inability to describe psychological suffering; the latter has a rich vocabulary accessible in literature and philosophy, whereas the former does not. Scarry compares psychological pain to an emotional, perceptual, or somatic state that takes an object, whereas physical pain does not take an object.

14. Martha Stoddard Holmes and Tod Chambers, "Thinking through Pain," *Literature and Medicine*. 24.1 (2005): 131.

15. DeShazer, *Mammographies*, 41.

16. Audre Lorde, "Uses of the Erotic: The Erotic as Power." *Sister Outsider*, 53.

17. Ibid.

18. Evelyne Accad, "Sexuality and Sexual Politics: Conflicts and Contradictions for the Contemporary Women in the Middle East." *Third World Women and the Politics of Feminism*. Eds. Chandra Talpade Mohanty, Ann Russo, Lourdes Torres (Bloomington, IN: Indiana UP, 1991), 237.

19. See Kenny Fries, ed., *Staring Back: The Disability Experience from the Inside Out* (New York, NY: Penguin Books, 1997).

20. See David Hevey, "The Enfreakment of Photography." *The Disability Studies Reader*. 2nd ed. Ed. Lennard Davis (New York, NY: Routledge, 2006), 367–78.

21. Hevey, "The Enfreakment of Photography," 367.

22. Shildrick, *Dangerous Discourses*, 5.

23. Ibid., 1.

24. Garland-Thomson, *Staring*, Kindle Edition.

25. Ibid.

26. Evelyne Accad, email message to author, October 24, 2009.

27. Some might continue to see Matuschka's or Accad/Enderlein's photographs as sexual, specifically belonging to a class of pornography that features mutilated women. However, my analysis focuses on those for whom the sexual gaze would be interrupted and refocused on cancer.

28. Given that publishers would have been concerned about the scandal of a half-nude, post-mastectomy black woman in 1980, the possibility for Lorde to have that cover would have been less than slim. Certainly, the ways in which Lorde as a racialized and gendered subject would have created such a scandal is worth exploration.

29. Susan Sontag, *Regarding the Pain of Others* (New York, NY: Farrar, Straus and Giroux, 2003), 10.

30. Patricia Hill Collins, *Black Feminist Thought: Knowledge Consciousness and the Politics of Empowerment* (New York, NY: Routledge, 1991), 72.

31. Ibid., 68.

32. Elizabeth Alexander, " 'Coming out Blackened and Whole': Fragmentation and Reintegration in Audre Lorde's *Zami* and *The Cancer Journals*," *American Literary History*. 6.4 (1994): 697.

33. Ibid., 697.
34. Garland-Thomson, *Staring*, Kindle Edition.
35. There is a great deal of conversation about the usefulness of pity within disability studies. Many scholars repudiate pity as a reaction that is infantilizing and not useful for changing social and political realities. Some view pity as a useful and necessary stepping-stone to begin discussions on disability and disability rights. My main concern with Accad's book cover is that it seems to shun pity and validate the embodied experience of her missing breast. Precisely what I discuss in relation to Sontag's argument is that pity positions the object thereof as outside oneself and has the ability to create a space to assist and hear the subject or create a space to ignore the subject, a space that exists with a façade of interest or feigned support. The woman on the cover inhabits her own body, beckoning engagement, not dismissal.
36. See Susan Sontag, *On Photography* (New York, NY: Anchor Books, 1989). This is Sontag's claim in *On Photography:* "Photographs are a way of imprisoning reality, understood as recalcitrant, inaccessible; of making it stand still. Or they enlarge a reality that is felt to be shrunk, hollowed out, perishable, remote" (163).
37. Karla F. C. Holloway, "Cultural Narratives Passed On: African American Mourning Stories." *African American Literary History*. Ed. Winston Napier. (New York, NY: NYU Press, 2000), 654.
38. Sarah M. A. Gualtieri analyzes the lynching of N. G. Romey in Florida, an event that brought to light the intertwining of xenophobia, violence, and erasure. See Sarah M. A. Gualtieri, "Strange Fruit? Syrian Immigrants, Extralegal Violence, and Racial Formation in the United States." *Race and Arab Americans before and after 9/11*, 147–69.
39. Sontag, *On Photography*, 20.
40. See Joseph Shapiro, *No Pity: People with Disabilities Forging a New Civil Rights Movement* (New York, NY: Three Rivers Press, 1994).
41. I am aware that some viewers are anesthetized to breast cancer images. However, as Garland-Thomson's book testifies, the cultural inclination to ignore or be horrified by illness is part of the current cultural moment. See Garland-Thomson, *Staring*, Kindle Edition.
42. I am aware that Sontag herself questions the ability of photographs to create sympathy and diminish in that ability over time in her text *Regarding the Pain of Others*. However, she questions that statement in light of the way that the television medium bombards viewers with images, which suggests that she believes photographs are different. Despite the fact that *Regarding the Pain of Others* ends on a note that suggests photographs lack the ability to create sympathy at all (though photographs still have the capacity to be powerful), this does not change my assertions about fear.
43. Sontag, *On Photography*, 99.
44. Ibid., 101.
45. Accad chronicles her psychological wrestling with pain, but that is not part of my discussion here.
46. Cheryl Toman makes this observation as well in her review of the book. See Cheryl Toman, Rev. of *The Wounded Breast: Intimate Journeys through Cancer, World Literature Today*. 76.2 (2002): 164–65.
47. Audre Lorde, *The Cancer Journals* (San Francisco, CA: Aunt Lute Books, 1997), 46.
48. Jeanne Perreault, " 'That the Pain Not Be Wasted': Audre Lorde and the Written Self," *Auto/biography Studies: A/B*. 4.1 (1988): 9.
49. Accad, *Wounded Breast*, 90.
50. Ibid., 91.
51. Ibid., 93.

52. Ibid., 90.
53. Ibid., 59.
54. Ibid., 16.
55. Ibid., 12–33. Accad's prologue, "The Price of Waste and Pollution: An Insidi-ous Massacre," powerfully indicts the medical establishment and stringently critiques silence.
56. Ibid., 283.
57. Ibid., 302.
58. Couser, *Recovering Bodies*, 50–51.
59. Lorde, *Cancer Journals*, 46.
60. Ibid., 47.
61. Cynthia Wu, "Marked Bodies, Marking Time: Reclaiming the Warrior in Audre Lorde's *The Cancer Journals*," *Auto/biography Studies: A/B*. 17.2 (2002): 249.
62. Accad, *Wounded Breast*, 58.
63. Lorde, *Cancer Journals*, 38.
64. See Bernie Siegel, *Bernie Siegel, M.D.* FSB Associates, 2009, last modified April 19, 2010. http://www.berniesiegelmd.com Accad feels the need to cul-tivate such inner peace based on the teachings of Bernie Siegel, a doctor who advocates inner peace as a method to thinking yourself well.
65. Scarry, *The Body in Pain*, 36.
66. Accad, *Wounded Breast*, 12–23.
67. Ibid., 46.
68. Ibid., 203.
69. Lorde, "Transformation," 41.
70. See Amira Jarmakani, "Arab American Feminisms: Mobilizing the Politics of Invisibility." *Arab American Feminisms: Gender, Violence, and Belonging*, 227–41. She uses this phrase to discuss the ways in which Arab American feminists and feminism are concealed by misinformation and yet highly visible in inaccurate form. I deploy it here to point to the ways that Accad's narrative draws on Arab (American) feminism as a praxis engaged with speaking truth to power regarding the multiple vectors of anti-Arab racism and sexism.
71. Accad, *Wounded Breast*, 72.
72. Lorde, *Cancer Journals*, 23.
73. Ibid., 39.
74. William Major, "Audre Lorde's *The Cancer Journals*: Autopathography As Resistance," *Mosaic (Winnipeg)*. 35.2 (2002): 39.
75. Lorde, *Cancer Journals*, 49.
76. See Abby Wilkerson, "Disability, Sex Radicalism, and Political Agency." *Femi-nist Disability Studies*, 193–217. Abby Wilkerson expands on Cindy Patton's definition of erotophobia as "the terrifying, irrational reaction to the erotic which makes individuals and society vulnerable to psychological and social control in cultures where pleasure is strictly categorized and regulated" as it relates to sexuality and disability.
77. Accad, *Wounded Breast*, 106.
78. Ibid., 106.
79. Lorde, *Cancer Journals*, 25.
80. David Morris, "Un-forgetting Asclepius: An Erotics of Illness." *New Literary History*. 38.3 (2007), 434.
81. See Audre Lorde, *Zami: A New Spelling of My Name* (Berkeley, CA: Cross-ing Press, 1982). For readers familiar with *Zami*, Lorde's meditation on her post-mastectomy body dialogues with her sexual experiences with a post-mastectomy lover, Eudora.
82. Alexis De Veaux, *Warrior Poet: A Biography of Audre Lorde* (New York, NY: Norton, 2004).

83. Herant A. Katchadourian and Donald T. Lunde. *Fundamentals of Human Sexuality, Second Edition* (New York, NY: Holt, Rinehart and Winston, 1975), 59.

84. American Chronic Pain Association. "Neuropathic Pain." *American Chronic Pain Association.* Medtronic Foundation, last modified 2013. http://www.theacpa.org.

85. Katchadourian and Lunde, *Fundamentals*, 58.

86. Lorde, *Cancer Journals*, 59.

87. Ibid., 60.

88. Accad, *Wounded Breast*, 150.

89. Garland-Thomson, *Staring*, Kindle Edition.

90. Garland-Thomson, "Integrating Disability Transforming Feminist Theory." *Feminist Disability Studies*, 27.

91. Accad, *Wounded Breast*, 151.

92. Anna Mollow and Robert McRuer, *Sex and Disability*. (Durham, NC: Duke UP, 2012), 1.

93. Shildrick, *Dangerous Discourses*, 5. Shildrick writes, "In emphasizing the problematics of subjectivity and sexuality, or more succinctly the question of the disabled sexual subject, I aim to interrogate related areas in which the normative is most firmly entrenched and therefore most challengingly deconstructed."

94. Diane Price-Herndl, "Our Breasts, Our Selves: Identity, Community and Ethics in Breast Cancer Narratives," *Signs: A Journal of Women in Culture and Society.* 32.1 (2006): 237.

95. Diane Price-Herndl, "Reconstructing the Posthuman Feminist Body Twenty Years after Audre Lorde's *Cancer Journals*." *Disability Studies: Enabling the Humanities*. Eds. Sharon L. Snyder, Brenda Jo Brueggemann, and Rosemarie Garland-Thomson (New York, NY: Modern Language Association of America, 2002), 149.

96. Ibid., 151.

97. Ibid., 152.

98. Liesch and Patton, "Clinic or Spa?," 4.

99. Lorde, *Cancer Journals,* 16, 28–29.

100. Leish and Patton, "Clinic or Spa?," 5–6.

Conclusion

Like other seasons before them, spring and summer 2013 weltered in the mud of cultural appropriation and state-sanctioned violence. On April 15, 2013, explosives halted the Boston Marathon. Reddit (an internet news website) and many journalists (including Perez Hilton) incorrectly identified one of the suspects as Sunil Tripathi, a missing Brown University student. The Tripathi family received threatening phone calls and messages marked by Islamophobic vitriol.[1] In May, President Obama justified the use of drones as a way to protect U.S. interests despite the acknowledgment of civilian casualties.[2] At the end of May, National Public Radio published an article that attempted to underscore Arab American visibility but did just the opposite by rehashing old conversations about Arab American representation in the census data.[3] In June, Paula Deen faced a civil lawsuit alleging racial discrimination and a racially hostile work environment (eventually settling out of court)[4] amid a media frenzy, involving a trending hashtag on Twitter (#PaulasBestDishes) that featured racialized and racist names for food (i.e., "Kale and Kabbage Kasserole or KKK for short," "Lynchables," "Emmett Tillapia").[5] Paula Deen desired a plantation wedding for her brother that called for middle-aged Black men as servants.[6] Also in June, North Carolina activists began 'Moral Mondays' to decry conservative measures taken by the legislature, including passing a voter ID law that ends same-day registration, terminating the earned income tax credit, rejecting federal funds for Medicare, and cutting teachers' pay.[7] During late June, the Supreme Court voted (5-4) to allow nine states to make changes to their voting laws without federal approval, a decision that "struck down the heart of the Voting Rights Act."[8]

The dog days of summer provided no relief. During mid-July, George Zimmerman was found not guilty in the murder of Trayvon Martin.[9] Defense attorneys depicted the 15-year-old Martin as the aggressor, charging that he weaponized the sidewalk.[10] At the beginning of August, Reuters published a poll declaring that "many Americans have no friends of another race."[11] Robin Thicke's song "Blurred Lines" topped the Billboard charts at number one[12] after being dubbed a rape anthem.[13] The video features nude models dancing while the crooner sings "I know you want it" in their

ears, and was backed by the liquor brand Rémy Martin.[14] In a *GQ* interview, Thicke joked, "What a pleasure it is to degrade a woman [. . .] I've
never gotten to do that before."[15] The interviewer quoted him and asked
readers to relax in the opening front matter.[16] Thicke filed, in what some
are calling a preemptive strike, a lawsuit against Marvin Gaye's estate,
requesting dismissal of future legal action that claims Thicke's song bor-
rows from Gaye's hit "Got to Give It Up."[17] During MTV's Video Music
Awards show in late August, Miley Cyrus performed her pop song "Can't
Stop" among a cadre of scantily clad Black women dancers.[18] Cyrus
gyrated in a manner she has elsewhere called "hood."[19] She simulated anilingus on one dancer's behind and patted it in a way reminiscent of Venus
Hottentot photos. Cyrus also used the women as props while she twerked,
a dance (primarily associated with Black women) requiring one to bend
over and shake her (usually ample) behind for an onlooker. Immediately
after, Cyrus performed a salacious duet of "Blurred Lines" with Robin
Thicke.[20] Perhaps the most disappointing aspect of these events from May
2013 until August 2013 is not just that they happened but that they've
happened so many times before.

These juridical battles, cultural appropriation, and state-sanctioned violence intimately connect as narratives of erasure and concretize the links
between Black and Arab American experiences. Following the logic of
Edward Said's *Orientalism*, what could be seen as Deen's, Cyrus's, and
Thicke's poor taste is actually more virulent. Their cooptation of Black
cultural forms—cooking, dance, and music, respectively—provides the
foundational disrespect of personhood required for avoiding intimate relationships, the legislation that sparked 'Moral Mondays,' and George Zimmerman's actions (and subsequent defenses thereof). In consonance with
the aim to midwife a cross-cultural conversation between Arabs and Blacks,
I should be clear that cultural appropriation is not an issue unique to Blacks
and Arabs within the United States. Arab American engagement with this
problem links to the history of colonization and imperialism that created
the Western world. Cooptation of Arab American culture, as Said's work
implies, created the groundwork for Western aggression in the Arab world
and invisibilization of Arab Americans within the United States. In short,
the drone strikes and Paula Deen's racial nostalgia; Cyrus's twerking and
the Tripathis' experience with Islamophobia, and 'Moral Mondays' and the
census article all operate according to the same logic. It is a logic that erases
and invisibilizes Blacks and Arabs for the purposes of sustaining a hierarchical racial order with whiteness as supreme, a gendered order where cis-
sexual straight masculinity resides at the apex, and an abled order where the
putatively healthy and capable reign.

I sought to dismantle these hierarchies by using disability studies as a
methodology and disability as an object of inquiry since disability as a social
identity raises suspicion about any standard of embodied normalcy. Since the
field has been slow to deal with issues of race and ethnicity, my exploration

about Black and Arab American experience also displaces the putative white center of disability studies and conversations about disability. Still, I contend that conversations about embodied experience fundamentally shift our thinking about racialized, gendered, sexualized, classed, and abled norms. Within this paradigm, the narratives I explore open up possibilities. One can follow Suheir Hammad's injunction to affirm life in June Jordan's dark. Danzy Senna and Alicia Erian confirm that each body is a home and it dare not be violated by or inscribed with the demands and desires of others. Rabih Alameddine brings to bear the urgency of revising commonplace definitions that prove destructive. Earvin Johnson's life experience critiques a belief in magic that makes political apathy permissible. Evelyne Accad and Audre Lorde coax us away from silence with the knowledge that it can't save us since we were meant to survive anyway. They invest in the frailty of the body, not as part of a merely sentimental celebration, but rather as part of a stark insistence on their/our commonality. These narratives remark upon what is utterly unremarkable as a way to negotiate having been made political flesh.

Keep in mind, this project was only meant to be a starting point. I examined a wide range of critiques and topics as an inroad to broadening the possible conversations about embodiment and Arab and Black experiences, broadly speaking. The preceding chapters could be reorganized and analyzed with an eye toward the commentary on contested citizenship for Blacks and Arabs in America. The Arab (American) *hakawati* and the Black (American) *griot* have much to tell each other. Arab American fantastic fiction (or speculative fiction) dovetails with the Afrofuturist impetus to question the machinations of power and contest the dismissal of embodied knowledge. African American and Arab American *bildungsromane* challenge the narrative of American exceptionalism that undergirds the formal impulse and the political implications of that genre. Arab and Black engagements with the so-called third world and global politics disrupt and complicate the belief and praxis of American solipsism. What new readings of African American texts might occur if one were to deploy an Arab American studies lens? What of the opposite?

To be accurate, the possibilities are not limited to literary scholarship. While this project was maturing, a colleague called my focus on narrative "ardently literary." I am extremely grateful for the description since it accurately represents this project's impassioned insistence that literature and narrative are a salient part of public discourse. As Moustafa Bayoumi says, "In ways that polemics and polls cannot, [stories] can reveal our conflicts within ourselves and our vulnerabilities to each other. Stories can describe why certain choices are made and others are passed over."[21] It is precisely because projects of domination are sophisticated and intertwined that the stories we tell need be also. Complex stories create an alternative cosmology that permits both possibility and praxis. To seek them, find them, create them, and tell them is not a luxury, but an obligation.

NOTES

1. Jay Caspian King, "Should Reddit Be Blamed for the Spread of a Smear?" *New York Times*, last modified on July 25, 2013. http://www.nytimes.com.
2. "Obama Speech on Drone Policy," *New York Times*, last modified May 23, 2013. http://www.nytimes.com.
3. Hansi Lo Wang, "Arab-Americans: A 'Growing' Community, But by How Much?" *National Public Radio*, last modified May 30, 2013. http://www.npr.org.
4. Meredith Blake, "Judge Approves Deal Dismissing Paula Deen Lawsuit," *Los Angeles Times*, last modified August 26, 2013. http://www.latimes.com.
5. "Paula's Best Dishes: Twitter Hashtag Pokes Fun at Paula Deen's Unsavory Side As Allegations of Racism Surface," *Huffington Post*, last modified June 21, 2013. http://www.huffingtonpost.com.
6. Hunter Walker, "Paula Deen on Her Dream 'Southern Plantation Wedding,' " *Talking Points Memo*, last modified on June 19, 2013. http://www.talkingpointsmemo.com.
7. See Mitch Weiss, " 'Moral Monday' Protest Held in Charlotte," *News Observer*, last modified August 19, 2013. www.newsobserver.com; Nick Wing, "Moral Monday Protests: 101 More Arrested, Two-Thirds Women, in Rally against North Carolina GOP," *Huffington Post*, last modified July 16, 2013. http://www.huffingtonpost.com; Nick Wing, " 'Moral Monday' Protest in North Carolina: 151 Arrested As Activists Decry 'Extreme' GOP Agenda," *Huffington Post*, last modified June 4, 2013. http://www.huffingtonpost.com.
8. Adam Liptak, "Supreme Court Invalidates Key Part of Voting Rights Act," *New York Times*, last modified on June 25, 2013. http://www.nytimes.com.
9. Chelsea J. Carter and Holly Yan, "Why This Verdict? Five Things That Led to Zimmerman's Acquittal," *CNN*, last modified on July 15, 2013. http://www.cnn.com.
10. Jelani Cobb, "George Zimmerman, Not Guilty: Blood on the Leaves," *New Yorker*, last modified on July 13, 2013. http://www.newyorker.com.
11. Lindsay Dunsmuir, "Many Americans Have No Friends of Another Race," *Reuters*, last modified on August 8, 2013. http://www.reuters.com.
12. Gary Trust, "Robin Thicke No. 1, Katy Perry No. 2 on Hot 100," *Billboard*, last modified on August 21, 2013. http://www.billboard.com.
13. Dominique Mosbergen, "Robin Thicke's 'Blurred Lines' Dubbed 'Rapey,' Hit Song under Fire from Critics," *Huffington Post*, last modified on July 11, 2013. http://www.huffingtonpost.com.
14. Mesfin Fedaku, "Robin Thicke Says 'Blurred Lines' Music Video Was His Wife's Idea," *Newsday*, last modified on August 23, 2013. http://www.newsday.com.
15. Stelios Phili, "Robin Thicke on That Banned Video, Collaborating with 2 Chainz and Kendrick Lamar, and His New Film," *GQ: Gentleman's Quarterly,* last modified on May 7, 2013. http://www.gq.com.
16. Ibid.
17. Kia Makarechi, "Robin Thicke Sues Marvin Gaye's Family to Protect 'Blurred Lines,' " *Huffington Post*, last modified August 17, 2013. http://www.huffingtonpost.com.
18. Lily Rothman, "4 Reasons You're Still Hearing About Miley Cyrus' VMA Performance," *Time*, last modified August 26, 2013. http://entertainment.time.com; Carly Mallenbaum, "Miley's VMA Performance Shocks Celebs," *USA Today,* last modified on August 27, 2013. http://www.usatoday.com.

19. Matt Diehl, "Miley Cyrus 2.0: The Billboard Cover Story," *Billboard*, last modified June 14, 2013. http://www.billboard.com.

20. Jim Farber, "VMAs 2013: Miley Cyrus Was Real Winner at MTV Video Music Awards, Getting Tongues Wagging with Her Risqué Moves," *New York Daily News*, last modified August 26, 2013. http://www.nydailynews.com; Phillip Mlynar, "Miley Cyrus Twerks, Gives Robin Thicke Some Tongue at VMAs," *MTV*, last modified August 25, 2013. http://www.mtv.com.

21. Bayoumi, *How Does It Feel to Be a Problem?*, 12.

Works Cited

Abdulhadi, Rabab, Evelyn Alsultany, and Nadine Naber, eds. *Arab American Feminisms: Gender, Nation, and Belonging*. Syracuse, NY: Syracuse UP, 2011.

Abdulrahim, Sawsan. "Whiteness and the Arab Immigrant Experience." *Race and Arab Americans before and after 9/11: From Invisible Citizens to Visible Subjects*. Eds. Amaney Jamal and Nadine Naber. Syracuse, NY: Syracuse UP, 2008.

Abu-Jaber, Diana. *Arabian Jazz*. New York, NY: W. W. Norton & Company, 1993.

———. *Birds of Paradise*. New York, NY: W. W. Norton & Company, 2011.

———. *Crescent*. New York, NY: W. W. Norton & Company, 2003.

Accad, Evelyne. "Sexuality and Sexual Politics: Conflicts and Contradictions for the Contemporary Women in the Middle East." *Third World Women and the Politics of Feminism*. Eds. Chandra Talpade Mohanty, Ann Russo, Lourdes Torres. Bloomington, IN: Indiana UP, 1991, 237–50.

———. *The Wounded Breast: Intimate Journeys Through Cancer*. North Melbourne, Australia: Spinifex, 2001.

Ahmed, Sara. *Queer Phenomenology*. Durham, NC: Duke UP, 2006.

AIDS Coalition to Unleash Power. Last modified August 2013. http://www.actupny.org.

Alameddine, Rabih. *The Hakawati: A Story*. New York, NY: Anchor Books, 2008.

———. *I, the Divine*. New York, NY: W. W. Norton & Company, 2001.

———. *Koolaids: The Art of War*. New York, NY: Picador, 1998.

———. *The Perv and Other Stories*. New York, NY: Picador, 1999.

———. "Transcontinental Detachment: What Shelf Are You On?" Interview with Carol Fadda-Conrey. *Al-Jadid*. 9.44 (2003): 38.

Alcoff, Linda. *Visible Identities: Race, Gender, and the Self*. New York, NY: Oxford University Press, 2005.

Alexander, Elizabeth. "'Coming Out Blackened and Whole': Fragmentation and Reintegration in Audre Lorde's *Zami* and *The Cancer Journals*." *American Literary History*. 6.4 (1994): 695–715.

Alsultany, Evelyn. *Arabs and Muslims in the Media: Race and Representation after 9/11*. New York, NY: NYU Press, 2012.

American Chronic Pain Association. "Neuropathic Pain." *American Chronic Pain Association*. Medtronic Foundation. Last modified 2013. http://www.theacpa.org.

Ammons, Elizabeth. "Black Anxiety about Immigration and Jessie Fauset's *The Sleeper Wakes*." *African American Review*. 42.3–4 (2008): 461–76.

Aptowicz, Cristin O'Keefe. *Words in Your Face: A Guided Tour through Twenty Years of the New York City Poetry Slam*. New York, NY: Soft Skull Press, 2008.

Associated Press. "Radio Station 'Regrets' Magic Johnson Remarks, Promises PSA." *ESPN*. Last modified October 10, 2008. http://www.espn.com.

Aswad, Barbara. "Attitudes of Arab Immigrants toward Welfare," *Arabs in America: Building a New Future*. Ed. Michael Suleiman. Philadelphia, PA: Temple UP, 1999, 177–92.

Aziz, Barbara Nimri. "Forward." *Scheherezade's Legacy: Arab and Arab American Women on Writing*. Ed. Susan Muaddi Darraj. Westport, CT: Praeger, 2004.

Ball, Alan, director. *Towelhead*. 2008; Burbank, CA: Warner Home Video, 2008. DVD.

"Basketball." *Ebony*. 47.10 (1992): 62–65.

Baynton, Douglas C. "Disability and the Justification of Inequality in American History." *The Disability Studies Reader*. 4th ed. Ed. Lennard Davis. New York, NY: Routledge, 2013, 17–33.

Bayoumi, Moustafa. *How Does It Feel to Be a Problem?: Being Young and Arab in America*. New York, NY: Penguin Books, 2008.

Beatty, Paul. *Tuff*. New York, NY: Anchor Books, 2000.

———. *White Boy Shuffle*. New York, NY: Picador, 1996.

Bell, Christopher M. "Doing Representational Detective Work." *Blackness and Disability: Critical Examinations and Cultural Interventions*. Ed. Christopher M. Bell. Berlin: Lit Verlag, 2011.

———. "The Problem with Magic in/and Representing AIDS." *Culture and the State: Alternative Interventions*. Vol. 4. Eds. J. Gifford and G. Zezulka-Mailloux. Edmonton: CRC Studio Publishers, 7–23.

Beltrán, Mary, and Camilla Fojas, eds. *Mixed Race Hollywood*. New York, NY: NYU Press, 2008.

"Blacks in Sports." *Ebony*. 47.10 (1992): 26.

Blake, Meredith. "Judge Approves Deal Dismissing Paula Deen Lawsuit." *Los Angeles Times*. Last modified August 26, 2013. http://www.latimes.com.

Blatty, William Peter. *The Exorcist*. 1971. Reprint, New York, NY: Harper, 2013.

———. *I'll Tell Them I Remember You*. New York, NY: Barrie & Jenkins, 1973.

———. *Which Way to Mecca, Jack?* New York, NY: B. Geis Associates, 1960.

Bourlaily, Vance. *Confessions of a Spent Youth*. New York, NY: Bantam Books, 1961.

Boudreau, Brenda. "Letting the Body Speak: 'Becoming' White in *Caucasia*." *Modern Language Studies*. 32.1 (2002): 59–70.

Bracey, Christopher A. *Saviors or Sellouts: The Promise and Peril of Black Conservatism from Booker T. Washington to Condoleezza Rice*. Boston, MA: Beacon Press, 2008.

Brantley, Ben. "Theater Review; Untamed Poetry, Loose Onstage." *New York Times*. 15 November 2002. Section E: 1.

Brooks, Daphne. *Bodies in Dissent: Spectacular Performances of Race and Freedom*. Durham, NC: Duke University Press, 2006.

Bruce, Dickson D., Jr. "W. E. B. Du Bois and the Idea of Double Consciousness." *W. E. B. Du Bois: The Souls of Black Folk*. Eds. Henry Louis Gates, Jr., and Terri Hume Oliver. New York, NY: W. W. Norton & Company, 1999.

Butler, Judith. *Bodies That Matter*. New York, NY: Routledge, 1993.

"Care." *Oxford English Dictionary*. Last modified August 2013. http://www.oed.com.

Carter, Chelsea J., and Holly Yan, "Why This Verdict? Five Things That Led to Zimmerman's Acquittal." *CNN*. Last modified on July 15, 2013. http://www.cnn.com.

Centers for Disease Control. "CDC Fact Sheet: New HIV Infections in the United States." *Centers for Disease Control*. Last modified 2012. www.cdc.gov.

Chang, Jeff. *Can't Stop Won't Stop: A History of the Hip-Hop Generation*. New York, NY: Picador, 2005.

Cobb, Jelani. "George Zimmerman, Not Guilty: Blood on the Leaves." *New Yorker*. Last modified on July 13, 2013. http://www.newyorker.com.

Cohen, Cathy. *Boundaries of Blackness: AIDS and the Breakdown of Black Politics*. Chicago, IL: U of Chicago Press, 1999.

Cohen, William A. *Embodied: Victorian Literature and the Senses*. Minneapolis, MN: U of Minnesota Press, 2008.

Cohn, David, et al. "Denver's Increase in HIV Counseling after Magic Johnson's HIV Disclosure." *American Journal of Public Health*. 82.12 (1992): 1692.

Comedy Central Roast of Flavor Flav. Comedy Central. August 17, 2007.

Couser, G. Thomas. *Recovering Bodies: Illness, Disability and Life Writing.* Madison, WI: U of Wisconsin Press, 1997.

Crenshaw, Kimberlé. "Mapping the Margins: Intersectionality, Identity Politics, and Violence against Women of Color." *Stanford Law Review.* 43.6 (1991): 1241–99.

Crimp, Douglas. *Mourning and Melancholia.* Cambridge, MA: MIT Press, 2002.

Crockett, Sandra. " 'Magic's' Book on Avoiding AIDS Gives Blunt Advice." *The Baltimore Sun.* 27 April 1992. www.baltimoresun.com.

Dangerous: The Short Films. Perf. Michael Jackson, Iman, Eddie Murphy, Earvin Johnson, Naomi Campbell. 1991; New York, NY: Epic Music Video, 1993. DVD.

Darwish, Mahmoud. *If I Were Another.* Trans. Fady Joudah. New York, NY: Farrar, Straus and Giroux, 2011, 9–15.

Daulatzai, Sohail. *Black Star, Crescent Moon.* Minneapolis, MN: U of Minnesota Press, 2012.

Davis, Lennard, ed. *The Disability Studies Reader.* 4th ed. New York, NY: Routledge, 2013.

———. *Enforcing Normalcy.* London: Verso, 1995.

De Moor, Katrien. "Diseased Pariahs and Difficult Patients." *Cultural Studies.* 19.6 (2005): 737–54.

DeShazer, Mary K. *Mammographies: The Cultural Discourses of Breast Cancer Narratives.* Ann Arbor, MI: U of Michigan Press, 2013.

De Veaux, Alexis. *Warrior Poet: A Biography of Audre Lorde.* New York, NY: Norton, 2004.

Diehl, Matt. "Miley Cyrus 2.0: The Billboard Cover Story." *Billboard.* Last modified June 14, 2013. http://www.billboard.com.

Dolan, Jill. "Utopia in Performance." *Theatre Research International.* 31.2 (2006): 163–73.

Du Bois, W.E.B. *The Souls of Black Folk.* New York, NY: W. W. Norton & Company, 1999.

Dunsmuir, Lindsay. "Many Americans Have No Friends of Another Race." *Reuters.* Last modified on August 8, 2013. http://www.reuters.com.

Dyer, Richard. "The Matter of Whiteness." *White Privilege: Essential Readings on the Other Side of Racism.* 4th ed. Ed. Paula Rothenberg. New York, NY: Worth Publishers, 2012, 9–14.

Ehlers, Nadine. *Racial Imperatives: Discipline, Performativity, and Struggles against Subjection.* Bloomington, IN: Indiana UP, 2012.

Elam, Michelle. *Souls of Mixed Folk: Race, Politics, and Aesthetics in the New Millennium.* Stanford, CA: Stanford UP, 2011.

Ellison, Ralph. *Invisible Man.* New York, NY: Vintage, 1980.

Erevelles, Nirmala. *Disability and Difference in Global Contexts: Enabling a Transformative Body Politic.* New York, NY: Palgrave Macmillan, 2011.

Erian, Alicia. *Towelhead.* New York, NY: Simon & Schuster, 2008.

Erian, Alicia, and Keya Mitra, "Defining Love, Enduring Brutality." *Gulf Coast: A Journal of Literature and Fine Arts.* 18.2 (2006): 237–50.

Fadda-Conrey, Carol. "Transnational Diaspora and the Search for Home in Rabih Alameddine's *I, the Divine: A Novel in First Chapters.*" *Arab Voices in the Diaspora.* Ed. Layla Al-Maleh. New York, NY: Rodopi, 2009.

Fanon, Frantz. *Black Skin, White Masks.* New York, NY: Grove Press, 1967.

Farber, Jim. "VMAs 2013: Miley Cyrus Was Real Winner at MTV Video Music Awards, Getting Tongues Wagging with Her Risqué Moves." *New York Daily News.* Last modified August 26, 2013. http://www.nydailynews.com.

Farred, Grant. "The Event of the Black Body at Rest: Mêlée in Motown." *Cultural Critique.* 66 (2007): 58–77.

Faulkner, William. *Absalom, Absalom!* 1936. Reprint, New York: Library Classics of the United States, 1985.

Fedaku, Mesfin. "Robin Thicke Says 'Blurred Lines' Music Video Was His Wife's Idea." *Newsday.* Last modified on August 23, 2013. http://www.newsday.com.

Feldman, Keith. "The (Il)legible Arab Body and the Fantasy of National Democracy." *MELUS.* 31.4 (2006): 33–54.

Foy, Anthony. "Joe Louis's Talking Fists: The Auto/Biopolitics of *My Life Story.*" *American Literary History.* 23.2 (2011): 311–36.

Fries, Kenny ed., *Staring Back: The Disability Experience from the Inside Out.* New York, NY: Penguin Books, 1997.

Gardner, Elysa. " 'Def Poetry Jam' Is All Relative." *USA Today.* 15 November 2002. 7.

Garland-Thomson, Rosemarie. *Extraordinary Bodies: Figuring Physical Disability in American Culture and Literature.* New York, NY: Columbia University Press, 1996.

———. "Feminist Disability Studies." *Signs: Journal of Women in Culture and Society.* 30.2 (2005): 1557–87.

———. "Integrating Disability Transforming Feminist Theory." *Feminist Disability Studies.* Ed. Kim Q. Hall. Bloomington, IN: Indiana UP, 2011, 13–47.

———. *Staring: How We Look.* New York, NY: Oxford University Press, 2009, Kindle Edition.

Garrigós, Cristina. "The Dynamics of Intercultural Dislocation Hybridity in Rabih Alameddine's *I, the Divine.*" *Arab Voices in the Diaspora.* Ed. Layla Al-Maleh. New York, NY: Rodopi, 2009.

Geha, Joseph. *Through and Through: Toledo Stories.* Syracuse, NY: Syracuse University Press, 1990.

Gomez, Michael. *Black Crescent.* New York, NY: Cambridge UP, 2005.

Griffith, Gabrielle. *Representations of HIV and AIDS: Visibility Blue/s.* Manchester, UK: Manchester University Press, 2001.

Grosz, Elizabeth. "Merleau-Ponty and Irigaray in the Flesh." *Merleau-Ponty, Interiority and Exteriority, Psychic Life and the World.* Eds. Dorothea Olkowski and James Moreley. Albany, NY: State University of New York Press, 1999.

———. *Volatile Bodies: Toward a Corporeal Feminism.* Bloomington, IN: Indiana University Press, 1994.

Gualtieri, Sarah M. A. *Between Arab and White: Race and Ethnicity in the Early Syrian American Diaspora.* Berkeley, CA: U of California Press, 2009.

———. "Strange Fruit? Syrian Immigrants, Extralegal Violence, and Racial Formation in the United States." *Race and Arab Americans before and after 9/11.* Eds. Amaney Jamal and Nadine Naber. Syracuse, NY: Syracuse UP, 2008, 147–69.

Hammad, Suheir. *Born Palestinian, Born Black.* New York, NY: Harlem River Press, 1996.

———. *Born Palestinian, Born Black and the Gaza Suite.* New York, NY: UpSet Press, 2010.

———. *Breaking Poems.* New York, NY: Cypher Books, 2008.

———. "Composites." *Signs: Journal of Women in Culture and Society.* 28.1 (2002): 471.

———. "In My Mother's Hands." *Essence.* 29.1 (1998): 70.

———. *ZaatarDiva.* New York, NY: Cypher Books, 2008.

Hammonds, Evelyn. "AIDS the Secret, Silent, Suffering Shame." *Still Brave: The Evolution of Black Women's Studies.* Eds. Stanlie M. James, Frances Smith Foster, and Beverly Guy-Sheftall. New York, NY: Feminist Press, 2009, 268–82.

Hartman, Michelle. "A *Debke* Beat Funky as P.E.'s Riff: Hip Hop Poetry and Politics in Suheir Hammad's *Born Palestinian, Born Black.*" *Black Arts Quarterly.* 7.1 (2002): 6–8.

———. " 'this sweet/sweet music': Jazz, Sam Cooke, and Reading Arab American Literary Identities." *MELUS.* 31.4 (2006): 145–66.

Haskins, James. "*Magic*": A Biography of Earvin Johnson.* Hillside, NJ: Enslow Publishers, 1982.

Hassoun, Rosina J. *Arab Americans in Michigan*. East Lansing, MI: Michigan State University Press, 2005.

Henzy, Karl. "Langston Hughes's Poetry and the Metaphysics of Simplicity." *Callaloo*. 34.3 (2011): 915–27.

Hermon, Aleksandar. "Changing the Subject." *PEN America: A Journal for Writers and Readers*. 9 (2008): 19–28.

Hevey, David. "The Enfreakment of Photography." *The Disability Studies Reader*. 2nd ed. Ed. Lennard Davis. New York, NY: Routledge, 2006, 367–78.

Hill Collins, Patricia. *Black Feminist Thought: Knowledge Consciousness and the Politics of Empowerment*. New York, NY: Routledge, 1991.

Holland, Sharon. *Erotic Life of Racism*. Durham, NC: Duke University Press, 2012.

Holloway, Karla F. C. "Cultural Narratives Passed On: African American Mourning Stories." *African American Literary History*. Ed. Winston Napier. New York, NY: NYU Press, 2000, 653–59.

Holmes, Martha Stoddard, and Tod Chambers. "Thinking through Pain." *Literature and Medicine*. 24.1 (2005): 127–41.

hooks, bell. "The Oppositional Gaze: Black Female Spectators." *Black Looks: Race and Representation*. Boston, MA: South End Press, 1992, 115–131.

Hout, Syrine C. "The Last Migration: The First Contemporary Example of Lebanese Diasporic Literature." *Arab Voices in the Diaspora*. Ed. Layla Al-Maleh. New York, NY: Rodopi, 2009.

———. "Memory, Home, and Exile in Contemporary Anglophone Lebanese Fiction." *Critique*. 46.3 (2005): 219–33.

———. "Of Fathers and the Fatherland in the post-1995 Lebanese Exilic Novel." *World Literature Today: A Literary Quarterly of the University of Oklahoma*. 75.2 (Spring 2001): 285–93.

———. "The Predicament of In-Betweenness in the Contemporary Lebanese Exilic Novel in English." *Literature and Nation in the Middle East*. Ed. Yasir Suleiman and Ibrahim Muhawi. Edinburgh: Edinburgh University Press, 2006.

———. "The Tears of Trauma: Memories of Home, War, and Exile in Rabih Alameddine's *I, the Divine*." *World Literature Today: A Literary Quarterly of the University of Oklahoma*. 82.5 (2008): 59–62.

Hughes, Langston. "The Negro Speaks of Rivers." *The Norton Anthology of African American Literature*. Eds. Henry Louis Gates, Jr., and Nellie Y. McKay. New York, NY: W. W. Norton & Company, 1996, 1254.

Irigaray, Luce. *An Ethics of Sexual Difference*. Trans. Carolyn Burke and Gillian Gill. Ithaca, NY: Cornell UP, 1993.

———. *This Sex Which Is Not One*. Trans. Catherine Porter with Carolyn Burke. Ithaca: Cornell UP, 1985.

Jackson, Michael. "Gone Too Soon." *Dangerous*. Sony Records, 1993. CD.

Jackson, Sherman. *Islam and the Blackamerican: Looking toward the Third Resurrection*. New York, NY: Oxford UP, 2005.

James, Jennifer. "Gwendolyn Brooks, World War II, and the Politics of Rehabilitation." *Feminist Disability Studies*. Ed. Kim Q. Hall. Bloomington, IN: Indiana UP, 2011, 136–58.

Jarmakani, Amira. "Arab American Feminisms: Mobilizing the Politics of Invisibility." *Arab American Feminisms: Gender, Violence, and Belonging*. Eds. Rabab Abdulhadi, Evelyn Alsultany and Nadine Naber. Syracuse, NY: Syracuse UP, 2011, 227–41.

Jarrar, Randa. *A Map of Home*. New York, NY: Penguin, 2008.

Jarrett, Gene Andrew. *Representing the Race: A New Political History of African American Literature*. New York, NY: NYU Press, 2011.

Jay, Martin. *Downcast Eyes: The Denigration of Vision in Twentieth-Century French Thought*. Berkeley, CA: University of California Press, 1993.

John, Elton. "Elton John's Letter to Ryan White, 20 years after His Death from AIDS." *Washington Post*. Last modified April 25, 2010. http://www.washingtonpost.com.

Johnson, Charles. "A Phenomenology of the Black Body." *Male Body: Features, Destinies, Exposures*. Ed. Laurence Goldstein. Ann Arbor, MI: U of Michigan Press, 1997, 121–36.

Johnson, Earvin "Magic". *What YOU Can Do to Avoid AIDS*. New York, NY: Random House, 1992.

Johnson, Earvin "Magic", with William Novak. *My Life*. New York, NY: Fawcett, 2009. Kindle Edition.

Johnson, Earvin "Magic" and Larry Bird with Jackie MacMullan. *When the Game Was Ours*. New York, NY: Houghton Mifflin, 2009.

Johnson, James Weldon. *Autobiography of an Ex-Colored Man*. New York: Penguin Group, 1990.

Jones, Sarah. "Your Revolution." *Russell Simmons Presents Def Poetry Jam: Season 1*. Directed by Russell Simmons. 2001; New York, NY: HBO Home Video, 2004. DVD.

Jordan, June. *Directed by Desire*. Eds. Jan Heller Levi and Sara Miles. Port Townsend, WA: Copper Canyon Press, 2007.

Jun, Helen Heran. *Race for Citizenship: Black Orientalism and Asian Uplift from Pre-Emancipation to Neoliberal America*. New York, NY: NYU Press, 2011.

Kadi, J. *Food for Our Grandmothers*. Cambridge, MA: South End Press, 1994.

Kahf, Mohja. *The Girl in the Tangerine Scarf*. New York, NY: Carroll & Graf Publishers, 2006.

———. "The Pity Committee and the Careful Reader." *Arab American Feminisms: Gender, Nation and Belonging*. Eds. Rabab Abdulhadi, Evelyn Alsultany and Nadine Naber. Syracuse, NY: Syracuse UP, 2011, 111–23.

Kalliel, Nora. "Al-Hajji Aliya Ogdie-Hassen: 1910–1190." *Arab Community Center for Economic and Social Services Newsletter*. 1.2 (1990): 1.

Katchadourian, Herant A., and Donald T. Lunde. *Fundamentals of Human Sexuality, Second Edition*. New York, NY: Holt, Rinehart and Winston, 1975.

Kayyalli, Randa. *The Arab Americans*. Westport, CT: Greenwood Press, 2006.

King, Jason. "Any Love: Silence, Theft, and Rumor in the Work of Luther Vandross." *The Greatest Taboo: Homosexuality in Black Communities*. Ed. Delroy Constantine-Sims. Los Angeles, CA: Alyson Publications, 2000, 290–315.

King, Jay Caspian. "Should Reddit Be Blamed for the Spread of a Smear?" *New York Times*. Last modified on July 25, 2013. http://www.nytimes.com.

Kittay, Eva Feder. "When Caring Is Just and Justice Is Caring: Justice and Mental Retardation." *Public Culture*. 13.3 (2001): 557–79.

Knopf-Newman, Marcy Jane. "Interview with Suheir Hammad," *MELUS*. 31.4 (2006): 71–93.

Kroll, J. "Smile Though Our Hearts Are Breaking." *Newsweek*. 18 November 1991: 70–71.

Langer, Monika M. *Merleau-Ponty's Phenomenology of Perception*. Tallahassee, FL: FL State U Press, 1989.

Liesch, John and Cindy Patton, "Clinic or Spa? Facial Surgery in the Context of AIDS-Related Facial Wasting." *The Rebirth of the Clinic*. Ed. Cindy Patton. Minneapolis, MN: U of Minnesota Press, 2010, 1–16.

Linton, Simi. *Claiming Disability: Knowledge and Identity*. New York, NY: NYU Press, 1998.

Lipsitz, George. *The Possessive Investment in Whiteness*. Philadelphia, PA: Temple University Press, 2006.

Liptak, Adam. "Supreme Court Invalidates Key Part of Voting Rights Act." *New York Times*. Last modified on June 25, 2013. http://www.nytimes.com.

Longmore, Paul. *Why I Burned My Book and Other Essays on Disability*. Philadelphia, PA: Temple UP, 2003.

Lorde, Audre. *The Cancer Journals*. San Francisco, CA: Aunt Lute Books, 1997.

———. "The Transformation of Silence into Language and Action." *Sister Outsider*. Berkeley, CA: Ten Speed Press, 2007, 40–45.

———. *Zami: A New Spelling of My Name*. Berkeley, CA: Crossing Press, 1982.

Loyd, Jenna. "Where Is Community Health? Racism, the Clinic, and the Biopolitical State." *Rebirth of the Clinic: Places and Agents in Contemporary Health Care*. Ed. Cindy Patton. Minneapolis, MN: U of Minnesota Press, 2010.

Ludescher, Tanyss. "From Nostalgia to Critique: An Overview of Arab American Literature." *MELUS*. 31.4 (2006): 93–114.

Lukin, Joshua L. "Disability and Blackness." *The Disability Studies Reader*. 4th ed. Ed. Lennard Davis. New York, NY: Routledge, 2013, 308–15.

"Magic Johnson's Full Court Press against AIDS." *Ebony*. 47.6 (1992): 108–11.

Majaj, Lisa Suhair. "Arab American Ethnicity: Locations, Coalitions and Cultural Negotiations." *Arabs in America: Building a New Future*. Ed. Michael Suleiman. Philadelphia, PA: Temple UP, 1999, 321–36.

———. "Arab Americans and the Meaning of Race." *Postcolonial Theory and the United States: Race, Ethnicity and Literature*. Ed. Amritjit Singh and Peter Schmidt. Jackson, MS: U of Mississippi Press, 2000, 320–37.

———. "New Directions: Arab American Writing at Century's End." *Post-Gibran: Anthology of New Arab American Writing*. Eds. Munir Akash and Khaled Mattawa. Syracuse, NY: Syracuse UP, 1999, 66–77.

Major, William. "Audre Lorde's *The Cancer Journals*: Autopathography as Resistance." *Mosaic (Winnipeg)*. 35.2 (2002): 39.

Makarechi, Kia. "Robin Thicke Sues Marvin Gaye's Family to Protect 'Blurred Lines.'" *Huffington Post*. Last modified August 17, 2013. http://www.huffing tonpost.com.

Mallenbaum, Carly. "Miley's VMA Performance Shocks Celebs." *USA Today*. Last modified on August 27, 2013. http://www.usatoday.com.

Massaquoi, H. J. "Ten New Dating Rules in the Post–Magic Johnson Era." *Ebony*. 47.4 (1992): 126–29.

Matar, Hisham. *Anatomy of a Disappearance*. New York, NY: Dial Press, 2011.

———. *In the Country of Men*. New York, NY: Dial Press, 2006.

Mattawa, Khaled, and Munir Akash. *Post-Gibran: Anthology of New Arab American Writing*. Syracuse, NY: Syracuse University Press, 1999.

Mays, Vickie M., et al. "Magic Johnson's Credibility among African American Men." *American Journal of Public Health*. 82.12 (1992): 1692–93.

McCallum, Jack. "Laying Down the LA Law: Playing with Conviction on Their Home Court, the Magic Johnson–Led Lakers Roared Back from a 17-Point Deficit to Beat the Boston Celtics." *Sports Illustrated*. 66.8 (1987): 20–23.

———. "Leaving a Huge Void." *Sports Illustrated*. 76.11 (1992): 20–24.

———. "A New Face, but the Same Old Magic with Magic Johnson." *Sports Illustrated*. 70.22 (1989): 16–20.

Meir, Golda. "Mrs. Meir Bars Any 'Deal' for Israel's Security." *The Washington Post*. 16 June 1969. Section A: 15.

Merleau-Ponty, Maurice. *Phenomenology of Perception*. Trans. Colin Smith. New York, NY: Routledge, 2008.

———. *The Visible and Invisible*. Trans. Alphonso Lingus. Evanston, IL: Northwestern University Press, 1969.

Mitchell, David, and Sharon Snyder. *Narrative Prosthesis, Disability, and the Dependencies of Discourse*. Ann Arbor, MI: U of Michigan Press, 2000.

Mlynar, Phillip. "Miley Cyrus Twerks, Gives Robin Thicke Some Tongue at VMAs." *MTV*. Last modified August 25, 2013. http://www.mtv.com.

Moallem, Minoo, and Iain A. Boal. "Multicultural Nationalism and the Poetics of Inauguration." *Between Woman and Nation: Nationalisms, Transnational*

Feminisms, and the State. Eds. Caren Kaplan, Norma Alarcón, and Minoo Moallem. Durham, NC: Duke University Press, 1999, 243–63.

Mohanty, Chandra Talpade. "Under Western Eyes: Feminist Scholarship and Colonial Discourse." *The Women, Gender, and Development Reader.* Eds. N. Visvanathan, L. Duggan, L. Nisonoff, and N. Wiegersma. London: Zed Books, 1997, 79–85.

Mollow, Anna, and Robert McRuer. *Sex and Disability.* Durham, NC: Duke UP, 2012.

Moraga, Cherríe. "Entering the Lives of Others: Theory in the Flesh." *This Bridge Called My Back: Writings by Radical Women of Color.* Eds. Gloria Anzaldúa and Cherríe Moraga. Berkeley, CA: Third Woman Press, 2002.

Morris, David B. "Un-Forgetting Asclepius: An Erotics of Illness." *New Literary History.* 38.3 (2007): 419–41.

———. *The Culture of Pain.* Berkeley, CA: U of California Press, 1993.

Morrison, Toni. Introduction. *Birth of a Nation 'Hood: Gaze, Script, and Spectacle in the O. J. Simpson Case.* Eds. Toni Morrison and Claudia Brodsky-Lacour. New York, NY: Pantheon, 1997.

———. "On the Backs of Blacks." *Time.* (Fall 1993): 57–58.

Mosbergen, Dominique. "Robin Thicke's 'Blurred Lines' Dubbed 'Rapey,' Hit Song under Fire from Critics." *Huffington Post.* Last modified on July 11, 2013. http://www.huffingtonpost.com.

Naber, Nadine. *Arab America: Gender, Cultural Politics, and Activism.* New York, NY: NYU Press, 2012.

Naber, Nadine, and Amaney Jamal. *Race and Arab Americans before and after 9/11: From Invisible Citizens to Visible Subjects.* Eds. Amaney Jamal and Nadine Naber. Syracuse, NY: Syracuse UP, 2008.

Nazario, Brunilda. "History of HIV/AIDS Slideshow: A Pictorial Timeline of the AIDS Pandemic." *WebMD.* WebMD, LLC. Last modified December 1, 2009. http://www.webmd.com.

Newman, Bruce. "Magic Faces the Music." *Sports Illustrated.* 62.19 (1985): 82–91.

Nussbaum, Emily. "In Conversation: Gloria Steinem and Suheir Hammad: A Feminist Rising Star on the Sexual Revolution, the Booty-Call Nineties, and the Superwoman Myth." *New York.* (2008). Last accessed 10 May 2012. http://www.nymag.com.

"Obama Speech on Drone Policy." *New York Times.* Last modified May 23, 2013. http://www.nytimes.com.

O'Brien, M., and C. Reid. "AIDS Book by Magic Johnson 'Self-Censored' by Three Retail Chains." *Publishers Weekly.* 8 June 1992: 17–19.

Orfalea, Gregory. *The Arab Americans: A History.* Northampton, MA: Interlink Books, 2006.

Oster, Judith. "See(k)ing the Self: Mirrors and Mirroring in Bicultural Texts." *MELUS.* 23.4 (1998): 59–83.

Pareles, Jon. "A New Platform for the New Poets." *New York Times.* 10 November 2002. Section 2: 1.

"Paula's Best Dishes: Twitter Hashtag Pokes Fun at Paula Deen's Unsavory Side As Allegations of Racism Surface." *Huffington Post.* Last modified June 21, 2013. http://www.huffingtonpost.com.

Perreault, Jeanne. " 'That the Pain Not Be Wasted': Audre Lorde and the Written Self." *Auto/biography Studies: A/B.* 4.1 (1988): 1–16.

Pflitsch, Andreas. "To Fit or Not to Fit. Rabih Alameddine's Novels *Koolaids* and *I, the Divine.*" *ArabAmericas: Literary Entanglements of the American Hemisphere and the Arab World.* Eds. Ottmar Ette and Friederike Pannewick. Madrid: Iberoamericana, 2006.

Phili, Stelios. "Robin Thicke on That Banned Video, Collaborating with 2 Chainz and Kendrick Lamar, and His New Film." *GQ: Gentleman's Quarterly*. Last modified on May 7, 2013. http://www.gq.com.

Pickens, Therí A. "'It's a Jungle Out There': Disability and Blackness in *Monk*." *Disability Studies Quarterly*. 33.3 (2013). Last modified August 28, 2013. http://www.dsq-sds.org.

———. "'Mic Check: Can You Hear Me?': Suheir Hammad and the Politics of Spoken Word Poetry." *Al-Raida*. 124 (Winter 2009): 8–14.

———. "To Be or Not to Be: The Question of Having a Body in Ethnic Studies." *Defying the Global Language: Perspectives in Ethnic Studies*. Eds. Cheryl Toman and Gilbert Doho. Amherst, NY: Teneo Press, Ltd., 2013, 19–44.

Price-Herndl, Diane. "Our Breasts, Our Selves: Identity, Community and Ethics in Breast Cancer Narratives." *Signs: A Journal of Women in Culture and Society*. 32.1 (2006): 221–45.

———. "Reconstructing the Posthuman Feminist Body Twenty Years after Audre Lorde's *Cancer Journals*." *Disability Studies: Enabling the Humanities*. Eds. Sharon L. Snyder, Brenda Jo Brueggemann, and Rosemarie Garland-Thomson. New York, NY: Modern Language Association of America, 2002, 144–55.

Rabih Alameddine. Last modified August 2013. http://www.rabihalameddine.com.

Randolph, Laura B. "The Magic 'Miracle': 'The Lord Has Healed Earvin.'" *Ebony*. 52.6 (1997): 72–76.

"Remarks by the President at Signing of the Ryan White HIV/AIDS Treatment Extension Act of 2009." *The White House*. 30 October 2009. Last modified April 16, 2010. www.whitehouse.gov.

Richardson, Lynda. "From Amman, Jordan, to Broadway, Via Brooklyn." *New York Times*. 14 March 2003. Section B: 2.

Rihany, Ameen. *The Book of Khalid*. 1911. Reprint, Charleston, SC: Nabu Books, 2012.

"Robin Roberts Personal Journey—Living with Breast Cancer." *Nightline*. New York, NY: ABC Studios, 2008. DVD.

Roberts, Robin. *From the Heart: Eight Rules to Live By*. New York, NY: Hyperion, 2008.

Rogers, Lynne. "Hypocrisy and Homosexuality in the Middle East: Selim Nassib's *Oum* and Rabih Alameddine's *Koolaids*." *Journal of Commonwealth and Postcolonial Studies*. 10.1 (2003): 145–63.

Rothman, Lily. "4 Reasons You're Still Hearing About Miley Cyrus' VMA Performance." *Time*. Last modified August 26, 2013. http://entertainment.time.com.

Rushdie, Salman. *Imaginary Homelands*. New York, NY: Penguin Books, 1992.

Said, Edward. *Culture and Imperialism*. New York, NY: Vintage, 1994.

———. *Orientalism*. New York, NY: Vintage Books, 1979.

———. *Reflections on Exile and Other Essays*. Cambridge, MA: Harvard University Press, 2002.

Salaita, Steven. *Anti-Arab Racism in the USA: Where It Comes From and What It Means for Politics Today*. Ann Arbor, MI: Pluto Press, 2006.

———. "Ethnic Identity and Imperative Patriotism: Arab Americans before and after 9/11." *College Literature*. 32.2 (2005): 146–168.

———. *Modern Arab American Fiction: A Reader*. Syracuse, NY: Syracuse UP, 2011.

Salamon, Gayle. "'The Place Where Life Hides Away': Merleau-Ponty, Fanon, and the Location of Bodily Being." *Differences: A Journal of Feminist Cultural Studies*. 17.2 (2006): 96–112.

Saliba, Therese. "On Rachel Corrie, Palestine, and Feminist Solidarity." *Arab American Feminisms: Gender, Violence, and Belonging*. Eds. Rabab Abdulhadi, Evelyn Alsultany and Nadine Naber. Syracuse, NY: Syracuse UP, 2011, 184–93.

————. "Resisting Invisibility: Arab Americans in Academia and Activism." *Arabs in America: Building a New Future*. Ed. Michael Suleiman. Philadelphia, PA: Temple UP, 1999, 304–19.

Samhan, Helen. "Not Quite White: Race Classification and the Arab-American Experience." *Arabs in America: Building a New Future*. Ed. Michael Suleiman. Philadelphia, PA: Temple UP, 1999, 209–26.

————. "Politics and Exclusion: The Arab American Experience." *Journal of Palestine Studies*. 16.2 (1987): 11–28.

Samuels, Ellen Jean. "My Body, My Closet: Invisible Disability and the Limits of Coming Out Discourse." *GLQ: A Journal of Lesbian and Gay Studies*. 9.1–2 (2003): 233–55.

Scarry, Elaine. *The Body in Pain: The Making and Unmaking of the World*. New York, NY: Oxford University Press, 1987.

Schrader, George Alfred, ed. *Existential Philosophers: Kierkegaard to Merleau-Ponty*. New York, NY: McGraw-Hill, 1967.

Seaman, Donna. "Symptomatic (Book)." *Booklist*. 100.15 (2004): 1349.

Senna, Danzy. *Caucasia*. New York, NY: Riverhead Books, 1998.

————. "Mulatto Millenium." *Half and Half: Writers on Growing Up Biracial and Bicultural*. Ed. Claudine Chiawei O'Hearn. New York, NY: Pantheon, 1998, 12–27.

————. *Symptomatic*. New York, NY: Riverhead Books, 2004.

Shaheen, Jack. *Reel Bad Arabs: How Hollywood Vilifies a People*. Northampton, MA: Interlink, 2001.

Shakespeare, Tom, and Nicholas Watson. "The Social Model of Disability: An Outmoded Ideology?" *Research in Social Science and Disability*. 2 (2002): 9–28. Centre for Disability Studies—Disability Archive. Last modified April 6, 2010. http://disability-studies.leeds.ac.uk/library.

Shakir, Evelyn. "Arab Mothers, American Sons: Women in Arab-American Autobiographies." *MELUS*. 17.3 (1991): 5–15.

————. "Mother's Milk: Women in Arab-American Autobiography." *MELUS*. 15.4 (1988): 39–50.

————. "Pretending to Be Arab: Role Playing in Vance Bourjaily's 'The Fractional Man.'" *MELUS*. 9.1 (1982): 7–21.

Shalal-Esa, Andrea. "Arab-American Writers Identify with Communities of Color." *Al-Jadid*. 9.42–43 (2003): 24–26.

Shanahan, Dervla. "Reading Queer A/theology into Rabih Alameddine's *Koolaids*." *Feminist Theology*. 19.2 (2011): 129–42.

Shapiro, Joseph. *No Pity: People with Disabilities Forging a New Civil Rights Movement*. New York, NY: Three Rivers Press, 1994.

Shildrick, Margrit. *Dangerous Discourses of Disability, Subjectivity and Sexuality*. New York, NY: Palgrave Macmillan, 2009.

Shryock, Andrew. "The Moral Analogies of Race." *Race and Arab Americans before and after 9/11: From Invisible Citizens to Visible Subjects*. Eds. Amaney Jamal and Nadine Naber. Syracuse, NY: Syracuse UP, 2008.

Siebers, Tobin. *Disability Theory*. Ann Arbor, MI: U of Michigan Press, 2008.

Siegel, Bernie Siegel, M.D. FSB Associates, 2009, last modified April 19, 2010. http://www.berniesiegelmd.com.

Simmons, Russell, director. *Russell Simmons Presents DEF Poetry Season 1*. 2001; HBO Home Video, 2004. DVD.

Smith, Andrea. "Heteropatriarchy and the Three Pillars of White Supremacy: Rethinking Women of Color Organizing." *The Colour of Violence: The Incite! Anthology*. Ed. Andrea Lee Smith. Cambridge, MA: South End Press, 2006, 66–73.

Sobchack, Vivian. *Carnal Thoughts: Embodiment and Moving Image Culture*. Berkeley, CA: U of California Press, 2004.

Sollors, Werner. *Neither Black nor White yet Both*. New York, NY: Oxford UP, 1997.

Solomon, Charles. "*What YOU Can Do to Avoid AIDS* by Earvin 'Magic' Johnson (Times Books: $3.99) and *The Complete Guide to Safer Sex* edited by Ted McIlvenna (Barricade Books: $6.95)." *Los Angeles Times*. 10 May 1992. www.latimes.com.

Sontag, Susan. *Illness as Metaphor and AIDS and Its Metaphors*. New York, NY: Picador, 1978.

———. *Regarding the Pain of Others*. New York, NY: Farrar, Straus and Giroux, 2003.

———. *On Photography*. New York, NY: Anchor Books, 1989.

Sorisio, Carolyn. "Introduction: Cross-Racial and Cross-Ethnic Collaboration and Scholarship: Contexts, Criticism, Challenges." *MELUS*. 38.1 (2013): 2.

Spillers, Hortense. "Notes on an Alternative Model—Neither/Nor." *The Difference Within: Feminism and Critical Theory*. Eds. Elizabeth Meese and Alice Parker. Philadelphia, PA: John Benjamins Publishing Company, 1989, 165–88.

Spivak, Gayatri. "Can the Subaltern Speak?" *Marxism and the Interpretation of Culture*. Eds. Cary Nelson and Lawrence Grossberg. Chicago: U of Illinois Press, 1988, 271–315.

Stevenson, R. W. "Magic Johnson Ends His Career, Saying He Has the AIDS Virus." *New York Times*. 8 November 1991. Section A: 1.

Toman, Cheryl. Rev. of *The Wounded Breast: Intimate Journeys through Cancer*. *World Literature Today*. 76.2 (2002): 164–65.

Touré. *Who's Afraid of Post-Blackness?* New York, NY: Atria Books, 2012.

Trust, Gary. "Robin Thicke No. 1, Katy Perry No. 2 on Hot 100." *Billboard*. Last modified on August 21, 2013. http://www.billboard.com.

U.S. Department of Health and Human Services. "A Timeline of AIDS." Last modified 2013. www.aids.gov.

Walker, Alice. "Alice Walker: Why I'm Joining the Freedom Flotilla to Gaza." *The Guardian*. Last modified August 17, 2012. www.guardian.co.uk.

Walker, Hunter. "Paula Deen on Her Dream 'Southern Plantation Wedding.'" *Talking Points Memo*. Last modified on June 19, 2013. http://www.talkingpointsmemo.com.

Walker, Rebecca. "Introduction." *Mixed: An Anthology of Short Fiction on the Multiracial Experience*. Ed. Chandra Prasad. New York, NY: W. W. Norton & Company, 2006.

Wang, Hansi Lo. "Arab-Americans: A 'Growing' Community, But by How Much?" *National Public Radio*. Last modified May 30, 2013. http://www.npr.org.

Ward, Patricia Sarrafian. *The Bullet Collection*. New York, NY: Graywolf, 2003.

Warner, Sharon Oard. "The Way We Write Now: The Reality of AIDS in Contemporary Short Fiction." *Studies in Short Fiction*. 30 (1993): 491–500.

Washington, Booker T. *Up from Slavery*. Boston, MA: Bedford–St. Martin's, 2003.

Weber, Rebecca L. "The Africana QA: Danzy Senna." *Rebecca L. Weber*. Last modified July 6, 2004. www.rebeccalweber.com/danzy.html.

Weiss, Mitch. "'Moral Monday' Protest Held in Charlotte." *News Observer*. Last modified August 19, 2013. www.newsobserver.com.

West, Kanye. "Roses." *Late Registration*. Roc-A-Fella Records, 2005. CD.

Wilkerson, Abby. "Disability, Sex Radicalism, and Political Agency." *Feminist Disability Studies*. Ed. Kim Q. Hall. Bloomington, IN: Indiana UP, 2011: 193–217.

Williams, Katt. *It's Pimpin' Pimpin'*. Dir. Troy Miller. Salient Media, 2008.

Wing, Nick. "'Moral Monday' Protest in North Carolina: 151 Arrested As Activists Decry 'Extreme' GOP Agenda." *Huffington Post*. Last modified June 4, 2013. http://www.huffingtonpost.com.

———. "Moral Monday Protests: 101 More Arrested, Two-Thirds Women, in Rally against North Carolina GOP." *Huffington Post*. Last modified July 16, 2013. http://www.huffingtonpost.com.

Wu, Cynthia. "Marked Bodies, Marking Time: Reclaiming the Warrior in Audre Lorde's *The Cancer Journals.*" *Auto/biography Studies: A/B.* 17.2 (2002): 245–61.

Young, Hershini Bhana. "Black 'Like Me': (Mis) Recognition, the Racial Gothic, and the Post-1967 Mixed-Race Movement in Danzy Senna's *Symptomatic.*" *African American Review.* 42.2 (2008): 287–305.

Index

Printed in Great Britain
by Amazon